RENAISSANCE DREAM CULTURES

This volume explores the dream cultures of the European long sixteenth century, with a focus on Italian sources, reflections and debates on the nature and value of dreams, and frameworks of interpretation.

The chapters examine a variety of oneiric experiences, since distinctions such as that between dreams and visions are themselves culturally specific and variable. Several developments of the period are relevant and consequently considered, from the introduction of the printing press and the humanist rediscovery of ancient texts to the religious reforms and the cultural encounters at the time of the first globalisation. At the centre of the narrative is the exceptional case of Girolamo Cardano, heterodox physician, mathematician, astrologer, autobiographer, dreamer and key dream theorist of the epoch. The Italian peninsula produced the first printed editions of many classical and medieval treatises and, particularly between the 1560s and the 1610s, was also especially active in the writing of texts, both Latin and vernacular, fascinated by the oneiric experience and investigating it. Given the role of the visual in dreaming, images are also analysed.

This book will be a recommended reading for scholars, students and non-specialist readers of cultural history, Renaissance studies and dream cultures.

Alessandro Arcangeli is Associate Professor of Early Modern History at the University of Verona. He is the author of *Cultural History: A Concise Introduction* (2012) and co-editor of *The Routledge Companion to Cultural History in the Western World* (2020).

Alessandro Arcangeli's new book is at once scholarly, wide-ranging and original.

Peter Burke, *University of Cambridge, UK*

RENAISSANCE DREAM CULTURES

Alessandro Arcangeli

LONDON AND NEW YORK

Designed cover image: Nicolas Dipre, "The dream of Jacob", Musée Du Petit Palais, Avignon (oil on panel transferred onto canvas, ca 1500) © Art Collection 2 / Alamy Stock Photo

First published 2025
by Routledge
4 Park Square, Milton Park, Abingdon, Oxon OX14 4RN

and by Routledge
605 Third Avenue, New York, NY 10158

Routledge is an imprint of the Taylor & Francis Group, an informa business

© 2025 Alessandro Arcangeli

The right of Alessandro Arcangeli to be identified as author of this work has been asserted in accordance with sections 77 and 78 of the Copyright, Designs and Patents Act 1988.

All rights reserved. No part of this book may be reprinted or reproduced or utilised in any form or by any electronic, mechanical, or other means, now known or hereafter invented, including photocopying and recording, or in any information storage or retrieval system, without permission in writing from the publishers.

Trademark notice: Product or corporate names may be trademarks or registered trademarks, and are used only for identification and explanation without intent to infringe.

British Library Cataloguing-in-Publication Data
A catalogue record for this book is available from the British Library

ISBN: 978-1-032-24671-0 (hbk)
ISBN: 978-1-032-24672-7 (pbk)
ISBN: 978-1-003-27970-9 (ebk)

DOI: 10.4324/9781003279709

Typeset in Sabon
by SPi Technologies India Pvt Ltd (Straive)

To Fabio, a dreamer

CONTENTS

List of Illustrations   ix
Preface   x

1   Introduction: Approaching the historical study of dreams   1

    1.1   Delimitations of subject, chronology and geography   1

2   Themes   5

    2.1   Dream as premonition   5
    2.2   Dream as deception   6
    2.3   Dream as (compensatory) escape   9
    2.4   Dreamworld and self-knowledge   9

3   *Les mots et les choses* (an intermezzo on vocabulary)   11

4   Contexts   15

    4.1   Night   15
    4.2   Sleep   17
    4.3   Dreams, visions and prophecy   20
    4.4   Imagination and the senses   22

5   Recovering and negotiating a long tradition   23

    5.1   Some key ancient sources   23
    5.2   Biblical and Christian doctrines and attitudes   32

5.3	Dreams and humoral complexions	34
5.4	Other sleep and dream pathologies	37
5.5	Dream and confession	40
5.6	Somnia Judaica	42
5.7	Other dreams	44

6 Girolamo Cardano, the dreaming scholar — 48

7 The sixteenth-century treatise on dreams: A quasi-genre — 57

8 A selection of sources on Renaissance dream cultures — 66

8.1	The linguistic invention and erotic imagination of a learned friar	66
8.2	Dreaming the powerful	69
8.3	Commerce with the classics: Aristotle and Macrobius	69
8.4	Some vernacular texts in odour of heterodoxy	71
8.5	Platonic theology	75
8.6	Oneiromancy between market square and menagerie	76
8.7	A theological commonplace	78
8.8	The interpretation of dreams as a form of entertainment	79
8.9	A dictionary of gesture	82
8.10	Popular interpretation	84
8.11	Dreaming the witches' sabbath?	88
8.12	The other half of the oneiric world	90
8.13	Pour (en) finir avec Descartes	91

9 A look at images — 95

10 Fragments towards a grand narrative — 103

11 The development of the studies in historical dream cultures — 111

12 A Coda on the oneiric present — 119

Appendix   A selection of dedicated printed sources, in chronological order of first edition — 121

Table of most notable topics — 128

Bibliography — 130
Index — 149

ILLUSTRATIONS

Figures

4.1	Michelangelo Buonarroti, "Allegory of The Night", Mausoleum of Giuliano de' Medici, Florence (marble statue, 1531). © Luisa Ricciarini / Bridgeman Images.	16
5.1	Nicolas Beatrizet. "Joseph Explaining his Dreams" (engraving on paper, 1541). The Wallace L. DeWolf and Joseph Brooks Fair Collections, the Art Institute of Chicago.	33
7.1	Peter Paul Rubens, "Decius Mus Relating His Dream" (oil on large canvas, 1616–1617). LIECHTENSTEIN, The Princely Collections, Vaduz-Vienna/SCALA, Florence. 2024 © Photo Scala, Florence.	62
8.1	Woodcut from the *Hypnerotomachia Poliphili* (Venice 1499), fol. d3v © Volgi archive / Alamy Stock Photo.	68
8.2	Giovanni Battista Cima da Conegliano, "Sleeping Endymion" (oil on panel, 1505–10). © Heritage Image Partnership Ltd / Alamy Stock Photo.	73
9.1	Albrecht Dürer, "Dream landscape with text" (pen and ink and watercolour on paper, 1525). © Bridgeman Images.	99

Box

6.1	Jung reader of Cardano	51

PREFACE

The purpose of this short book is to raise awareness on the importance that a proper consideration of the oneiric experience – the meaning and value people from the past tended to give to what they dreamt – must have in any plan for a historical anthropology of their lives. Research on historical dream cultures is developing rapidly, and yet there seems to be room for a survey of the major issues concerning the European long sixteenth century. I have confined most of my reconstruction of the existing historiography to a dedicated final chapter, which is also to serve as a guide for further reading; the impression that the scholarly scene gave me is to have produced slightly more on the literary field, as well as on the tradition of individual linguistic areas, than on a transnational historical mode. Some of my emphasis will rest on Italian (Latin and vernacular) sources; I hope, however, that it will be regarded as useful, both on its historical merit and as an addition to the existing territories which have already been significantly explored. Something more on chronology and geography will be said towards the beginning of the book's Introduction. In end-matter tools, the reader will find a chronological description of a selection of printed sources, which does not aspire to completeness, but should give some idea of the wealth of material that circulated during the period. The index will permit, inter alia, to see where they are presented and discussed. To a more traditional index is added a sample table of the sort provided by the Renaissance printing press, which intends to give back some of the flavour that the consultation of the books in question offered at the time.

Of the diverse and potentially elusive range of source material available, I have concentrated on reflections and debates on the nature and value of dreams, rather than on a phenomenology of what we are told was dreamt. This preference – partly due to restrictions of time and space, partly to my personal reading and writing habits – may position the present contribution in a grey zone between cultural and intellectual history as they are usually understood. On the other hand, I had the opportunity elsewhere to advocate a fusion between these two perspectives (Arcangeli 2012: 78–9), and studies in culture have long done with fences between (sub)disciplines.

The present study does not primarily concern the dream as a literary form. Its aim is, in the fashion of cultural history, to help approaching the dream as it was experienced, interpreted and evaluated by men and women of the time span considered. Understandably, this enterprise would demand the examination of a wide range of sources, and this survey cannot aspire to be in any way exhaustive. Still, there is no point in excluding literary sources, and the question whether a narrated dream was actually experienced by someone in their sleep is, to some extent at least, *mal posée*. The dream narrative as we know it is not simply what happens to us while asleep, but at the very least a subsequent re-elaboration, whose rhetoric has been the subject of study by a major intellectual tradition (of which the Freudian episode is only a fairly recent one and the best known).

The fact that work on this book has to a good extent taken place in the era of the Covid-19 world pandemic has offered the subject for a coda. Since that concluding section deals with the present, it is the only part of the book where reference may be given to modern frameworks of understanding of the oneiric experience. For the rest, following the defining attitude of cultural history, the emphasis will rather be on the way contemporaries perceived it and thought about it.

An audience present at a conference in Helsinki and participants at a virtual seminar in Montreal have listened to partial presentations of material I have reworked here: I thank them and the organisers of the two events for the opportunity and for their comments and suggestions. I thank for their support my own Department of Cultures and Civilisations at the University of Verona and the Faculty of History at the University of Cambridge, which welcomed me repeatedly as a visiting scholar over the past few years. I owe my familiarity with the source and critical material to many physical and online resources; as ever, for me, a special role has been played by the Warburg Library in London.

Many friends and colleagues have provided valuable hints, comments and encouragement: I thank them all and would like to mention at least James Amelang, Lucio Biasiori, Anna Bognolo, Vincenzo Borghetti, Umberto Cecchinato and Antonella Fenech. Peter Burke – with whom I have been sharing thoughts and bibliographies on dreams over a few years – has read a first draft of the manuscript and provided highly valuable feedback. The editorial staff at Routledge and anonymous readers of the book project have also offered me vital help and encouragement.

* For sources marked with an asterisk, see appendix, in order of date of first printed publication.

When not otherwise stated, translations from other languages are mine.

1
INTRODUCTION

Approaching the historical study of dreams

The idea of dream has strong associations with the modern imagination of the Renaissance, and a reference to "Renaissance dreams" – whether intending the historical epoch or supposed/desired re-enactments of it – can be easily found as a shorthand for renewal, imagination and self-conscious fashioning of individuals and communities. In this book, however, metaphor is given a minor part, and the focus is on actual dreaming. A preliminary intellectual positioning is however necessary to clarify what is meant here by "actual". As Douglas Cairns (2022) has convincingly claimed for the case of emotions, all historical sources are representations of events, rather than events. If we can know dreams (as well as emotions) only via the fact that someone wrote about them (or left another sort of documentation, such as visual or material), that also applies to revolutions, battles and plagues. If anything, a peculiarity of dreams is that the very psychological process by which – according to most theories, ancient as well as modern – we experience them is intrinsically narrative and/or pictorial, involving subsequent processes of remembering and reassembling oneiric material. Rather than diminishing the documentary value of any writing or drawing about dreams, however, this peculiarity makes such documentation the only available evidence from the perspective of historical research, that is, what historical dreams *are* (in absence of oral reports from the distant past), rather than a pale image of them, or what one must settle for.

1.1 Delimitations of subject, chronology and geography

This book does not attempt an interpretation of past experience in terms of modern psychological paradigms. It will not adopt such terms as unconscious (unless expressly illustrating and discussing twentieth-century psychoanalysis), which would underpin the anatomy and physiology of the dreaming experience with an ontology unrequired in historical research. It is of course entirely legitimate to outline a history of the notion of unconscious, a task that implies, for epochs and cultures preceding/other than Western modernity, reconstructing varying forms of anthropological understanding of the human mind and experience (Mazurel 2022). Less epistemologically sound is to attempt a psychoanalysis (or apply any alternative psychological doctrine) to the lives of people from the past – an undertaking that does not belong (in my opinion) to the discipline of history, and has not proved particularly successful in the attempts to implement it.

A critique of the psychoanalytic approach for the fact that it concerned the individual and/or humankind but ignored anything in between, that is, a social or cultural dimension, was powerfully put in 1973 by Peter Burke, on the grounds particularly of the findings of psychological anthropology (Burke 1997a, 23–27; for an anthropological perspective, see also Lanternari 1981a and 1981b). It has been confirmed and reinforced more recently based on a fresh sociological approach by Bernard Lahire (2020). Lahire, who acknowledges to have been inspired by an earlier seminal article supporting the development of such perspective (Fine and Fischer Leighton 1993), compares psychoanalysis to the thorns and dragon that impede access to the fairy-tale castle, meaning that it operates as an actual obstacle to the dream as an object of study. This is, inter alia, because the Freudian paradigm interprets dreaming solely as the fulfilment of an unsatisfied wish or desire, whereas dreams express much else: from present or anticipated fears, to the revisiting of past traumatic experiences or the facing of problems in daily life (Lahire 2020: 237–42; Mazurel 2022: 509). And this is also because it assumes a generalised operating of systems of self-censorship, while oneiric self-expression may offer individuals potentials they would not enjoy in other ways.

Building on the viewpoints and findings of both Burke and Lahire, Hervé Mazurel (2022: 498–535) has recently discussed the case of dreams within his more ambitious reflections on the history of the unconscious. He is no less critical than his predecessors of psychoanalysis's essentialism; however, with the inclination to historicise the question more than a sociologist would do, he cannot rule out that the Freudian combination of desire-cum-repression may prove to effectively interpret the human experience in a specific context and at a given time, while being inadequate if generalised.[1]

Distinctions such as those between dreams and visions, as well as any other articulation of the notion of dream in subcategories, are clearly culturally specific; therefore, a cultural analysis of the phenomenon cannot exclude any of them categorically, as most neighbouring experiences will have to be considered in order to establish definitions, verify differences, similarities and overlaps of meaning and/or value (Van Deusen 2010).

As I anticipated, the focus of this study is the written culture produced and circulating in Western Europe, with particular emphasis on the material that became available after the introduction of the printing press, until the first quarter of the seventeenth century. Chronologies have necessarily to be kept slightly fuzzy, considering the interlacing and overlapping of cultural phenomena across areas and disciplines, and adapted to the object of one's enquiry. Both ends of a chosen timeline require some degree of justification. The "Gutenberg galaxy" offers itself fairly easily as a turning point that, even if not substituting oral and manuscript communication altogether, intervened to significantly reshape the materiality of written texts, their audiences, uses and reception. Combined with the development of humanist practices – the search and passion for ancient texts and reinforced philological skills in reconstructing and interpreting them – the printing press offered to the ensuing generations of writers and readers a powerful platform on which to develop and also share information and opinions on the dreamworld. The Renaissance of this book's title, therefore, is not just a traditional (and potentially outmoded, if not controversial) name for a period in general history, but rather a more specific reference to a cultural milieu in which Classical texts and monuments provided powerful intellectual inspiration and cultural models. A hypothetical subtitle "from Ficino to Descartes" would carry excessive emphasis on philosophy, thus giving a wrong impression of the content, but would indicate a working chronology and rationale of the chronological termini, as the Neoplatonists made an impact by circulating influential classical texts, whereas the birth of early modern rationalism engages with epistemological questions concerning the truth and reliability of vision that are indebted to tradition while renovating it. The Reformation offers another obvious landmark as the religious renewal and controversies that followed it inevitably impacted on the evaluation of the prophetic value of dreams that had accompanied the Western tradition, among others, since Antiquity. There will be the opportunity to discuss the relationship that this story had with other major historical developments of the time – voyages and discoveries, just to mention one of the most obvious.

As centuries of historiography have by now attested and debated, the story (of humanism and the Renaissance) found a special cultivation medium in late fourteenth- and fifteenth-century Italy. However, this role of a geographic area in the Mediterranean only emerged due to the connections that it entertained with other parts of the world, and in particular with Byzantine and Arabic traditions, which had transmitted and re-elaborated much knowledge from Antiquity; and its subsequent diffusion, to form the shared culture of much of sixteenth-century Europe in a variety of social milieus, can be properly appreciated if due importance is given to adaptation and the interactive nature of cultural exchanges, rather than imagining it as passive reception (Burke 1998; Brotton 2006). The circulation of oneirological texts will provide yet another example of such cultural dynamics. For the purpose of this book, exceedingly technical language will be avoided. Nevertheless, as well as speaking repeatedly of dream cultures, I will make use of the terms (and related adjectives) *oneiromancy*, to refer to the practice or discipline of interpreting dreams, and *oneirocritics* (or *oneirology*), for the writing about it. On the notion of dream culture itself, the reader will also find some background information in the final historiographical section.

Note

1 For a recent critique of Sigmund Freud's *Interpretation of Dreams*, see Sugarman 2023; on the questions arising from the difference between modern and ancient dream interpretations, see Price 1986.

2
THEMES

Leading emotion historian Barbara Rosenwein has arranged her book on *Love* (2022) around "five fantasies" – that is, like-minded union, transcendent rapture, selfless giving, obsessive longing and insatiable desire – which she encountered and followed across epochs and cultures. The present book is organised along different lines. Nevertheless, it is tempting to wonder what narratives about dreams could prove promising if adopting a structure inspired by Rosenwein's choice of themes. Some that seem plausible would presumably include the following.

2.1 Dream as premonition

As it is regularly mentioned in the relevant literature, a paradigm shift that separates the modern, particularly post-Freudian, understanding of the meaning of dreams from that which preceded it, is that we tend to conceive of them as potentially informing us about the past, whereas our ancestors took them seriously as signs alerting about the future.[1] This forward orientation presented various facets, usually widespread in both learned and popular culture, such as medical prognosis (the dream as a way of identifying an illness and/or predicting its outcome) and prophecy (future telling in general and the dramatic developments of its religious forms, in particular in an age of crisis and reformation as the sixteenth century – Niccoli 1990). Much scholarly debate, in a long philosophical tradition that had its roots in Ancient Greece and continued over the centuries between the Near East and Europe, concerns a distinction between true and false dreams that presented themselves as potentially prophetic, the conditions that affected their reliability and the rules that governed their deciphering. We will encounter several attempts to tackle these interconnected challenges. Whatever their recognised epistemological status, prophetic dreams and dreams of death enjoyed also a life as theatrical stratagems from Classical Antiquity to Italian Renaissance drama and Shakespeare's plays, with cultural variations that were affected by the emerging religious divides (Montanari 2022, with a scheme of a standard sequence, including the anxiety expressed by a character about their recent dream, its recounting and the subsequent acceptance or denial on the basis of a general rejection of the reliability of night visions – a pattern that Shakespeare effectively challenged; for a psychologist's reading of Shakespearean dreams: Bulkeley 2020; the literature on the Bard is predictably extensive).

2.2 Dream as deception

The fact that the oneiric experience resembles real life and deceives the dreamer to believe that it is all actually happening has brought the term to work as a synonym for falsehood and deceit. There was also a theological tradition, partly due to overlapping and confusion with classical elements, that explained such deception as the working of the devil. Congruently, false dreams could be regarded as the effect of enchantment. If academic debates were not interested in the subject, the connection was explored by medieval literature, since the condition of being enchanted may offer a useful plot, being comparable to the deceptiveness of being in a dream without realising that what one senses is not true (Olsan 2010).

A variation on this theme is the ubiquitous commonplace stating that life is but a dream, meaning deceit. Since one of its most programmatic assertions in Western literature is Pedro Calderón de la Barca's play *La vida es sueño* (1636), literary criticism on this masterpiece of Spanish drama has a tradition of reconstructing the intellectual history of the idea and its cultural metamorphoses. Already a century ago, it has been claimed that the topos has oriental origins in ancient India and in the notion of maya, a concept that became familiar in the Western tradition particularly after its adoption within the philosophy of Arthur Schopenhauer, to indicate the veil behind which reality hides. More recent studies have traced it possibly even further back to shamanism (Farinelli 1916; Domínguez Leiva 2007). The late medieval re-elaboration of classical and Christian traditions (including the *contemptus mundi*, the debasing of this vale of tears as not the real world, part of a Catholic pastoral of fear: Delumeau 1990) found one of its most programmatic expressions in Francesco Petrarca. It is found at the end of the opening sonnet of his *Canzoniere*, with which Petrarch reinvented Western love poetry ("as I clearly know/that what we love of life is but a dream"), and in the stoic moral philosophy of his *De remediis*, extremely influential dialogues, widely translated and read for centuries. Here, Book 1 (Remedies for prosperity) includes a chapter (90) on tranquillity, in which Joy keeps repeating to have toiled the whole life and deserve rest, whereas Reason highlights the risks that this may bring; Book 2 (Remedies for adversities) has chapters on insomnia and nightmares (86–7), with Sorrow complaining of losing sleep and Reason praising what can be done in wakefulness. Rather than to life, by the way, sleep here, in compliance with another commonplace, is equated to death: "sleepe is a short death, and death a long and everlasting sleepe" (Elizabethan translation in Petrarca 1579: 269r).

Calderón's plot has been told as follows:

> since childhood, Sigismond has been imprisoned by his father, the king of Poland, in an isolated tower. His father makes him drink a certain drug which puts him to sleep. He is then carried into the royal palace where he wakes up luxuriously dressed and, by order of his father who wishes to put him to the test, is treated as a sovereign by all the courtiers. Sigismond at first wonders whether he is not perhaps dreaming; then, taking confidence, he quickly shows himself to be brutal and headstrong, cruel and tyrannical. The proof is conclusive: the young man – being given once more the same narcotic – finds himself that same day back in his prison, dressed in his accustomed rags. His warder has no difficulty in persuading him that he has only dreamed the miraculous interlude. A popular uprising later sets him free and for the second time he is given unlimited power. However, he believes that now for the second time he is only experiencing a dream, that the glittering show will vanish away, and he will find himself once more in his dungeon. This time, of course, nothing of the sort is true, but now Sigismond knows that all of life is only a dream and dreams themselves are also dreams.
>
> *(Caillois 1963b: XXVI–XXVII)*

Among the parallels and precedents of this deliberate playing with the confusion between dreamworld and reality, one could cite the tale – retold, among others, by Marco Polo – of Hassan-i-Sabbah ("the Old Man of the Mountain"), the founder of the Isma'ili sect (aka the Assassins), who allegedly drugged his most devote followers with hashish, let them experience sensual delights, only to subsequently convince them that it had only been a dream, and they had sensed in anticipation the pleasures that were waiting for them in Paradise. Roger Caillois, from whom I have taken the above summary of *La vida es sueño*, wondered if Calderón had been inspired by the reading of Polo, or else an even more remarkable similarity had occurred without direct influence.

Arguably the most popular of the Italian *novelle*, the tale of a *beffa*, or practical joke, also resorts to a similar stratagem. The fact that the prominent Florentine artists Filippo Brunelleschi and Donatello appear as participants may well have contributed to its fame. The victim is the woodcarver Manetto, nicknamed as "fatty" (*il grasso legnaiuolo*), who once failed to turn up at a dinner with his mates, who therefore plan their revenge. The group sets up a day-long misidentification of *il grasso* with another person, with accuses of wrongdoing that end him up overnight in jail. Since nobody believes his statements of his real identity, the unfortunate ends up having himself doubts. When the next day he is universally recognised for himself, he at first thinks of having dreamt the bad experience, until it becomes clear that it was a hoax. Pretty vicious to modern sensitivities, the joke allegedly upset its victim so much that, embarrassed for having fallen for it, he left Florence the next day (Martines 2004: 169–241; Rochon 1974). The tale was very popular, circulating orally and in writing in different versions, including as an independent publication in print. Whatever degree of "reality" we may attribute to it, the anecdote fits nicely in, and corroborates, a number of cultural practices of the epoch: from the strength of the (male) companionships, not indifferent to class (while the brigade comprises people from different social ranks, it has been noticed that the victim of the joke is an artisan at the bottom of that range; to confirm the hierarchical distance, he and Brunelleschi even address each other with different pronouns), to the role and frequency of practical jokes, a key dimension of Renaissance ludic cultures (Burke 2021: 40–73). Also, it has been intriguingly and effectively cited as a telling tale of the complexities of personal identities in an age that had limited means to attest them formally (Groebner 2004: 13–16). For our own scope here, it may testify to the fuzziness of the distinction between dreamed and real world, as well as to contemporary awareness and forms of negotiation with it.

The commonplace can also be found, for instance, in Michel de Montaigne's *Essais*, where the author poses the rhetorical question: "Why make we not a doubt whether our thinking and acting are but another dream; our waking, some other species of sleep?" (II.12, "An apology for Raymond Sebond", Montaigne 1603: 347; Mathieu-Castellani 1990). Its tradition was entangled with others, such as the fugitivity of time or the vanity of all things (both a biblical and a Neoplatonic topos: Gandolfo 1978: 138–58). It further reverberated in literary and theatrical forms, by transporting on the scene or plot the ontological doubts on the possibility to detect reality and distinguishing it from fiction – doubts that, as is known, René Descartes was going to exploit at the heart of his epistemological foundation of modern thought and science (Cavaillé 2003; Domínguez Leiva 2007). Considering that demonology, the literature concerning witchcraft, was the field of early modern scholarship in which reflections on the value of dreams and preoccupation on the reliability of sensual perception converged more significantly than elsewhere. I will return to the topic, in Section 8.11, when addressing that theme and genre of sources.

2.3 Dream as (compensatory) escape

On the other hand, the attractiveness of some dreamt visions may be in sharp contrast with the hardness of ordinary life and so, in a variety of cultural forms (as, just to mention one, the imagery of the Land of Cockaigne), offer itself as a surrogate substitution, psychological satisfaction of needs and wishes that remain unfulfilled. In this topos, some degree of interchangeability between dreamworld and reality exists as in the previous one; however, emphasis is on contrast, on the imagined life as one we would willingly swap with the real one. Utopias of various strands – political and religious, among others – offer obvious examples. But their relationship with the real does not stop there, as ideas can lead people to action and contribute to change the world, in an attempt to make (collective as well as individual) dreams come true ("I have a dream …"). Thus, Johan Huizinga's influential study of forms of life and thought of the fourteenth and fifteenth centuries in France and the Low Countries defined the chivalric component of those forms as "the heroic dream";[2] Guido Ruggiero has spoken of the Italian Renaissance society's utopian reconfigurations in term of dreams, and even "re-dreams" when, as in the case of Niccolò Machiavelli and Baldassarre Castiglione early in the sixteenth century, the return to past virtues and glories of a culture in time of crisis had already taken the nostalgic connotation of the praise of an irretrievable lost world (Ruggiero 2015: 438–88); and, witnessing an evocative though perhaps more vague use of the term, a prominent art historian has entitled "Renaissance dream" her commentary on the sexual imageries of Titian and Michelangelo (Goffen 1987).

If in Thomas More's invention of the genre the man-made island is visited by way of traveling, there are sixteenth-century utopias where the described alternative world is instead reached via dreaming. This is the case for *I Mondi* (The Worlds, 1552) by the humanist Anton Francesco Doni, who few years earlier had edited the Italian translation of More; his work later circulated also in French. The text inherits from Erasmus the game play between a wise and a fool interlocutor. What may matter more here, however, is the fact that the oneiric access to a better world is not played to create cognitive confusion, but rather by warning the reader and carefully monitoring the boundaries between real and unreal, rational and irrational (Sellevold 2016).

2.4 Dreamworld and self-knowledge

Although a specific and deeply rooted sense in which today we tend to assume that the content of the oneiric experience reveals something significant about the dreamer only dates to modern psychoanalysis, there are various other ways in which past cultures did that also. One of the obvious, as we will see, was the medical discourse. But the period has good reasons to be regarded as one in which metamorphoses of the notion and practices of the self, which had to do with a multiplicity of contemporary social and cultural developments, also influenced people's dreamlife and came to entrust it with renewed meanings and importance. This could prove an interesting addition to the already-rich palette of the development of the individual and of identity, which has been at the core of the historiographical concept of the Renaissance since its nineteenth-century invention (Farr 2020; Giglioni 2022).

The development of a sense of some complex and distinguished individuality that appears to have moved some steps forward during the period under examination should not be confused and identified with the fact that much earlier doctrines and procedures, including oneirocritics, already distinguished the meaning and effect that anything had on people according to their legal and social status, gender, humoral complexion and the rest. All such dichotomies were applied separately – say, by Artemidorus – and the person in question would be positioned in the right box in each case; but they did not sum up to make a whole multifaceted identity (Thonemann 2020b: XX).

Notes

1 For a challenge to this neat distinction, suggesting that elements of the dream experience ordinarily associated with modernity – subjectivity and a reconsideration of the past – were already present in the early modern period, see Hodgkin 2008 (based on sources from the English Civil War).
2 The title of Chapter 3 in the first editions of *Autumn of the Middle Ages* (Huizinga 1996: 61–125); subsequently, the author split the book's content differently and "Dreams of Heroic Deeds and Love" became the title of the new Chapter 5 (Huizinga 2020: 106–21). I am grateful to Graeme Small for detailed information on the editorial history of the text; he also provides it in Small 2020: 574.

3
LES MOTS ET LES CHOSES (AN INTERMEZZO ON VOCABULARY)

As for many other domains within cultural history, if not in cultural history in general, the study of dreams needs to consider the historical semantics of the very vocabulary with which we name the object and define the nature and limits of our analysis. Thus, it will be worth saying something about the vocabulary of dreams in a sample of ancient and modern European languages, to help identifying – more accurately than one does by mere common sense – the spectrum of human experiences they used to define, as well as the cultural attitudes they tended to associate with them. This consideration for words and meanings, and their dynamics in historical contexts, will also help in defining what this book takes into consideration, what else it excludes or leaves at the margins of analysis. The distinction between dreams and visions is one of the first and most important that comes to mind. A caveat: definition is not a precise science, semantics a fuzzy field, and although it is appropriate to distinguish some concepts from one another, it may be unwise to consider them independently, for their story is to a significant degree symbiotic.

If we begin with Greek and Latin, we find that ancient authors of dream literature adopted a terminology that reflected some cultural distinctions. Firstly, we should be aware that we think of dreams as "series of events with a loose narrative structure" (Gregoric and Fink 2022: 9), whereas ancient terms tended to refer and apply to individual images: "this explains why a dream is described as an appearance (*phántasma*)" (ibid.). Also:

> while in English we would naturally speak of having a dream, the Greeks instead speak more with emphasis on the visual rather than the possessive, i.e. I see a dream … or it seems a dream appears … In this way, the subject

DOI: 10.4324/9781003279709-3

of the dream is implicitly separated from the individual themselves; the dream is witnessed, not created, by the dreamer.

(Holton 2022: 12)

In archaic and Classic Greek, sleep was expressed by the noun *hýpnos*, also personified as the name of the god responsible for it. Three main terms for dream were largely interchangeable: *óneiros* (the standard word for "the Homeric dream, looming over the sleeper to deliver a message"), *enýpnion* (the term preferred by the Hippocratic writers and by Aristotle), and *ónar* (ibid. 10–12). Among late-antique sources, Artemidorus noticeably introduced a distinction between *enýpnia*, dreams that merely expressed anxieties and desires of a person unable to control their thoughts, therefore only referring to the present, and *óneiroi*, that preannounced the future either explicitly or allusively – and it was the latter case that offered the cultural justification for an art of deciphering symbols. A couple of centuries later, another author who subsequently, in the sixteenth century, enjoyed a renaissance, Synesius, showed a different orientation by adopting as his key term *enýpnia*, which his predecessor had marginalised as meaningless.

One of the most influential texts in the Western tradition was Macrobius's commentary on the *Dream of Scipio*, reported by Cicero at the end of his *Republic*. It used the umbrella term *somnium*, only to apply it to a variety of phenomena that bore specific names and values. Consistently with the bipartition we have found in the Greek vocabulary and critical tradition, a group of them was regarded as meaningless: the *insomnium* of physical or psychic origin, expressing bodily needs or wakeful concerns; *visum*, a borderline experience between wakefulness and deep sleep; and similarly *ephialtes*, a nightmare provoked by a demon (not categorised as a species of dream, but as a distinct phenomenon). Conversely, truthful dreams comprised *somnium* proper, which was symbolic; *visio*, clear prefiguration of reality; and *oraculum*, advice or instruction provided by a respectable persona (Kruger 1992: 23). Of these terms, modern languages have retained derivatives of *somnium* (as in French, Italian and Spanish), the only family of words that has kept a relation of meaning with the oneiric experience, while *vision* and *oracle* have lost it (Demaules 2016b: 9–10; see also Schalk 1955). While Byzantine text of oneirocritics tended to use the key terms as interchangeable (Timotin 2016: 51), Macrobius's terminology and classification was again standard in the Renaissance. In fact, sixteenth-century vernaculars struggled to translate classical terms and concepts, since they had not yet developed adequate equivalents and subtle nuances.

In sixteenth-century French, *songe* is the all-inclusive noun referring to every mental activity that takes place during sleep, as well as the images produced during such activity. For extension, it was used metaphorically to refer to activities and products that were understood to share characteristics with the oneiric experience; this metaphorical sense had negative connotations, implying precariousness and fallibility. *Rêve* emerged during the seventeenth century to satisfy the need to refer to oneiric phenomena without such connotations. Meanwhile, *rêverie* was abandoning an original pathological value that connected it to delirium, to acquire, already in the writing of Michel de Montaigne, a sense of disorderly but free and potentially deep wandering of the mind (Gautier 1988b: 9; Bokdam 2012: 9–13).

The Italian vocabulary, following the Latin *somnium*, resorted mainly to the noun *sogno* and the verb *sognare*. Some of their connotations may be noted by looking at their attested values beyond the most obvious literal meaning. The noun could stand for "fallacious, illusory appearance", or "fanciful hypothesis, thesis without foundation; unfounded news"; the verb could stand for "to imagine unreal, non-existing things, people and facts; to glimpse them with one's imagination; to presume they may exist or happen", as well as "to follow images created in one's own fantasy; to confuse reality with imagination; to fantasize, to rave". Thus, John Florio's 1611 *Queen Anna's New World of Words* translates *sogno* as "a dreame, a vision or raving in ones sleepe, a vanitie not likely to be true" (Arcangeli 2024).

Neighbouring vocabulary included, for instance, the Italian *chimera*, which Florio in the first 1598 edition of his dictionary registers in the plural (*chimere*), and in the expanded one of 1611 renders as "a chimere, a monster, a foolish imagination, or castle in the ayre", in an entry paralleled by a related verb ("*chimerizzare*: to rave or build castles in the aire").

In the Germanic languages, German *Traum*, Duch *droom* and English *dream* (with noun and verb both attested from c. 1200 CE) are etymologically connected to a root referring to "phantom, illusion".

As Macrobius's classification has already allowed us to surmise and appreciate for its implications on the evaluation of oneiric experiences, the condition of being asleep does not necessarily present a clear-cut distinction from wakefulness. Languages and literatures show awareness of the existence of a grey zone, the state of being half-asleep – a liminal position which plays a paramount role in allowing the consciousness, while emerging from the torpor of the senses, to grasp the desirable yet fugitive dreamt images, before they vanish for good. The fourteenth-century poet and composer Guillaume de Machaut, among others, called it *dorveille* (Schmitt 2007: 234); current Italian retains the equivalent hybrid *dormiveglia*. It may be worth mentioning in passing that research on sleep is related to, though wider and distinguishable from that on dream. In fact, specialists of the former tend to lament that dream monopolises scholarly and general attention. Still, the topic is probably an understudied treasure trove. In the medical discourse, the correct alternation between sleep and wakefulness represented one of the six non-naturals, the lifestyle conditions to be kept under control if one wanted to remain in good health (on which see below).

The case of nightmare is particular. The French term *cauchemar* appears in the fourteenth century to indicate a nocturnal ghost, a demon, an aetiology that moved on, over the subsequent two centuries, to be applied to witches (Closson 2016). Nevertheless, some scholars observed that from this lack of specific name we cannot infer that the experience of stressful dreams dominated by anguish was absent (Demaules 2016b: 9). Others, instead, emphasise the fact that the affective state of the dreamer came to work as a differentiating factor in our distinction between dream and nightmare only two centuries ago, thus suggesting that it was not estimated as a significant element in classification before modern times.

To sum up, a whole spectrum of activities from dreams to wakeful thinking and various neighbouring sensorial phenomena need to be considered by dream research, as the way they are divided into discrete realities and evaluated has shown much cultural variation.

In addition to the elements of classification and evaluation that were attached as connotations to the use of particular terms, classification may differentiate between different types of oneiric experiences, whatever their names. We will encounter physicians and philosophers distinguishing between different varieties. Such categories too reveal tradition and innovation.

4
CONTEXTS

4.1 Night

Despite references to daytime visions and other dreamlike experiences, the story told by this book took place predominantly at night. Unsurprisingly, the alternating of light and darkness is not simply a given natural fact: it is embedded in human history, both in the sense that technology and social practices in general have affected the way they have appeared and been perceived by women and men throughout the centuries and, more specifically, in the sense that meanings and values have been attached to them, and the night has been the locus of specific experiences in a variety of contexts. It is very helpful, therefore, that its cultural history has been fruitfully explored. If over the whole early modern period a process of progressive "nocturnalisation" has been identified, with an expansion of socially approved activities later in the day, ultimately permitted by the adoption of artificial light (Koslofsky 2011), one should not infer that attitudes towards darkness had been invariably negative and it was only question of conquer and enlighten it. The vision of the unpolluted starred sky was – and must still be, somewhere – an experience inspiring awe and reflection. If the classical (and, later, humanist) tradition tended to polarise between the fears and transgressions associated with night time and the worth entrusted on light and clarity, at least the influence of the Bible is understood to have introduced a more balanced evaluation: both day and night were a divine creation and therefore enjoyed an equal status; furthermore, they did not need to be understood in opposition, but rather as complementary, in a cyclical succession that required both. The night was also perceived as a particularly apt time for self-perception and reflection, prayer, study and artistic creativity (Ekirch 2005; Ménager 2005).

16 Contexts

Sculpture would appear to allow to represent more easily a sleeping figure rather than their dreams. The complexity of the cultural meanings that the world of the Renaissance could symbolically attribute to the night is aptly exemplified by a statue created by Michelangelo and so entitled by himself (see Figure 4.1). It is part of the funerary monuments he designed and realised (though partly left unfinished) for some of the Medici rulers of Florence by the mid-1530s in the Sagrestia Nuova of San Lorenzo – in particular, the tomb of Giuliano de' Medici, Duke of Nemours and brother of Pope Leo X (1479–1516). In the lack of a fully documented plan, both the overall iconographic design and the meaning of specific details are open to interpretation. Nevertheless, contemporary commentaries suggest that the pairing of representations of day and night allude to the inexorable passing of time; and the attributes the sleeping female figure is endowed with carry several symbolic connections. On a diadem on her head, she bears the crescent moon and a star, whereas the reclining male Day at the other end of the tomb has the rays

FIGURE 4.1   Michelangelo Buonarroti, "Allegory of The Night", Mausoleum of Giuliano de' Medici, Florence (marble statue, 1531). The image became the subject of a tradition of copies, both in sculpture and in painting – a practice helped by the fact that in the 1560s the Sagrestia Nuova hosted the Florentine Academy of the arts of drawing, whose pupils had the opportunity to observe the masterpieces (Rabbi Bernard, Cecchi and Hersant 2013: 62–7). © Luisa Ricciarini/ Bridgeman Images.

of the sun. The allegoric implications of the cosmologic iconography of the whole room have been connected to the world of Renaissance Neoplatonism. Despite traditional dualist associations of positive and masculine qualities to the day, negative and feminine to the night, the latter connotation is not convincingly at stake here. The Night is accompanied by an owl, the nocturnal bird sacred to Minerva, which contemporary emblem books associated with reason; by poppy pods, which procure sleep and were recommended for that purpose in the Orphic hymns translated by Marsilio Ficino; and by a mask, the most complex of the symbols. It has often been alleged to represent the deceptive nature of dreams but was not necessary implying that: its classical connection with funerary rituals would suggest that it alludes to death, though not quite in negative terms. In one of his sonnets, Michelangelo described the night as a "sweet time" (*dolce tempo*); even a reference to death may point at a mystical and magical image of renewal and rediscovery of the divine (Gandolfo 1978: 113–38). In parallel, for instance, hymns to the night and winter echoed in French poetry (Ménager 2005).

Night, sleep and dreams had traditionally ways to be of some relevance in legal matters too. In late medieval Italian towns, the night is defined by convention, not by nature, as the interval between two instances of bell ringing; and during that time things follow different regulations, some activities normal in daytime are not permitted, or else doing them at night automatically acquires the stigma of an aggravating circumstance – a suspicion on the part of local disciplining authorities that will last for the whole seventeenth century (Sbriccoli 1991b). As in folklore and short stories, a dream could reveal events or the location of things to be found significant to the outcome of a trial. Also, a recognised status of been asleep or dreaming had a direct impact on the culpability of a suspect. The French jurist (and friend of François Rabelais) André Tiraqueau accepted the received thesis that, if someone committed a crime while asleep, they were not punishable, their condition being assimilable to that of a person insane or deprived of mind. The logic of this exclusion from culpability, derived from theology, was that every sin is such as the result of a rational decision, and someone who is asleep is in no condition to make one (Tiraqueau 1986: 59–61; Boulet-Sautel 1988).

4.2 Sleep

Sleep was the object of philosophical and medical attention, from Antiquity to the Renaissance (Leroux, Palmieri and Pigné 2015). Its proximity to the subject of sleep is witnessed also by the similarity of the two Latin terms, *somnus* (sleep) and *somnium* (dream), and consequent relative ambiguity of which of the two is in question. The amount of sleep appropriate to each category of person was assessed depending on variables, the principal one being age – children needing more, the elderly less. Despite disapproving of it, Cipriano Giambelli (1589*: 29), the author of a vernacular dialogue, which will be described in Chapter 7, quotes a popular saying (*opinione del vulgo*), according to which "the student sleeps six hours, the workman seven, the sleepyhead (*dormiglione*) eight, the lazybones (*poltrone*) nine". Napoleon is accredited with the variation "six for a man, seven for a woman and eight for a fool" (Edwards 2018: 202).

In the Hippocratic-Galenic tradition, sleep and wakefulness represented one of the so-called six non-naturals, the others being air (a label for environment in general), food and drink, retention and evacuation, exercise and rest, and the passions of the mind. The logic of this list, the produce of medieval Arabic re-elaboration of Galen's thought, was to provide a comprehensive picture of factors that affect an individual's health, and that he or she could control, considered that a balanced regimen would insure a good physical condition and therefore prevent the onset of any pathology (Cavallo and Storey 2013). Within the context of humoral physiology, with the dominant role it tributed to what was ingested in, and expelled from, the body as factors influencing health and illness, sleep too was assessed primarily in relation to digestion, on matter of its timing as well as for many other conditions. The dominance of this preoccupation over the medical advice on good health brought not only a prevailing recommendation to sleep on one's side but also the suggestion on which side to start with, and when to swap overnight, in order to best facilitate the process. The humoral body is one in serious danger if digestion is interrupted or not completed properly.

There is evidence that cultural practices concerning sleeping underwent significant shifts during the epoch considered. On the basis of diaries and images from Continental Europe, Roger Ekirch has claimed that it was customary at the time to split night-time sleep in two parts, separated by a pause in which it was common to tell one another's dreams; documentation from elsewhere has not corroborated the diffusion of such a practice (Ekirch 2001, 2005; Gantet 2021: 127). Most people still slept in the nude, although a shift or nightshirt was coming into use (Dannenfeldt 1986: 426). With focus on late Renaissance Rome, and combining information derived from a variety of sources, including the seventeenth-century correspondence of a specific family that had recently climbed into the local elite, Spada-Veralli, Sandra Cavallo and Tessa Storey have offered proof of a series of developments that appear to have taken place over a comparatively brief period, while being able to compare the instructions provided by prescriptive literature with testimony of their actual implementation. In general, sleep seems to have attracted increased attention and from the mid-sixteenth century also became the object of dedicated works by humanist scholars. Its regulation, the definition of what constitutes a healthy sleeping environment, came to be a matter of concern. Traditional advice warned against daytime sleep, which in general was allowed only for people of feeble constitution or in specific circumstances, as the long summer days. By the late sixteenth century, some degree of deregulation – on bedtime, the length of sleep and sleeping positions – seems to develop: naps are tolerated and, contrary to a previous tabu versus daytime horizontal resting, special furniture and rooms are set to allow it. Furthermore, a choice based on generations seems to enter the scene, with the young more prone to daytime laziness; also, by the beginning of the seventeenth century habits that are first documented at elite level appear to have spread down the social ladder to be taken up by their domestic servants. Despite medical and moral concerns for the risk of sleeping too much or too comfortably, the number of mattresses increase and the structure of the bedroom evolves: with the successful diffusion of the canopy, "the evolution in layout and furnishings of the bedroom testifies to its gradual transformation from a space for sleeping but also for family meals, musical performances, and social gatherings to a more private and individual space" (Cavallo and Storey 2013: 113–44, at 140; Cavallo 2021).[1]

The most extensive medical treatise of the period on sleep and wakefulness (350 pages in quarto) was published in 1556 by Giovanni Argenterio, a university physician who had recently moved from a teaching position in Pisa to one in Naples. From his preface, the author qualifies his topic as a complex one that had never before been assessed systematically and had not found past authorities in agreement: as well as to Aristotle and Galen, he refers to the tenets of comparatively early Greek philosophers and physicians, such as Alcmaeon of Croton, Empedocles, Diogenes (all of which related sleep to variations in the flux or temperature of blood), Plato and the stoics (who instead connected it to the spirits). The author proceeds from his authorities (Aristotle above all) and the interpretative tradition also when subsequently discussing a range of details of sleep and wakefulness: their definition, natural or preternatural causes, the differences between long and short sleep, as well as deep vs light, tranquil vs turbulent, continuous vs interrupted, with or without snoring, or else related phenomena such as coma and lethargy. In the second, slightly shorter part (book), Argenterio takes issues with the fact that the philosophical and medical tradition discussed the precise location of sleep and wakefulness within the body, whereas in his opinion such conditions affect it all and do not origin or reside in specific parts or functions.

It has been suggested that a process of medicalisation in the aetiology of dreams was also, by the late seventeenth century, the result of a decline in the belief in the supernatural, and search for natural causes, even if still within a predominantly traditional, humoral paradigm (Andries 1988, with reference to French pedlars' publications, though the comment could have wider application). If this was the case, medicine had an old and rich interpretative tradition to offer to new users.

4.3 Dreams, visions and prophecy

Throughout various ways of segmenting the oneiric experience by articulating it in more than one type and distinguishing it from neighbouring phenomena, the differentiation between dreams and visions has been one of the most widespread. Specialists have acknowledged, however, that it is not always easy to tell them apart (Freedberg 1999). One elementary way to do it is by locating the former at night, the latter in daytime. Albeit reductive (to state the obvious, one can dream during the day), it plays part in the more elaborate definitions that were provided through time.

A study of dream in the life and thought of Augustine suggests that both in the Bible and in Classical Antiquity the distinction was not clear; both forms were understood to be clearly inferior to the direct revelation such as that expressed by God to Moses and shared an enigmatic value. The terms appear interchangeable also in early Christian writing. Augustine classified them together as spiritual visions, inferior to the intellectual one. Differences however do emerge. In the ascetic experience of the early monasticism of the eastern Mediterranean world, mystics are alleged to have visions rather than dreams, visions being more commonly acknowledged as a divine gift, endowed after praying and fasting; there are also examples of physical exercises aimed at preventing them from falling asleep, although the resulting imagery could be interpreted as hallucination. But a clear statement of a hierarchy between the two would have to wait for Aquinas (Dulaey 1973: 49–55). Echoes of contrasting values associated with dreams and visions can be found in the Italian literary discourse where, in the 1570s and 1580s, a series of attacks on Dante criticised his poetry, inter alia, as the mere relating of a dream, whereas the erudite Jacopo Mazzoni repeatedly intervened in his defence and offered an elaborate exposition of what has to be understood for phantasy, vision and dream in the *Commedia*, which he denied could be dismissed as an oneiric experience (2017: 437ff.).[2]

Among the scriptural passages that encouraged comparative reflection on the two notions, Joel 2:28 reads in King James Version: "And it shall come to pass afterward, that I will pour out my spirit upon all flesh; and your sons and your daughters shall prophesy, your old men shall dream dreams, your young men shall see visions". The verse was the subject of sixteenth-century commentaries, prolonging an exegetic tradition. The interpreters tended to downplay the hierarchical difference between the two experiences: after all, they both worked as forms of communication between God and his prophets. Also, the distinction between ages (the old have dreams, the young visions) tended to be nuanced as a question of relative rather than absolute age. Others still read the passage allegorically. Thus, for Martin Luther, the list was a rhetorical figure of generality, suggesting that faithful of all ages are endowed with grace (Fragonard 1990).

Jean-Claude Schmitt has exposed the way the difference is remarked by Hildegard of Bingen. Interrogated about the nature of her visions, the twelfth-century mystic from Rhineland replied:

> that her spiritual visions have nothing in common with the dreams experienced in sleep and the dark of the night. She mistrusts dreams that are inspired by the devil, *fantasmata*, diabolical illusions that enter into the mind during sleep when the vigilance of reason lets down its guard. And she also insists on the fact that she received her visions in "open" places, not secret ones: she has witnesses.
> *(Schmitt 2010: 110–13)*

Hildegard further distinguished a third form of experience, "ecstasies of the mind", which she did not claim to have. Her refuse of dream offers a glimpse also of a potential gender divide in the medieval monastic relationship between autobiography and ecstasy: while nuns are described as only passive receivers of visions, monks dream, aware of the grace they are offered in their nocturnal experiences (Schmitt 2002a: 336–8).

The reference to ecstasy evokes altered states of consciousness. As we will see, authors differed in their attribution of a capability to experience truly prophetic dreams either to anyone or to selected few. When philosophers in the Neoplatonic tradition emphasised the peculiarity and exclusivity of the gift, as Iamblichus did in Late Antiquity (c. 300 CE) and Marsilio Ficino while exposing him in Renaissance Florence, dreamlike conditions that could facilitate the revelation of forms of divine knowledge could be identified in such experiences as "possessions of the eyes" or a "seizure similar to a blackout"; it has been noticed how the list closely resembles a potential one of symptoms of mental disorders (Giglioni 2016: 99).

Introducing a different element, a Renaissance source could argue that, if while dreaming we are aware to be dreaming, it means that not only the senses but also the intellect is operating, and that more properly qualifies as vision (Dottori 1575*: 11v).

A distinction can be made between dream and prophecy. In the tradition of biblical monotheism, and consequently also in Islam, the figure of the prophet, envoy and spokesman of God emerged. If in ancient Judaism prophecy maintained elements of prediction of future events, its focus was *kerygma*, the annunciation of the divine will and call. In contrast with the obscurity and enigma of dreams and omens, the prophetic word is clear: a call for deliberation. This does not mean, however, that prophetic dreams disappeared or lost all their value. Seventeenth-century rationalism undermined the reliability of both (Miegge 2005: 43). The metamorphoses of early modern prophecy in relation with religious and political developments have been noticeably reconstructed by Reinhart Koselleck (1985).

4.4 Imagination and the senses

The Renaissance has been identified as a period during which the concept and attributes of the imagination underwent fairly dramatic changes. In the combined philosophical and medical tradition – for which the most influential authorities were Aristotle, Galen and Ibn Sina (Avicenna, 980–1037 CE) – the imagination was one of the five internal senses, which were located in the cerebral ventricles. By the mid-sixteenth century, however, following advances in anatomy that challenged ancient beliefs in the location of faculties, and as a result of a process of simplification, it emerged as a unique mediator between body and soul, the material and the immaterial, acquiring major importance as a faculty that governs many human affairs. As by Aristotelian definition imagination is the faculty which retains absent objects and presents them as if they were present, it was acknowledged both with significant powers (of varying extension according to the individual writer) and the capability of error and deceit – a process that is clearly exemplified by the dream's appearance as reality (Park 1974). As the survey below will show, Aristotle and the Hippocratic tradition held different views on the strength of sense perception as experienced in dreaming. By the late sixteenth century, following Galen, imagination returned also to indicate, somewhat confusingly, together with reason and memory, one of the three parts of the rational soul.

Scholarship on the philosophical tradition of Neoplatonism has attracted attention to the difference it posited between what could be called *phantasia* and *imaginatio* (even though usage of the two terms varied): while the former defined the evanescent appearing of things as derived from the senses, the latter was intended to offer a stable vision of the intelligible forms, that is, of reality beyond sense-perception. In the complex interplay that the medical and philosophical traditions had identified between human faculties, Guido Giglioni has proposed an articulated set of three "laws" that tended to prevail, despite individual, disciplinary or school variations on the theme: an inverse proportionality between sentient and vegetative life, with the body understood the more vital the more the senses were dormant; an inverse proportionality between the senses and the intellect, which posited that the mind was sharper when the senses were less active; and a direct proportionality between imagination and desire, with phantasmatic representations making appetites more vigorous (Giglioni 2016: 96–7; on these concepts and vocabulary in Marsilio Ficino, Giglioni 2011; on their *longue durée*, Fattori and Bianchi 1988).

Notes

1 Handley 2016 focuses on developments the author dates at the mid-seventeenth century.
2 I owe this reference to an ongoing research project by Valentina Serio.

5
RECOVERING AND NEGOTIATING A LONG TRADITION

5.1 Some key ancient sources

The Renaissance inherited from Classical Antiquity a variety of myths and attitudes concerning dreams that amounted to a shared oneiric culture. The prophetic value of dreams took among others the form of the royal dream, which originated in the Ancient Near East and, via the Bible, was transmitted to medieval and Renaissance rulers, and normally accepted by contemporary intellectuals (Berriot 1990). At the heart of the whole textual body was an image that occurs in a passage from Book 19 of the *Odyssey*. Penelope tells her disguised husband a dream of hers, asking him to interpret it. When Odysseus suggests that it predicted his own imminent return and slaughter of the suitors, she is reluctant to accept it and tells him that dreams come through two different gates, either one of ivory that lets through false dreams, or one of horn that conveys true ones. Retold by Virgil and cited, among others, by Macrobius, the idea of the two gates could be found in many Renaissance authors, including Rabelais.[1] The interpretation of the passage proved enigmatic since Antiquity: Where did dreams come from, then? To what reality did the gate open? What was the precise value of dreams? At a more basic level, the story suggests a neat distinction between reliable and unreliable dreams: the prophetic nature of some of them is thus influentially attested, while at the same limiting it to some. The two materials of which the gates are made offer the matter for the differentiation: horn having the capability of being made so thin to be transparent, ivory always maintaining an intrinsic opacity; opacity, however, serving here not to mean concealed truth, but rather falsehood (Auger 2021). The materials have been noted also for reversing, in this role, their value as goods: the poor element is truthful; the

DOI: 10.4324/9781003279709-5

rich one deceives. Many other readings have been suggested, including the idea that the two materials may allude metonymically at an opposition between words and deeds – though this would lead us away from dream theory (Haller 2009).

At the level of transfer of knowledge, one of the reasons for the focus on the Renaissance is the fact that the humanist passion for everything ancient, the hunt for classical books and their subsequent ample circulation in their original languages and in translations, as well as prolonging the shelf life and widening the familiarity of texts that had been already available throughout the Middle Ages, allowed for nearly forgotten ones to re-emerge and come to occupy centre stage in the public perception and discussion of the theme. This is exactly the case for Artemidorus and his sixteenth-century revival. His book of dreams was, however, neither the earliest nor the only ancient text on the subject to exercise significant influence on the Mediterranean and European medieval and early modern cultural traditions. A representative selection of a wider family of sources, some of which circulated as groups or coupled with one another, originally written between c. 400 BCE and 400 CE, should enlist at least the following:

1   Considering that medicine was since Antiquity one of the most prominent disciplinary areas that dealt with the understanding of the nature and functioning of the human body, it will not come as a surprise to acknowledge that the earliest extant treatise about dreams is Book 4 of the Hippocratic *On Regimen* (text and translation in Hippocrates 1931). Often regarded as a spurious addition to the rest of the work or disputed in its authorship and relevance, it can instead be regarded as an important and systematic early assessment of the significance of sleep and dreams for health. Its Renaissance circulation as an autonomous tract owes something to the period's interest for the subject but also to some characteristics of the manuscript tradition (Roselli 1995: 141–2). The fact that it treats sleep and dreams together is a common feature of ancient Greek natural philosophy, which will be inherited by the ensuing tradition; the text has been the object of renewed scholarly attention in the context of a reappreciation of the importance of the theme in early Greek thought, Presocratic as well as Hippocratic (Holton 2022).

    Datable to the end of the fifth or the beginning of the fourth century BCE, the book, as the whole treatise and the Hippocratic approach in general, marks a move away from the entrusting of health care to specialists, by exposing a doctrine that may guide the educated readers to self-help: as we already mentioned, following a correct regimen may effectively allow one to prevent the development of illnesses. Dreams in particular may prove useful in early diagnosis. The departure from traditional reliance on magico-religious men and healers is made explicit by distinguishing clearly the medically prognostic dream from those that may have divine nature and consequently be open to correct interpretation by a specialisation in dealing with the sacred. The physiology supported by the book is particular in claiming that, detached from the body, the sleeping and dreaming soul is exposed to freer and enhanced sensory experience.

The author further differentiates between different subgenres of dreams. Since *On Regimen* is a unique Hippocratic text in recurring to a theory of correlation between micro- and macrocosm, some of these categories (dreaming of cosmologic bodies, or of the natural environment) are explained on the basis of such connection (Jouanna 1998). The emphasis on star dreaming was still perceivable in the most extensive sixteenth-century commentary on the Hippocratic text, written by Julius Caesar Scaliger (La Garanderie 1990). If one dreams of heavenly bodies according to the appearance, disposition and movement they normally have, that signals good health; if otherwise, it indicates some psychological problems that may be redressed by watching comic or delightful things.[2]

Other dreams are understood as day residue: thus, reviving in dream daily activities, including thought, is regarded as a good sign, at least if the order of the events is maintained (a reverse ordering, instead, signals trouble). Dreaming of clothing ("possessing white clothes and the most beautiful shoes, is good") or of the dead (also, according to their attire) is interpreted symbolically; dreaming one's ordinary activities is a sign of desire and of eating ordinary food the symptom of insufficient nutrition. In addition, the tradition attributed to Galen a short treatise (sometimes labelled as a fragment) *On Diagnosis from Dreams*, which, summarising in Late Antiquity the medical knowledge of his predecessors, also read the dreams understood as originating from the body in terms of the physical condition they may reveal or of the cure they may suggest, while acknowledging the divine origin of some of them (Oberhelman 1983; Pigeaud 1995: 34–40; Barras 2016). Galen's own choice to study medicine, apparently, had been determined by a dream of his father's, who believed in them.

2 Next, chronologically – approximately a couple of generations later – as well as logically, came the assessment given to the topic by Aristotle. Of his seven small treatises on natural philosophy (*Parva naturalia*), three dealt, respectively, *On Sleep and Waking*, *On Dreams* and *On Prophecy Through Sleep*, thus testifying to a significant interest to the overall topic (Aristotle 2018: 104–25). They form a rather coherent group, to the extent that they have occasionally been regarded as three parts of a sole book. In the first instance, the philosopher defined who experiences sleep (humans and animals) and what purpose it serves. Aristotle's method guided him to define, from the beginning, which part of the soul is protagonist of the experience:

it is the perceptual part, and in particular the "common sense" that coordinates all the specific ones. He placed it in the heart, and his aetiology of sleep linked it to the daily flow of blood from and to centre and periphery and its renovation by nutrition; the scope or function of sleep was to rest the body and restore its consumable capability of movement and perception. Aristotle never quite stated an equivalent functional reason behind dreaming, which he identifies as the perception of earlier appearances when the senses are almost entirely inactive. Contrary to the Hippocratic author, Aristotle regarded these non-actually sense-perceived appearances feebler than normal and, consequently, in the absence of inputs from other cognitive capacities, potentially vague or deceptive. A central argument of his on this front is the doubt on the actual existence and reliability of prophetic dreams. He rejected the popular conviction of the divine origin of prophecies, claiming boldly that, if the gods wanted to send a message, they would select worthy recipients and not choose the night as the most apt time to communicate, and distinguished between different ways in which a dream may come true. A dream can be the cause of the event that makes it true, as in the case in which we are reminded to do something. Or it can be a sign, as with the first perceptions of a developing illness. They are both explained in terms of natural philosophy without leaving anything mysterious or requiring resorting to the supernatural. More ambiguous is the case of a third type, the coincidental match between dream and event, which as such does not allow prediction. Here the Greek philosopher admitted that there is room for strangeness, while statistically assigning to individuals who sleep a lot – a habit correlated to a melancholic complexion – higher chances to have such sort of dreams; images by which Aristotle expressed this simple notion of probability were the increasing likelihood to win by someone who plays repeatedly games or chance, or by an archer to hit the target after many attempts (the latter, subsequently reproposed by Cicero and Schopenhauer: Pigeaud 1995: 46–8).[3] Another telling parallel Aristotle made, which links his physiology to themes explored by the medical tradition, is that between the images that appear in dreams and those an ill person can see while awake (Bolzoni 2013).

The treatises were the object of a medieval Arabic and Latin tradition of commentary and adaptation, the main alteration being the reinstating of the possibility of divinely inspired prophetic dreams. They were regular object of lectures within the arts curriculum of European universities until at least the end of the fifteenth century, and therefore familiar to anyone trained in philosophy (Gregoric and Fink 2022).

3 The variety of contexts in which classical culture confronted the range of questions at stake is revealed by Cicero's *Republic*, a dialogue written

in ideal conversation with the one by Plato with the same title, which has come down to us only fragmentarily, including, in its sixth and last book, a "Dream of Scipio" (*Somnium Scipionis*). Scipio Aemilianus hosts the fictional gathering that forms the setting for the conversations, and plays a dominant role, by advocating the superiority of practical life (civic duty in the service of the commonwealth) over the theoretical one. This may also be regarded as the key message of his narration of the appearance in sleep of his adoptive grandfather, Scipio Africanus, who foretells the grandson's future conquest of Carthage, encourages service to one's homeland as the highest goal and mentions eternal glory as its reward. The text, however, contains considerable other material, as cosmology, also in imitation of some of Plato's most ambitious myths, as the two Scipios discuss the structure of the universe, and much else, such as the immortality of the soul and the harmony of the spheres, a topos that was due to fascinate the imagination of Renaissance Neoplatonism. To add complexity to the source, in case it needed, one should add that Cicero was unusual in rejecting any predictive value of dreams in his *On Divination*.

Around 400 CE (i.e., nearly half a millennium later), the Neoplatonist writer Macrobius, one of the key figures in the late antique transmission of digested classical knowledge to the Middle Ages, wrote an extensive commentary to Cicero's dream. Following the text, it also dealt with a variety of scientific matters, including geography. There is a manuscript tradition of transmitting text and commentary together, and it is partly due to the success of Macrobius's work if the "Dream of Scipio" was the only part of Cicero's *Republic* known during the Middle Ages. If the dream itself is just a literary device, Macrobius's exegesis comprised a discussion of the nature and different types of dreams (see Chapter 3). His classification was not original, depending on Artemidorus and, possibly, on a Neoplatonic source that may now be lost, a circumstance which does not help any firm identification. By the end of the Middle Ages, Macrobius's classification and evaluation of dreams – partly via intermediaries including Isidore of Seville – had become the reference one in European culture (Macrobius 1952: 87–8).

4 The last two items in this list were the objects of rediscoveries and made their first appearance on the book market hand in hand. Written around 200 CE, Artemidorus's *Oneirocritica* (*Interpretation of Dreams*: Artemidorus 2020) is the only complete dream-book to have survived from Graeco-Roman Antiquity. It is the work of a professional dream interpreter based in Ephesus, a major port in the eastern Mediterranean, and intended to serve as a reference book for his colleagues; in fact, Books 4 and 5 are dedicated to his son and aim at training him in the father's art.

The author – who, according to the Byzantine lexicon *Suda*, also wrote a treatise on divination by the observation of birds – was only interested in dreams that foretell the future and do so cryptically, rather than plainly, thus requiring decodification. Symbolism may work in various ways, quite often by puns (homophony between the signifier and the signified). The book contains much detailed guidance to the interpretation of specific dream contents. However, there is not an automatic correspondence between the dreamt image or event and their meaning; interpretation needs to carefully weigh the status of the dreamer – their gender, age, marital status, social and health conditions: the same dream foretells very different outcomes to different people. Among the general rules that Artemidorus outlines and applies, a dominant one has to do with how much the dreamt situation appears to follow a norm. A dreamt reality may be highly bizarre, but if at least some of its conditions (time and place, or appropriateness in one way or another to the dreaming subject) respect the order of nature, it may be taken as a good omen, the contrary otherwise. The book left no trace in the centuries immediately following but re-emerged in ninth-century Baghdad and in the subsequent Byzantine culture, from which it was brought to Italy by Greek émigrés; its twentieth-century fame owes more than something to the homage paid to him by Sigmund Freud (Thonemann 2020a and 2020b).

5   The Greek text that complements the first edition of Artemidorus, printed by the Aldine press in Venice (although the publication of its Latin translation, *De insomniis*, had preceded it), is the *Peri enypniōn* (Concerning dreams) written at the very beginning of the fifth century by Synesius of Cyrene, who after its composition was to be elected bishop of Ptolemais in today's Libya (roughly a contemporary of Macrobius). In contrast with the character of Artemidorus's institution of a professional technique, it is said to have been written by its Neoplatonic author at night time, in a state of inspiration. While also distinguishing between different types of oneiric experiences, according to how clear or obscure their message is, it assumes the bold and unusual stance of declaring all dreams true. The question is how to interpret them correctly, and in this view the author recommends a spiritual path that will accompany the dreamer to an inner self-comprehension (Russell and Nesselrath 2014; Wagner 2019). That Girolamo Cardano, the author of the largest Renaissance treatise on dreams, declared from the very title of his work to be mostly inspired by this comparatively small and idiosyncratic text, is a choice that will require some comment below. Meanwhile, a striking difference between the two late antique sources should be noted: while Artemidorus writes a manual for professional dream interpreters, Synesius offers the dreamers a way to do it themselves. In addition, intriguingly the latter also recommended one to keep dream diaries.

Without denying the importance of other ancient authors and texts, as well as of those who followed their footsteps in the Middle Ages, including the scientific ecumene of the Near East, the significance of the five above-mentioned authors in their later revivals will appear evident from what follows. Nevertheless, the chronology of the actual availability of some of these texts must be kept in mind if we want to reconstruct the story of their comparative effects with any accuracy. In particular, Greek manuscripts of Artemidorus's text were acquired or copied at the requests of fifteenth-century Italian patrons and intellectuals: the oldest extant manuscript, dating from the eleventh century, was bought by the Greek scholar Janus Lascaris for Lorenzo the Magnificent in Crete in 1491–2 (therefore, now it is held at the Laurentian Library in Florence); even before that, still in Fiesole near Florence, the outstanding classical scholar and poet Agnolo Poliziano must have had access to a different codex, since in 1482 he was able to transcribe some passages; the copy from which the first printed edition was derived had been made by the Byzantine theologian, rhetorician and copyist Michael Apostolius for Cardinal Bessarion (and is still kept at the Marciana National Library in Venice). A handful of other copies were made between the fifteenth and the sixteenth century (Blum 1941). Before that, other sources had been better known, and one should have a closer look at the role played by Byzantine scholarship.

One way of accessing a less-known, influential source, a medieval addition to the above-mentioned ancient quintet, is by looking up Robert Burton's *Anatomy of Melancholy*. Burton's oeuvre can serve in many respects as a key to the bookcase of the late Renaissance scholar. While we will have to return to the book's overall treatment of the subject, the bibliographical references he offers his reader on the subject of dreams are telling and intriguing. When first introduced, in a subsection concerning "the Inward Senses", the topic is presented in the following terms. Sleep and waking are the affections of such senses, sleep being a rest both of the outward senses and of the common sense:

> The Phantasie alone is free, and his Commander, Reason; as appears by those Imaginary Dreames, which are of divers kinds, *Naturall, Divine, Dæmoniacall, &c.* which vary according to humors, diet, actions, Objects &c. of which Artemidorus, Cardanus, and Sambucus, with their severall Interpretations, have written great volumes.
>
> *(1.1.2.7 in Burton 1989–2000: I, 153)*

Artemidorus and Cardano (on whom more later) can be expected and taken for granted. But who was Sambucus and what is the text Burton regarded as an obvious and necessary reference on the subject? János Zsámboky was a Hungarian humanist and physician, who studied medicine in Padua and served as court physician to Emperor Maximilian II. The publication Burton refers to is his edition, in Frankfurt in 1577, of *Apomasaris apotelesmata, sive De significatis et eventis insomniorum, ex Indorum, Persarum, Agyptiorumque disciplina*. Translated by the German humanist and Orientalist Johannes Löwenklau (Leunclavius), the text was that of (pseudo-) Achmet's *Oneirocriticon*, the most important Byzantine work on dream interpretation, itself an incorporation of partially Arabic material into the Greek tradition, possibly dating from the tenth century. The name of the author was a pseudonym (as it was customary), assigning the text to the son of a Calif's dream interpreter, and presenting the work as a mere Greek translation. Some medieval manuscripts of the treatise had circulated under the attribution to the ninth-century Arab astrologist Abû Ma'sar al-Falakî, known in the West under the name of Albumasar or Apomasar, and so the name of the supposed author is stated both in the Frankfurt edition and in the French translation that followed four years later (*Apomazar des significations et evenemens des songes, selon la doctrine des Indiens, Perses et Egyptiens*). The two, however, had been preceded, and by half a century, by an Italian one (*Espositione de gli insomnii secondo la interpretatione de gli Indi Persi et Egyptii*, reprinted in Venice by three different publishers between 1525 and 1551); this was based on the earliest extant Latin translation, made in Byzantium in the twelfth century by Leo Tuscus, a Pisan interpreter in the imperial chancery of Manuel Komnenos (Camozzi Pistoja 2014) and turned into vernacular by the Mantuan Dominican friar, mathematician and astrologer Patrizio Tricasso. As all the titles suggest, the Byzantine redactor introduces the voice of fictional Indian, Persian and Egyptian experts to expose their respective traditions; however, the redactor mixes in clear Christian elements – a practice that perhaps could be compared with the adaptation of the Quran that brought to Italian readers, including the miller Menocchio, the *Alcorano di Macometto* (Ginzburg 1980; Tommasino 2018). Achmet's *Oneirocriticon* – which Nicolas Rigault in 1603 re-edited in Paris together with Artemidorus and other Byzantine oneirocritic material – is the only surviving Greek source comparable to Artemidorus for size and importance and follows the structure of the keys of dreams (see below); in fact, it was much more influential than Artemidorus until the latter's rediscovery (Lamoreaux 2002: 140–54; Mavroudi 2002; Bernardi 2011).[4] Even apart from vernacular and printed editions, the manuscript circulation of Tuscus's Latin translation was very successful among both Italian Renaissance intellectuals and prominent ruling families (Camozzi Pistoja 2014).

The fact that the authoritative texts on the subject that an academic in early seventeenth-century Oxford would recommend without hesitation to his readers – rather as a matter of fact, hardly in need to be mentioned, let alone described – had been originally written, respectively, in the second, possibly tenth and sixteenth, century CE suggests something about authority and continuity in Renaissance culture. It may also be considered as evidence in favour of one historiographical approach to the effect of the printing press: the idea, characteristically put forward by Lucien Febvre and Henri-Jean Martin (1976), that the technical innovation flooded Europe with old, if not backward, material, rather than encouraging innovation. The least one might learn from Burton's selection is that 1,500 years had passed between the oldest and newest of his references without the fact mattering too much: the reliability of the content and guidance offered by successful reference books appears to annul the passing of time. And yet one should avoid jumping to the conclusion that there was no significant development. It would be anachronistic to apply later notions of originality to a world whose preferred and most esteemed form of practice was variation on a tradition.

A genre of texts that did not need reviving because it had been there all along the Middle Ages, in fact dominating the oneirocritic textual production of that millennium, were the "keys of dreams", lists of correspondence between signifier and signified in dreams, often in alphabetical order. Their model was a text known as "Daniel's Dream" (*Somniale Danielis*), with a mythical attribution to a prophet (alternatively, Joseph), whom the Scripture associated with the interpretation of dreams. The original Greek text appeared in Byzantium around 400 CE, was translated in Arabic and Hebrew, and began to circulate in Latin versions in the West circa 800. By the later Middle Ages, it was available in vernacular adaptations in many European languages, from the British Isles to Russia (Berriot 1989 and 1990; Bach 2007). As in Artemidorus, its logic of combination of oneiric images with meanings followed such patterns as word play (by phonetic resemblance), analogy and antinomy – that is, birth symbolising death, and so on (Timotin 2016). I will return to this material when addressing the popular interpretation of dreams. For the moment, it may be worth clarifying that, in contrast with the alleged attribution to a biblical prophet, the medieval Church was hostile against both the text and much oneiromancy (Semeraro 2002).

Contrary to our expectations, only some of the oneiromantic tradition considered the dream's content while offering an interpretation. Three genres of medieval dream-book have been distinguished. Only the keys were based on content. The other two were alphabetical books, in which a meaning was attributed to each letter, and one was supposed to open a book at random and pick the first letter of the page; and *lunaria*, in which what was relevant was the timing of the dream in relation to a lunar calendar, with the consequence that different dreams that people had on the same day shared their alleged predictive value (Kruger 1992; Schmitt 2016). The fact that biblical references appear rather generically within this literature has suggested that it transmitted pre-existing material that was only superficially Christianised (Timotin 2016: 56). How much (as well as which) people actually used this reference books should not be taken for granted. In fact, medieval biographic and autobiographic narratives tend to offer more articulate descriptions of dreams and nuanced interpretations, which consider the context of the dreamer's condition (Schmitt 2016: 68–71).

Achmet and Pseudo-Daniel did, like Artemidorus, suggest interpretation according to some of the dreamer's characteristics. Their texts were the two longest in a wider Byzantine tradition that comprised several others, which were shorter and provided automatic correspondence between dream content and predicted event. A cluster of them resuscitated during the first century and a half of printing (Oberhelman 2008).

5.2 Biblical and Christian doctrines and attitudes

Against this classical tradition of medical and philosophical texts, Judeo-Christian religious writing produced its own, though no less ambivalent in its assessment of the oneiric experience. It requires a rapid survey, considering its lasting influence and its revival in the Age of the Reformation. Old and New Testament alike contain examples of visions and dreams used by God to convey messages and prescriptions, with prophets and patriarchs also displaying skill in interpreting someone else's dream – typically, following a Near Eastern pattern, the oneiric life of rulers (Daniel Nebuchadnezzar's in *Daniel* 2, Joseph the Pharaoh's in *Genesis* 41: see Figure 5.1); but also warnings against the illusory nature of most dreams and the idolatrous implications of granting them predictive value (Légasse and Dulaey 1990; Bar 2001).

Although the early Christian Church had to face heresies that – as in the case of early modern enthusiasts – saw in oneiric experiences a privileged means of communication with the divine, Church Fathers (including Augustine) emphasised the role of Revelation but often appreciated the prophetic nature of other dreams and visions, partly under the influence of currents of contemporary secular philosophy, such as Neoplatonism; medical knowledge could also guide their classification.

In his own style, Aquinas crowned medieval reflection by harmonising Aristotle with the Bible. He distinguished between three types of predictive dreams. One is natural forecast, allowed by processes within the human body and cosmological influences, which experts can decipher to a reasonable degree as predicting medical or meteorological developments (in line with Aquinas's tolerance of some forms of astrology). A second, divination, is inspired in our sleep by demons who share with us their conjectural knowledge of the future: it is a sin to try to consciously interpret them. Thirdly, though rarely, truly prophetic dreams may be sent to humans by God via angels (Goris 2012). Thus, when a sixteenth-century French physician, Auger Ferrier, claimed that he was rejecting medieval taxonomies and proposed a tripartition between natural, divine and diabolic dreams (Cooper

Recovering and negotiating a long tradition 33

FIGURE 5.1 Nicolas Beatrizet. "Joseph Explaining his Dreams" (engraving on paper, 1541). A reversed copy of a print after the fresco painted by the workshop of Raphael (c. 1517–19) in the vault of the seventh bay of the Raphael Loggia in the Vatican. The engraver, from Lorraine, was active in Rome and derived the drawing from work by the school of Marcantonio Raimondi; the print was published by Tommaso Barlacchi. All this circle was also engaged in the reproduction of monuments from Antiquity. A couple of years before his death in 1520, Raphael undertook the monumental papal commission of Old Testament paintings to decorate private apartments in the Vatican Palace, Rome, in an antique style inspired by recent archaeological excavations. They have since been reproduced in drawings and engravings for centuries. The Wallace L. DeWolf and Joseph Brooks Fair Collections and the Art Institute of Chicago.

1990: 58–9), he was in substance copying Aquinas's (and others') categories. Aquinas's interpretative scheme was popularised by dedicated pastoral literature including the *Trattato dei sogni* of the fourteenth-century Dominican preacher Jacopo Passavanti, where the model was expanded with emphasis on the derivation of dreams from passions and humours, and adapted to a different audience and purpose by adopting a humorous mode (Abbruzzetti 1997).

To give an idea of the *longue durée* of some cultural attitudes from the perspective of moral theology, in an encyclopaedic work of the age of the Enlightenment, one could still read that sleep results from original sin (Zedler's 1745 *Universal-Lexikon*, cit. in Engel 2003: 26).

A specific set of practice and beliefs that Christianity inherited and reinterpreted from the Ancient Near East and the Classical world was incubation, whose specificity is that the oneiric experience in that case is actively sought after. Sleeping in Christian sanctuaries in order to experience oracles, in the form of the apparition of a saint, usually for therapeutic purposes, is attested at least from the early fifth century CE. That the dreamer was understood to be the passive receiver of the supernatural visit justified the fact that more than one person might claim to share the same vision. Incidentally, some of these stories postulate a distinction between vision and dream and described the apparitions as presenting themselves to vigilant believers. Narratives of miraculous healing had, in turn, the effect of generating forms of ritual practice such as dedicated cults and pilgrimage to holy places (Canetti 2010 and 2011; cf. Dodds 1951: 110–16).

5.3 Dreams and humoral complexions

The philosophical and medical tradition associated some characteristics of people's oneiric life with their humoral balance. Descriptions of the type of dreams more frequently associated with one or the other temperament are often generic, sometimes more expanded (Fattori 1985; Levin 2008: 40–3).[5] An example can be taken from the vernacular treatise by the Bolognese canon regular Giovanni Battista Segni:

> Therefore, sanguine persons, who are dominated by blood, dream of red, beautiful, cheerful and dreamy things, of dancing, running, jumping: they often even feel as they fly, because blood is very similar to air. Choleric people ordinarily dream of disputes, discords, quarrels and wars; for choler gives rise to these affections ... and since choler is very much in tune with fire, they often dream of fire, to become inflamed and burn. Phlegmatic persons, in whom water predominates, most often dream of being near fountains, rivers, lakes and seas, washing themselves in them, swimming, sailing and drowning. And particularly children dream of getting very wet, of treading on snow and slipping on ice, and this happens because of the abundant dampness that is natural in them. Melancholic people, as they have a great symbiotic affinity with the earth, so they ordinarily dream that they are under some cliff, and oppressed by some falling ruin of a bank or mountain; they dream of talking with the dead, of standing over cemeteries, and even of being buried; in short, the simulacra that represent themselves to them in their sleep are dark, caliginous, and dreary things. It seems to them to wander through wild, wooded, and frightening solitudes; and finally to be among sulphur, stench, and horrid screeching with demons in hell.
>
> *(Segni 1591*: 14–15)*

The list is followed by an indication of the dreams caused by the suffering of specific medical conditions, such as the corruption of the blood or a perturbation of the brain.

An extended presentation is included in a treatise by the Italian Giuseppe Rosaccio (1600). In the frontispiece, the multitalented author – a heterodox physician and charlatan, astrologer and rhetorician from Friuli, particularly capable as a publisher – is described as a cosmographer. The long title explains that the book "deals briefly with the vegetative, sensitive and rational soul; with man, his complexions and physiognomy; and with the infirmities that arise in all parts of the body and their treatment". The exposition comes at the end of Chapter 5, devoted to the head and to the reason why the five senses are positioned there. When Rosaccio discusses diseases affecting the nerves, these include the experiencing of nightmares, which he associates with melancholy and informs that common people (*il volgo*) mistakenly call them *incubi*, believing they are caused by devils (Rosaccio 1600: 77–8). The author then touches upon solutions that may help falling asleep or waking up, according to one's needs: to fall asleep, the recommendations vary according to specific conditions, one of them involving poppy seeds (that is, inhaling opium); as for waking up from enduring deep sleep, one should burn some man's hair, macerate it in vinegar, and put the resulting ointment up their nostrils.

After this, Rosaccio presents dreams regrouped according to each of the four complexions:

> Those who, while sleeping, dream of seeing red things or doing weddings or dancing or eating sweet food, sensing wind, seeing meat or blood and similar things, denote in them excess of blood. Those who dream of seeing blazing fire, a burning house, burning coals, sparks of fire, thunderbolts, the sky turned red, flaming stones, shrieks or noises, the colour yellow, brass, gold, copper, blond hair, eating bitter things and other such things, denote that in these the yellow bile (*la colera*) dominates.
>
> When one dreams of seeing rain, hearing rivers, the sea, waters, springs, wells, lakes, ships going, fish, nets, washing white things, seeing white colouring, such as lime, cottonwool, milk, cask and other things, falling into water, tears, spittle, urine, syrup, butter, swimming, washing one's head and other similar things, it means phlegm reigns in them.
>
> If one dreams of seeing black or gloom or smoke, darkness, burials, the sick, the bones of the dead, dead bodies, sadness, helplessness, being in prison, obliged or drowned, seeing monstrous things, hearing noises from afar, smelling foul things and similar things, it denotes dominating melancholy.
>
> *(ibid. 78–9)*

Beyond the characterisation of the main four complexions, dreams may also reveal an alteration of the humours that produces evil ones and shows itself in the dreaming of wanting to go somewhere and not being able to, of going to dirty and stinking places, of handling mud or dung, feeling exhausted, have little appetite out of the ordinary and many other things – infirmities which require purgation (ibid. 79–80).

A particular humoral mix is not, in Hippocratic-Galenic thought, necessarily a pathological condition. It may become so only if at some point humours become particularly unbalanced. However, if there is one of the four key temperaments that is close to being classified as problematic in itself, this undoubtedly is the melancholic – even though, over the millennia, it has also presented valued associations with the person gifted with genius, and consequently sought after for self-fashioning. Melancholics have many dreams, suggests Benedetto Dottori, one of the sources I will describe in a next section, and this gives them a higher chance to receive premonitions (Dottori 1575*: 28v). It will not come as a surprise, therefore, if one of the most striking lists of subjects of pathologic dreams comes from a treatise on the diseases of the hypochondriac. At the chronological limit of the present investigation, but consistent with a long tradition, Paolo Zacchia, an Italian physician who is credited with laying the foundations of legal medicine, offered a meaningful list of the themes of nightmares experienced by the melancholic (as cited by Piero Camporesi and translated by David Gentilcore):

> Finding oneself among the dead in graves and among the limbs of quartered men and not being able to get out; seeing oneself in the hands of the ministers of justice, condemned to execution; seeing the sky burst, and from it pour down fire and lightning with the most frightening appearance of strange figures; being deep inside very high and dark towers, with no way of finding the exit, and being restricted and distressed between two walls and not being able to breathe for the suffering; beholding oneself immersed in mountains of mud or other dirt and filth; finding oneself placed on some terrible precipice with the inevitable danger of falling; being surrounded by a multitude of serpents ready to devour one; or seeing oneself chased by very fierce and mad dogs or by other most ferocious animals, waiting from moment to moment to be lacerated and devoured by them; seeing oneself before one's dearest friends, either dead or in death's agony, or to have lost them and not be able to find them ever again. These and a thousand other dreams, of which more frightening cannot be imagined, are so disturbing to suffer and such horrors to see that man would rather choose death, or at least to never close his eyes in order to sleep …
>
> Many, judging themselves to be dead and because of this not wanting to eat or drink, have run the very manifest risk of dying; others not only think they are dead but, in fact, condemned to hell; there are those who believe themselves to be pursued by great potentates, and for this lock

themselves in their own houses, and do not want to move for any reason; others think they have some animal living inside their bodies, and others [think they have] an illness or a putrid and incurable wound on some part; others [think] their heads [are] of the most fragile glass or clay or stone, or have been transformed into some kind of animal.

(Camporesi 1989: 129–30)

The passage constitutes a paragraph within a chapter of the second book of Zacchia's *De' mali hipochondriaci* (1639), which is preceded by one mentioning sleeping disorders, and followed by the discussion of hypochondriac melancholy, delirium and madness. The physiology of the production of these terrifying oneiric images was rooted in the materialistic aetiology characteristic of Galenic medicine (Gowland 2011; on early modern hypochondria: Haskell 2011b). We have contemporary reports of people described as suffering from such conditions and experiencing similar nightmares. A notable example comes from the notebooks of the early seventeenth-century London artisan Nehemiah Wallington, well known for providing some access to the inner lives of contemporary Puritans. "Dreams were a source of both spiritual comfort and anxiety, serving to reveal his inherent sinfulness as well as God's mercy and grace" (Rivière 2017: 116–19, at 116).

5.4 Other sleep and dream pathologies

Dream-books in the astrological vein left the hermeneutics of the oneiric experience relating to health to the care of the specialists. In the Hippocratic tradition, sleep and dreams continued for long to be assigned some role in medical prognosis as well as to represent the sphere of manifestation of specific health conditions (Dandrey 1988). Among the latter we find somnambulism. It is discussed within Renaissance scholarship on sleep and dreams (Ponzetti 1515*: 105v). Tiraqueau mentions it explicitly, with reference to a long literary tradition, as a case for exclusion from culpability (Tiraqueau 1986: 61).

A variation on neighbouring phenomena such as sleepwalking was offered in 1605 England by the case of a preacher who appeared to deliver his most articulated and elaborate sermons while asleep: in the end he was exposed by King James I as a fraud, although the same divine, Richard Haydocke, composed, apparently at the request of the king, a learned medical treatise in English on the nature of sleep and dreams, which remained manuscript (Levin 2008: 13–19; Marr 2016).

The question of the relationship between the physic and mental being in the production and effects of dreaming reaches a climax in the case of erotic dreams. Ancient Greek medicine had a special terminology for labelling the dreams that accompany or may be regarded to cause pollution. The phenomenon was distinguished from the ordinary pollution that can occur without the accompaniment of mental images, even if not actually produced by the senses, but rather illusory. The case therefore convoked problems of perception, of hallucination and of the power exercised by dreams. A distinction could be made between the dreaming of sexual intercourse without the emission of sperm (*oneiropolesis*) and the one with it (*oneirogmos*). The latter was not automatically pathologic, though it could become so. The matter proved of significance in defining mind–body relationships, as it involved the power of images that could cause direct physical effects. The direction of the causal influence, on the other hand, could be understood differently: according to the Hippocratic treatise *On generation*, it was the pollution that produced the imagined sexual intercourse, rather than vice versa (Caelius Aurelianus 1950: 956–65; Pigeaud 1981; Pigeaud 1995: 27–34). The medical knowledge that filtered down to a late medieval pastoral treatise such as the one by Jacopo Passavanti could include advice against sleeping in a supine position, understood as physiologically encouraging the accumulation of sperm in the genitals and consequently phantasies of satisfaction of sexual desire (Abbruzzetti 1997: 78–9). Within the Hippocratic Corpus, there is also a reference to female pollution while dreaming, and Aristoteles and Galen expressed contrasting views on the relationship between women's erotic dreams and the contribution of the female seed to generation (Andò 2009).

It may be worth adding that the erotic dream has been found underrepresented in Western literature and art. Manfred Engel, who has explored the issue, notes the difficulty in defining the object, let alone the division between eroticism and pornography, with all its aesthetic and moral variables. It gets more complicated than that, as the image may be sexual but not its attributed meaning, or vice versa. When Artemidorus discusses dreaming of incest with one's mother, he judges it quite simply as a good omen (see Foucault 1986: 22–3; Grottanelli 1999). So did, incidentally, an Assyrian dream-book of the seventh century BCE about dreaming of copulating with wild animals (Thonemann 2020b); something similar could be argued for the sexual explicitness of much mystic imagery, which could be intended to stand for purely spiritual meanings. On the other hand, Freud, to pick the most obvious counterexample, offers plenty of cases of dreams considered to symbolise sex, even if their narrative or visual content appears unrelated. Another dimension to be considered, which has its, however limited, functions within the production of literature and art, is the deliberate scope (of fictional dreams) to arouse sexual desire (Engel 2022).

Burton returns to dreams in the second section of the first partition of his *Anatomy*, which deals with the causes of melancholy. There, in a subsection devoted to "the force of the imagination", the author points at "the wonderfull effects and power of it", raging particularly in melancholic persons, in which the impressions (species) made by objects are amplified by long meditation:

> And although this *Phantasie* of ours, be a subordinate facultie to reason, and should bee ruled by it, yet in many men, through inward or outward distemperatures, defect of Organs, which are unapt or hindered, or otherwise contaminated, it is likewise unapt, hindred, and hurt. This we see verified in sleepers, which by reason of humours, and concourse of vapours troubling the *Phantasie*, imagine many times absurd and prodigious things, and in such as are troubled with *Incubus*, or Witch ridden (as we call it) if they lie on their backes, they suppose an old woman rides, and sits so hard upon them, that they are almost stifled for want of breath; when there is nothing offends, but a concourse of bad humours, which trouble the *Phantasie*.
>
> *(1.2.3.2 in Burton 1989–2000: I, 250)*

The cure for it, as a relevant passage in the second partition exposes, consists chiefly in a regimen:

> Against fearefull and troublesome dreames, *Incubus* and such inconveniences, wherewith melancholy men are molested, the best remedy is to eat a light supper, and of such meats as are easie of digestion, no Hare, Venison, Beefe, etc. not to lie on his backe, not to meditate or thinke in the day time of any terrible objects, or especially talke of them before hee goes to bed.
>
> *(2.2.5.1 in Burton 1989–2000: II, 98)*

These dietary prescriptions are followed by a cluster of classical quotations, mainly confirming that the choice of daytime occupations will affect the oneiric experience (according to a line attributed to Petronius, "As a dogge dreames of an Hare, so doe men, on such subjects, they thought on last", ibid. and commentary in Burton 1989–2000: V, 189). The passage closes with a renewed invitation to read "*Artemidorus, Sambucus* and *Cardan*" (Burton 1989–2000: II, 99). In a subsequent section, where the cure concerns more specifically head melancholy, Burton's dietary recommendations for having pleasant dreams are taken from a chapter of Giovan Battista Della Porta's *Magia naturalis* (2.2.5.1 in Burton 1989–2000: II, 98).[6]

There also existed a medical tradition suggesting that a soul's capability to correctly predict the future occurred in some pathologies that made human sensitivity sharper, as well as in the proximity of death (Pigeaud 1995: 40–2).

5.5 Dream and confession

The late sixteenth-century academic literature on dreams tends to reserve a space, often towards the end, to assessing the belief in the prophetic value of dreams. This discussion fully belongs to the Aristotelian tradition; furthermore, in the context of the century's religious reforms and conflicts, it may take on the specific nature of an evaluation in terms of Christian moral judgement. One of the treatises in particular, Segni's, which we have already quoted for its depiction of complexions, devotes the last chapter or lecture to the authority of the Holy Scripture that appears to condemn the observation of dreams. After explaining why not everyone is endowed with the gift of interpreting dreams and citing a cluster of biblical passages, its last point concerns cases in which "observing" dreams – that is, trusting them and behave accordingly – is sinful. The act of dreaming not being voluntary, it cannot itself be a sin and consequently does not require confession. It is what one does subsequently in consequence of the dream, in terms of thoughts and/or deeds, that comes under moral scrutiny. In the mode of the contemporary literature for confessors and penitents, Segni examines the situations and behaviours that qualify for either a mortal or a venial sin. It can be venial, considering that it does not produce serious consequences, if someone judges rashly on the causes (and consequent reliability) of a dream, despite it being uncertain. It would turn into mortal if as a consequence someone omitted some obligatory action or acted contrary to what is required in view of "salvation". Segni's source is a specific manual for confessors, the *Summa, quae Aurea Armilla inscribitur* by the Dominican friar Bartolomeo Fumi, an alphabetic guide to over 500 entries published for the first time in Piacenza in 1549 and subsequently reprinted numerous times, including in an Italian translation. Both the Latin *salus* and the Italian *salute* present, in the sixteenth century, the ambiguity of potentially referring to either, spiritually, the perspective of eternal life or, down to earth, health. In a theologian here, a concern for the latter would seem less congruous, if not in force of the long tradition of association between oneiric life and medicine. Whatever the case, Fumi's casuistry, copied and pasted by Segni, continues with the specification that such trusting dreams will represent only a mortal sin if it turns beneficiary, rather than harmful. However, this attenuating circumstance ceases if someone falls in the vice of superstition, which is accompanied by diabolic illusion and a silent company of the devil: the person who falls for this will increasingly turn to rely so much in dreams that they use them regularly as a guide for action, ending up committing a variety of wicked deeds (Fumi 1561: 279v, "somnium"; Fumi 1588: 281v; Segni 1591: 62–4).

If Fumi may have been unusual in setting dreams apart in a dedicated confessional entry, his discussion is rooted in a century-old scholastic tradition. The key text that dominates it, having acquired an aura of theological authority on the matter, is the already-mentioned question 95 of Aquinas's *Secunda secundae* (completed in Paris around 1270), which deals with various forms of divination, and devotes a specific section to divination via dreams. In the dialectic form typical of medieval Scholastics, Thomas also resorted to the evidence of physicians as a source for his argumentation (cf. Cameron 2010: esp. 98–100). Aquinas is also the authority on which another extremely popular early sixteenth-century *summa* for confessors, the *Sylvestrina* by Silvestro Mazzolini – a Dominican who was among the first polemicists to attack Martin Luther and died in the Sack of Rome – included a discussion of divination by dreams under the broader headline "De superstitione" (Mazzolini 1518: 437v–438r). In the even more widespread manual of the theologian from Navarra Martín de Azpilcueta, the topic is treated much more cursorily among the transgressions to the First Commandment (Martín de Azpilcueta 1573: 29v).

The Iberian cultural environment had already produced critiques of superstition and witchcraft before the Counter-Reformation, as in the case of the philosopher and theologian Pedro Ciruelo, who in a treatise on the subject ended a chapter on dreams with the recommendation that "every good Christian must abandon this preoccupation with interpreting dreams" (Ciruelo 1977: 163). A systematic attack on the "fallacious and superstitious arts" was later launched by the Spanish Jesuit Benedictus Pererius (Benito Pereira), professor of rhetoric, philosophy and theology at the Collegio Romano, with a treatise whose first book was devoted to magic, the second (which occupies 40 pages in octavo) "on the observation of dreams", the third on astrologic divination, first published in Ingolstadt in 1591 and reprinted several times over the turn of the century. In a series of clearly articulated questions, the author summarises the doctrine on the subject, from the ancient authors to Christian authorities, such as Gregory the Great. He affirms the truthfulness of the dreams recorded in the Bible and confirms the existence of divinely inspired dreams, together with three other sources: bodily affects, life habits and the perturbations of the mind, and demonic influxes. Contrary to the elitism typical of classical authors, Pererius believed that even ignorant people, who may prove especially innocent and pious, may receive divine communication in dreams. Segni (1591: 58) agreed by suggesting against the Aristotelians that God sends dreams both to the good and to the evil (*a' tristi*), and this is not a shortcoming of divinity. While Pererius accepted that Christians "observed" dreams that may help diagnosing their health condition or orienting their behaviour, he warned that they should not do so for the prediction of the future, a superstitious practice in his eyes even worse than divination via astrology. In terms of literary genre, the section on dreams stems from an appendix to the author's commentary on the first book of *Daniel*: as we will find later in the case of the reformed commonplace by Pietro Martire Vermigli, the biblical commentary offered itself at the time as an important platform for cultural production that could subsequently be reused for different audiences and functions; and Pererius's agenda in reproposing his critique here was his worry for the use the advocates of Renaissance magic could make of some scriptural references (Pererius 1592: 125–64; Blum 2007: 357–60; Paoli 2011: 55–6).

This concern for superstition found a new area of expression on the missionary frontier of the newly discovered worlds. Both in Mexico and in Peru, Catholic confessors asked their indigenous flock whether they believed in their dreams; they often associated the question whether they trusted any other traditional form of divination, among which the listening to bird songs featured prominently. Birds – owls and condors, for instance, on the Andes – also haunted South American dreamers with their oneiric appearances. The confessors' questionnaire could further comprise an inquiry whether the penitents had related their dreams to others or asked others to tell theirs, the sharing of oneiric imagery and narratives being evidently regarded as a fundamental building block towards the conservation of pre-Columbian beliefs and practices. Implicit in such inquisitory interest, in a campaign to eradicate idolatry, was the possibility that oneiric experiences were shared with professional interpreters, employed in indigenous cultures, while the conquerors read these experiences in terms of witchcraft and demonology. They also practised an equivalent to Mediterranean incubation and used coded associations between dreams and meanings in the style of the keys of dreams (Azoulai 1993: 145–56).

The charge of superstition had particular resonance in the decades in which the Catholic Church had won the battle against the Reformation in the Italian Peninsula and consequently turned its predominant inquisitorial attention towards the world of magic. In this area, however, dangers arose much closer home than across oceans. An internal frontier was represented by the oneiric culture of the Jews, whom Christians also charged with superstition. Even though Judaism is a separate religion, the Roman Church adopted the tactics of considering it a heresy, because it shared belief in the Old Testament, but diverged on the New: this excuse was brought to justify the competence of the Inquisition – a tribunal that by definition could only judge Christians – in prosecuting Jews (Caffiero 2012). The expertise of Jewish interpreters of dreams – as well as in all other fields of the occult – was well known. All in all, Jews and Christians shared much oneiric culture, having their roots in a biblical series of authoritative passages that included both the telling and interpreting of dreams that were thought to be of divine inspiration, and others warning against the trust in those that were not. This proximity made the traffic by Christians with Jewish experts the more problematic.

5.6 Somnia Judaica

While sharing beliefs in the nature and origin of dreams with the Greek medical and philosophical textual heritage, the Jewish tradition had also its own characteristics. The Talmud took the matter clearly seriously and regarded all dreams somewhat meaningful and true, an idea summarised in the saying that "a dream which is not interpreted is like a letter which is not read" (Niehoff 1992; Storper Perez and Cohen-Solal 1997).[7] Jewish dream-lore added a way of understanding how this happened:

> While the body is asleep, the spirit, or soul, leaves its corporeal prison and wanders over the face of the earth, reporting back its experiences to the sleepless mind. When one dreams of meeting a friend who is far distant, it is the souls of the two, annihilating space, which have made contact. Some men, of a higher spiritual capacity, behold these visions clearly and well defined; for most men they are confused and obscure.
> *(Trachtenberg 2004: 234)*

At the beginning of the sixteenth century, roughly at the same time as when the Venetian press rediscovered the classics of ancient Greek oneirocritics, the Turkish Jew Shelomo Almoli published in the Ottoman Empire a Hebrew treatise on the interpretation of dreams that is regarded as the most systematic in the Jewish tradition. It was subsequently reprinted (in Istanbul as well as in Poland) and, at the end of the seventeenth century, translated into Yiddish, thus exercising a lasting impact on the popular culture of the Ashkenazi diaspora. It combines material of the Jewish tradition with other non-Jewish, thus confirming the proximity and porosity of all the relevant texts and practices. It is articulated in three parts: the first deals with the classification of dreams and the general principles of interpretation (discussing whether to rely on them, distinguishing the reliable ones and describing the rules for decoding them, which include consideration of the dreamer's status); the second offers a comprehensive glossary of dream symbols, from inanimate matter to higher beings; the third elucidates the methods of counteracting the effects of ominous dreams, discussing such practices as the "dream-fast", which has rich ethnographic parallels (Almoli 1998; Trachtenberg 2004: 230–48; Schmitt 2010: 67–113; Caffiero 2012: 86–93).

Another area of interaction between Jewish and Christian oneiric cultures was opened by the humanist passion for the Kabbalah and the syncretic tradition this encounter produced. An example is offered by Heinrich Cornelius Agrippa von Nettesheim's *De occulta philosophia*, whose Chapter III, 51 cites the Talmud, which among other information offers the author yet another classification, according to which there are

> four kinds of true dreams: the first matutine, which is made betwixt sleep and awaking: the second, which one seeth concerning another: the third, whose interpretation is shown to the same dreamer in the nocturnal vision:

the fourth, which is repeated to the same dreamer, according to that which Joseph saith to Pharaoh, "but that thou hast seen the dream belonging to the same thing the second time", it is a sign of confirmation.
(Agrippa von Nettesheim 1993: 634, with reference to Genesis 41: 32; cf. Agrippa von Nettesheim 1992: 559)

The Jewish dream culture was considered so distinctive of that religion that, when Jean Bodin in his *Colloquium of the Seven about Secrets of the Sublime* has some of the speakers, representing the world's religions, touching on the subject of dreams and visions, the persona standing for Judaism is the most consistent advocate of their divine origin and meaningfulness (Holland 1999: 137–8).

5.7 Other dreams

The impact of the printing press in facilitating and encouraging the production and circulation of written material on the matter of dream interpretation, along with many others, should be evident by now. While the gunpowder has little to do with this story, the third celebrated technological innovation of the era, the compass, in a way played its role too, at least in the sense that intensified traveling and contact with other parts of the world gave Europeans increased familiarity with different oneiric cultures (and vice versa), and this aspect of alien customs and believes contributed to the renewal of Western anthropologic thought.

By reading their classics, Europeans had been aware all along of the cultural variation of the dreaming experience. In the first of his *Ragionamenti* (1613*: 1–2), while stating "that dreaming is natural to humans", Paolo Grassi – the author of one of the treatises presented in Chapter 7 – signalled rare, recorded exceptions that confirmed the rule, concerning individuals or entire peoples. According to Herodotus (4.184.3–4), near mount Atlas in north-western Africa lived a people called Atlantes, who "are reported not to eat any living thing, and never to have any dreams"; the information is confirmed in Pliny's *Natural History* (4.45), although in his testimony, Grassi comments, it is not affirmed they do not sleep at all, but rather that "when they are asleep they do not have dreams like the rest of the mankind", a phrasing that may leave open the possibility that they do it otherwise (that they do things differently is indeed suggested by Pliny's immediately preceding statement: "The Atlantes have fallen below the level of human civilization, if we can believe what is said; for they do not address one another by any names, and when they behold the rising and setting sun, they utter awful curses against it as the cause of disaster to themselves and their fields"). The exception, thus, does appear to confirm the rule, if it pertains to a community whose belonging to civilisation is in question. As for individuals, Suetonius informs us that Nero only dreamt after killing his own mother. All in all, these combined evidences of non- (or otherwise) dreamers do not stop the author from developing his argument in favour of the naturality of this human experience. In a way, at the opposite end of the spectrum we find a legend concerning people who go into hibernation every winter (when, even more paradoxically, the narrative turns into one of collective yearly death and resurrection). It came originally from the *Rerum Muscoviticarum commentarii* (1549) of Baron Sigismund von Herberstein, who translated material from a Russian travel book and expressly doubted the credibility of the story; but subsequent texts that borrowed it from him not always questioned it, and among others we find it in works by Johannes Kepler, including his notes to the *Somnium*, where the protagonists are cited as "the people of Lucumoria, a province of Scythia in the far north" (Kepler 1967: 133, 236–9).

The imagined Indian, Persian and Egyptian dream interpretation of Achmet's text introduced the reader to another form of exoticism. However, the representation of those esoteric tradition in the text is fictional. In the first chapters, three nominal representatives of the three oneiromantic schools are introduced. The illustration of their principles, however, remains generic and quickly switches to biblical attestations of divine dreams. The supposedly Persian representative spends some words in praise of oneiromancy, in contrast with astrology (Bernardi 2011).

The already-considered otherness of the Jews worked also in the case of magic books and spells, for which for instance early modern Venetians regularly resorted to the recognised knowledge and power of some inhabitants of the ghetto (Barbierato 2002: especially 304ff.). Among other bans, the Tridentine Index of prohibited books forbade the circulation of all books of astrology. When in 1569, with the bull *Hebraeorum gens*, pope Pius V, former head of the Roman Inquisition, expelled all Jews from the Papal States (apart from the cities of Rome and Ancona, where they were confined to ghettos), it included allusions to their divinatory and magical practices (Valente 2022: 176).

Early modern cultural encounters in particular allow a comparative perspective and lessons from the anthropological gaze. The work Ann Marie Plane did on native Americans at the time of the English colonisation offers a fruitful example of the potential represented by the analysis of cultural difference and of the way this operates on the sense each group makes of its own and the other's oneiric experience, as well as the perhaps unexpected uses that can be made of dreams within power conflicts. In diaries, letters, court testimony, missionaries' accounts and conversion narratives, Plane found a wealth of references to the dream practices of both New England colonists and native Algonquians. Dreams and dreamlike experiences – such as visions and trance – were central to both cultures, on the native side being related to shamanic practice and offering an entry to invisible worlds not accessible by other means. "Above all else, dreams and visions represented a means through which individuals in the quotidian realm of the everyday might enter into contact with manitou, emanations from spiritual power that pervaded places, animal spirits, spiritually potent individuals, and natural features, such as the sun" (Plane 2014: 43). The Europeans' attitude was inevitably ambivalent, considering that, while suspicion towards the likelihood of deceit was strong, visions could potentially represent true revelation: therefore, "the English could never completely dismiss the meaning of dreams, whether their own or those of the indigenous people they encountered" (Plane 2014: 13). However, suspicion prevailed, and they quickly came to cast indigenous dream belief and practice as wholly diabolical. Conversely, among the surviving native population the recuperation of their own dreaming turned into a form of cultural resistance. Of the Spanish New World, something was said above in connection with the sacrament of penance and superstition. In general, although Native American dream cultures differed from one another, and we have limited written sources to testify to their historical variation, European colonialists and missionaries were frequently impressed by the importance they were given in indigenous societies (Plane and Tuttle 2013a). In particular, a seminal study showed how among seventeenth-century Iroquois a dream culture not so distant from Freud's theory regarded dreams as wishes of the soul and allowed periodically their satisfaction, even via the fulfilment of sexual desire with acts not ordinarily permitted, thus exercising a social function comparable to the "escape valve" role of European carnivals (Wallace 1958).

Ronnie Po-chia Hsia has studied the case of China, where, in the context of Jesuit missionary enterprise, holy dreams came to play a more significant role than they had at home, primarily functioning, among the converts, to affirm the sanctity of the person in question. He also compared recorded Buddhist and Christian Chinese dreams with one another and found that both the Buddhist and the Jesuit reports of the Christian mainly served to reinforce doctrine. However, Buddhist dreams presented some distinct characteristics:

> many are double dreams, in which two or more people dreamed similar dreams; still other dreams unfold in actions in the wakeful state. Compared with Christian dreams, with their strong distinction between real life and dreams, as it were, Buddhist dreams are framed by porous boundaries, allowing uninhibited passage through time and space, and between experiences in different modes of existence.
>
> *(Hsia 2005 and 2010: 115)*

Overall, an era of cultural encounters in which at least some Europeans dreamt of the existence or attainability of forms of universal language, including believing in the communicative power of gesture (Knox 1990), the respective oneiric experiences, while altogether taken rather seriously, did not seem to offer much ground for intercultural understanding.

Notes

1 For an example of sixteenth-century discussion of the Homeric passage, which also considers the tradition of literary criticism, see Mazzoni 2017: 534–42, 555–7.
2 Girolamo Cardano also dreamt of the starred sky: for a consumed natural philosopher, this must have been a very common experience, and in fact when he relates one of such occasions, the emphasis is on what is wrong with the dreamt disposition of the celestial bodies. In his style of decodification with reference to his own life and career, the stars represented a college of physicians who denied him entrance (Cardano 2008: 606–7). In the following century, Thomas Browne observed: "the phantasies of sleepe do commonly walk in the great roade of naturall & animal dreames; wherein the thoughts or actions of the day are acted over & echoed in the night. Who can therefore wonder ... that Cardan whose head was so taken up about the stares should dreame that his soul was in the moone!" (Wiseman 2008: 1).
3 Pietro Martire Vermigli brings a common example of this coincidental type: "Even as when we talke of anie man, if happilie the same partie come in the meane while, we saie *Lupus in fabula*, The woolfe is in presence. And yet the talking with him was neither cause, nor token of his comming. So therefore, these things are said to be joined by chance, and also seldome have successe. For this is the nature of things that come by chance; to happen but seldome" (Vermigli 1583: 34).
4 Jean-Claude Schmitt's conclusion is therefore that, if by 1500 and beyond Macrobius was providing the key rationale for enumerating and judging the types of dreams, this had not been the case throughout the Middle Ages (Schmitt 2010: 84); on Macrobius's medieval and Renaissance *fortuna*, however, see Desrosiers-Bonin 2020.
5 Descriptions of dreams according to complexion can be found in Ponzetti 1515: 107rv; Giambelli 1589: 43–5; references to several other sources in Fretz 2020: 12.
6 As indicated in the commentary to the Clarendon edition (Burton 1989–2000: V, 307), Burton indicates the wrong book and chapter of the work of the Neapolitan author. The passage can be found, however, in Book 8, chapter 3 (Latin text in Della Porta 1589: 152–3; Italian translation in Della Porta 1560: 98–100, where the material appears at the beginning of Book 2, chapter 26 – perhaps the version Burton had at hand). On Della Porta's take on dreams, see Paoli 2011: 38–9.
7 On ancient Hebrew sources, see also Kottek 2009; on the medieval tradition, Michelini Tocci 1985.

6
GIROLAMO CARDANO, THE DREAMING SCHOLAR

Discussing dreams, even in the discursive context of a learned commentary to someone else's text – Scaliger on Hippocrates – could offer the opportunity for some slightly incongruous autobiographic references (Roselli 1995: 147–50). The analysis of the self is much more systematically interlaced with academic enquiry in the work of the key Renaissance writer of oneirocritics.

In Lin-Manuel Miranda's *Hamilton*, the musical's emotional climax is reached when, in "It's quiet uptown", Alexander and Eliza describe their life after the loss of their son, Philip, who died in a duel: the mourning couple, whom the tragedy helped to feel closer, has to learn to deal with the "unimaginable". Girolamo Cardano lost his elder son too, although in totally different circumstances (he was executed on the charge of having poisoned his own wife); still, the parallel may help perceiving how devastating the event may have been in the father's life and, consequently, how dominating in his oneiric imagination.

In approaching the key figure in sixteenth-century European dream theory, it may be wise to aim for the golden mean and avoid the extremes, on one side, to feel him as our contemporary, and on the other, to regard him from safe distance as a man stuck in the world of magic. If the concept of Scientific Revolution has by now been at least qualified, it may still be suggested that Cardano's approach to dream interpretation reasonably represented for him – and in historical perspective – a science, in the sense that he aimed at proposing a systematic and rational approach to the establishing of connections between the dreams and their "outcome" (Boriaud 2012). The discipline in his opinion could not aim at precision: in the company of the other forms of divination – astrology, physiognomics, metoposcopy or chiromancy – it could give only some idea of the future; otherwise its capability of prediction would have erased free will.

DOI: 10.4324/9781003279709-6

Overqualifying as a polymath, whatever the definition one adopts (see Burke 2020), Cardano, with the richness of his autobiographical writing, allows us to learn both a wealth of details of his oneiric life and the way he classified and understood it. Two key places, though not the only ones, in which he listed and commented on his own dreams are a dedicated part of the treatise on the interpretation of dreams and a shorter section within his autobiography. To contextualise Cardano's relationship with his dreams, perhaps it will not be superfluous to mention that he regarded insomnia as his main health problem and described in some detail the methods he adopted to try to fight it (Cardano 2002: 23, 27). He listed variously the natural gifts he thought he was endowed with; but when he wanted to single out a special one of his choice, it was for a divine gift of premonition. The dream section of the autobiography, which is set within a wider description of his gifts, opens with the statement: "Does there not seem to be that about dreams – the fact that they have been so real – which can be worthy of admiration?" (Cardano 2002: 138)[1]. Towards the end of his life, he claimed to have benefited for over 30 years a type of clear dreams of premonition, which warned him about immediate events. Into this category can be conflated also his idea of having had the content of many of his books – including the most comprehensive and ambitious of them all, the *De subtilitate* – anticipated when not literally dictated in dream. He declares to have learnt the art of deciphering complex and symbolic dreams only later on in life. Nancy Siraisi (1997: 174–91) distinguishes between two main uses Cardano made of his dream recollections, one autobiographical and the other as *exempla* for his dream theory, while acknowledging that the two may often overlap and interact (see also Grafton 1999: 178–98).

Cardano also tells us that he experienced repetition or continuation of some dreams, as in TV serials (repetition and recurrency in fact appear as categories within Book Two of his *Somnia Synesia*). Of some of his most elaborate dreams, he has left in different books slightly different reports. In his autobiography, in his treatise of dreams and elsewhere in his writing one of his recurrent themes is an emphasis on a selection of "fatal" dreams, warning him about crucial points in his life and career, or a series of unfortunate events. As well as premonitions of the tragedy that was to cut short the life of his son (with little pity for the daughter-in-law), this shortlist includes the complex narrative of his escape from a crowd heading for death by the arduous climbing of a hill, on top of which he is welcomed by a boy: he reads this as an early premonition of his future academic "glory". In another, he dreams that his disembodied soul is alone in the heaven of the moon and hears his father predicting the time Girolamo will spend in each of the heavens – a clear metaphor, in his interpretation, of the many disciplines in which he was to become expert. In one of the few cases, in his long career as a physician, of failure of a cure he prescribed to a young patient, he has a premonition of having got the wrong prescription and subsequently tries, though with poor result, to amend it (the father of the boy, a member of the aristocratic Borromeo family, will consequently try to murder Cardano); the actual dream, or rather nightmare, having consisted in the terrifying view of a huge snake, its deciphering had required some work, to such extent that Cardano tells us that it was the dream that convinced him to study oneirocritics thoroughly and publish a treatise on it (Siraisi 1997: 174; Boriaud 2012: 26–33).

The memory of the dramatically lost son constantly returned to Cardano throughout his subsequent life (Maggi 2009; on the role of Cardano's father in his thought, instead: Giglioni 2010a). In a dream of particular importance, considering that the author believed that it anticipated, in a nutshell, much of the future course of his life, he met his future wife as a young girl, before her family, in real life, moved next door. The details of the imagined scene are not all promising, and in fact, retrospectively, Cardano appears to conclude that his marriage was the source of most of his troubles (Cardano 2002: 80–1). An oneiric appearance of his mother telling him off for his lifestyle, instead, acts as a warning of his coming first serious health threat (Cardano 2008: 634–7). In many cultures, dreams offer some kind of opportunity for communication between the living and the dead.[2] This is also the case for Cardano (Maggi 2010, also presenting Catholic theology and Marsilio Ficino's tenets on the matter; Bokdam 2016). The section on personal dreams within his treatise contains a particularly relevant story. On 2 October 1537, two hours before dawn (traditionally, a particularly appropriate timing for true dreams), Cardano dreams of a dear friend who had died the year before, Prospero Marinoni (he will dream of him again). He looked cheerful and Cardano took notice of the bright colour of his cloak. Since the friend approached him trying to kiss him, Cardano asked him whether he knew that he was dead. He said he did, and so Cardano allowed him to kiss him on his mouth. Cardano's curiosity did not stop there, though, and he seemed eager to exploit this oneiric experience to find out more about the mysteries of the afterlife. He therefore asked his friend if he remembered who he was, and he replied yes; if death was painful, and he learnt that as long as you feel pain you are still alive; what sort of pain it was, and it was compared to an acute fever; whether he would rather be still alive, and the answer was no. Further questions, beginning with "is death similar to sleep?", went unanswered, consequently leaving the dreamer in a state of sadness. Incidentally, this was one of Cardano's dreams on which Carl Gustav Jung made comments (see Box 6.1). Cardano provides his own deciphering: the friend represented his beloved city of Pavia, and his loss the imminent interruption of his position there (Cardano 2008: 604–5; Maggi 2010: 479–80).

While in the making, the treatise underwent varying plans; in the book reconstructing his literary career, Cardano declares to have first drafted it in the mid-1530s and then revised it in the early 1560s (Boriaud 2012). It was

BOX 6.1 JUNG READER OF CARDANO

In his 1940–41 Zürich seminar, which belonged to a series devoted to children's dreams, Carl Gustav Jung analysed a selection of personal dreams from the last book of Cardano's *Somnia Synesia*. His method was selecting some dream narratives while deleting the author's reference to the events he believed the oneiric experiences prophesised. Thus, the first move of modern psychoanalysis is to undress past cultural life of its own interpretative framework, a necessary step towards imposing a new one. This is after all not scandalous and the logical consequence of an epistemological posture, according to which the examined subjects did not have the adequate framework to understand themselves and their world. After all, this is precisely what a cluster of "masters of suspicion" – Marx, Nietzsche and Freud – had successfully done, in the definition of French philosopher Paul Ricoeur (1970). From the perspective of cultural history, however, historical frameworks of understanding are essential if we want to go somewhere in the direction of reconstructing past experiences.

Jung found that Cardano was in error in interpreting his dreams by referring them to his life and world. According to the Swiss psychoanalyst, their correct understanding required instead the acknowledgement of an archetypical and timeless set of associations. For the purpose, he selected Cardano's dream objects consistent with his own interests and symbolic theory. In his first example, Cardano dreamt of a monkey he interrogated about how long he had left to live (answer: four years). Jung (who also thought he had repeatedly anticipated the duration of his life in dreams) discarded Cardano's astrological discussion of the reply, and only focused on the presence of the talking animal, whom he regarded as an intrusion of the real, as distinguished from consciousness. Animals also feature elsewhere in the selection: they are given standard meanings as in the medieval tradition of the keys of dreams – and occasionally misidentified (as Freud did by taking a kite – mentioned in a memory from Leonardo's childhood – for a vulture), which leads him to even more doubtful symbolic associations (a *lupus domesticus*, that is, a dog, with somewhat different implications than a wolf). The oneiric apparition of the dead (an acquaintance, the mother) also is read as a substitute for the unconscious. A third subject area is offered by astronomical imagery, which Jung deciphers in light of his own alchemic beliefs. Overall, the exercise tells us more of the limits of twentieth-century essentialism than of the rich sixteenth-century cultural experience. As it has been observed, this is a paradox if we consider that Jung – contrary to standard narratives of the Renaissance, and in particular to Jacob Burckhardt's, who saw alchemy as an obstacle to the fulfilment of the humanistic ideal – was personally much closer to a past worldview that gave the "occult sciences" full credit as paths to access truth (Jung 2014; Freud 1957; Boriaud 2010; Prins 2017; Gantet 2021: 284–8).

published stating in the title that it owed much to Synesius (*Somniorum Synesiorum omnis generis insomnia explicantes libri quatuor*). This could confuse prospective readers, who will not find themselves reading a commentary. In fact, specialist scholarship does not agree whether his stronger debt is to Artemidorus or Synesius. It clearly owes to Artemidorus some of the treatment by systematic survey of the dreamt matter, including the choice of dedicating the last section to his own dreams. His position, instead, has been regarded "Synesian", in relationship to the focus on prophecy; and for the key fact, central to our assessment of the position of the book in the cultural history of dream interpretation, that he is not addressing professional interpreters (Artemidorus's son and colleagues), but rather suggests the reader tools for self-understanding, emphasising the need for individualised strategies of decoding (Browne 1979; Mancia 2003; Giglioni 2010b; Bokdam 2012: 420–39). Cardano blames his predecessors for lack of clarity and rationale in their organisation of the matter and abandons original plans that structured his book in the fashion of the traditional keys and comes out in the end with a wealth of material to which it is not that easy to orient ourselves.

In the end the work consists of four books. According to a summary of his own, in the first book Cardano exposes the variety of the things we dream, in the second the way we dream them, in the third the different genres of dreamers and in the fourth he offers examples of dreams and their correct interpretation. Throughout the text, he also provides the reader with several lists of recommended ways to use the book. The most synthetic one includes aspects treated in all four books, and therefore again the subject of the dream in all its causes, details and circumstances, by looking up the meaning of each of them and, in lack of one specific, proceeding by analogy to something similar, as well as all the characteristics distinguishing the dreamer. The latter point necessarily and explicitly implies that the same dream has different meanings for different people. It has also different meanings in different circumstances. Therefore, and somewhat frustratingly, in establishing a correspondence between a given dream and the sense of its prediction, Cardano (who in this anyway is not alone) may well suggest that it may announce one outcome or its exact opposite. From the complex of the *Somnia Synesia*, it may be worth extracting some of his classification of the different types of dreams, and the logic of the criteria he recommends in order to interpret them (on his overall method: Le Brun 1994).

Cardano – whose explicit target for the most systematic criticism is Cicero's denial of the prophetic value of dreams – was only seriously interested in dreams he regarded as of supernatural origin. The ways in which he split them into different types are multiple. Some are perfect, some obscure, some never get forgotten, some are unfinished, in others still one believes to be awake (the reader of Borges and Foucault will be reminded of a "certain

Chinese encyclopaedia"). A key term for him, *idola* (whose complex semantic history included, among its precedents, the ancient atomists' theory of perception), conceptualises visions of intelligible reality so that, strictly speaking, they are not dreams; however, they can affect the human imagination in quasi-oneiric experiences: in this form, they replicate reality faithfully. Incidentally, it has been pointed out that when Cardano uses *idolum* to refer to a specific type of oneiric phenomenon, this is understood as primarily an aural form of experience and memory. The intriguing context in which he sees it most intrinsically set is the state of ecstasy, as distinguished from both sleep and wakefulness, a condition which offers those who experience it the chance to hear prophetic words in the clearest way. Cardano considered hearing subtler than sight. Moreover, in line with the interpretation of biblical passages, and with a tradition of medieval mysticism, his idea was that during ecstasies external senses are at rest, but sounds have a transcendent nature, and the intellect is intensified, thus reaching higher (Corrias 2018).

It is, instead, the category of visions, complex type of dreams whose meaning is expressed obliquely, that require expert decoding. A further species, though again not properly speaking dreams, are *oracula*, the comparable experiences one can have in daytime (Boriaud 1999; Giglioni 2010b). The criteria for interpretation begin with the whole typology of subject matter: from the divine to the whole of nature and the human, including actions, trades and objects, clothes, lodgings, acquaintances, travels and even troubles with justice. But then, as we saw, it matters significantly who dreams them, and thus it depends on their status, marital condition, temperament, age, gender and health, as well as ancestry. Cardano adds, in Book One, instructions on how to identify truthful dreams, and recommendations on the way to ensure you have them: these consist in a regimen, which also implies purgation, as if you were keeping your house clean; but a prayer and a gem may also help. Some of the correspondences he establishes in the theoretical part of the book can be found in action in his personal examples: thus, a dream concerning a part of his body has to do with a member of his household (a servant).

Cardano's retelling of many well-known dreams of others, and in particular classical (including Calpurnia, Caesar's wife), served the purpose to ennoble the recent oneiric experience by inscribing in a long, uninterrupted and prestigious line; others come from his contemporaries and acquaintances, and in this case, it is he who acts as witness guaranteeing their truthfulness (Boriaud 2008). Corroboration of stories, insisting that he has not invented them, is a constant concern of his, a deontological and epistemological issue he cares for, as well as an obvious line of defence against many adversaries. Aware that he was challenging his readers' disposition to believe, Cardano periodically warned them that they must trust him, despite the exceptionality of the narrated stories (actual events, not dreams). The surprising nature of some of them puts to test even his own trust in the reality of what happened to him – an occasion for evoking the troubled question, "am I awake or am I dreaming?" An example is offered by an assault by a vicious dog while the author was travelling on his mule; he narrowly avoided to be hurt by lowering his body while the beast jumped over him. Not easily believing what had happened, he asked a boy who was travelling just behind him, who confirmed the veracity of the scene (Cardano 2002: 95–6). Apart from this convenient presence of a witness, Cardano's general criterion of verification of his extraordinary personal memories is that he luckily took notes and repeatedly referred to them, so that he could be sure that he had not just made them up. Travelling was a common experience that understandably made frequent appearance in the oneiric mirror. Cardano says he owned a small horse; but on another occasion he apparently dreamt of being riding on a large mule and seeing above him a naked woman urinating and defecating while laughing. He apologises for the rudeness and in deciphering the scene concentrates on the mount (Cardano 2008: 632–5).

Beside the more complex narrative of his key dreams, what does Cardano tell us that he dreamt? Himself in various situations and conditions (including ailments), family and acquaintances, clearly (or else people and facts he believes represent them). But also historical figures (Alexander the Great), animals (quite a range of them including a young elephant and a biting rat), starry nights and rainbows, and of course a variety of locations, more or less known and recognisable in their oneiric appearance. A scholar's dreams are also, inevitably, "bookish": so, in one of them, he dreams that half of his own library, the part which did not contain books of medicine, collapsed (Cardano 2008: 622–3). A scholar also needs writing implements, so another time he dreams to capture an owl to pluck some useful feathers (ibid. 624–5). Career (with his frequent clashes with the medical establishment, not to mention his trouble with the Inquisition), wealth and health concerns feature prominently. To satisfy the curiosity of psychoanalysts, sex and genitalia are not missing – from a woman sterilising another woman who is castrating bitches; to Cardano dreaming of himself as adolescent, happily serving a king and showing his loyalty by resisting the sexual temptation of a king's young lover (ibid. 648–9, 640–3). Other sexual matter is found in other people's dreams for whose interpretation he has been consulted.

Towards the end of the description of the selection of his own dreams, Cardano (2008: 656–7) warns that, in a dream, we should clearly distinguish what is memory of past events and what is premonition of the future, and comments that people tend to concentrate too much in identifying the former, thus risking missing completely the latter, which is what matters. The interaction between living people he dreams of and later encounters of them in real life offers him the opportunity for reflections on notions of reality, copies and diverging details. Cardano's summaries of individual dreams may end with an annotation concerning the result of having experienced and interpreted them. With the concentration being on his life and career, this may mean that, of a dream that he found gave him confidence, he regards it as a factor that, by boosting his morale, actually helped him succeed – a sort of self-fulfilling prophecy. Dreams may also have warned him that someone else, as well as himself (as is the case with one of his sons), is getting ill and in serious danger, and thus make him rush to help them and save their lives.

The already-mentioned dream in which Cardano reports to have met his father, and which has been referred to the whole series of heavens of ancient cosmology, had a reprise in a separate imaginary dialogue between himself and his father, which he wrote later on in life ad can qualify as a re-elaboration of the scheme offered by the *Dream of Scipio*. In fact, his reworking of the model offered by Macrobius's commentary has been contrasted with that which, a few generations before, had been proposed by Marsilio Ficino. In one of his letters, the Florentine magus played with the thought of enchanting to sleep the King of Naples Ferdinand of Aragon and telling him of the experience Ficino's own disembodied soul had had by visiting the heavens and meeting the king's father Alfonso; in the oneiric experience, Ficino had subsequently met and informed cardinal Giovanni, son of Ferdinand and grandson of Alfonso – thus mirroring, even if by interposing himself as the go-between dreamer, the relationship between the two Scipios. The moral message was that the royal rule should aim at restoring peace by giving up insignificant earthly ambitions. By contrast, Cardano's reworking of the model ignores a philosophy of life based on detachment and expectations cast in the afterlife, while facing the troubles of his own real life. In his reappearance in the dialogue, Cardano's father comforts his son by distracting him from an anxiety for his future, reminding him of his life achievements and recommending him to divert his mind by concentrating on practical tasks. It has been noticed that the dream discourse and utopian ideals here are negotiated in two strikingly different social contexts and with consistently diverging outcomes: Ficino is the man of the establishment advising the world's rulers, Cardano the heterodox scientist never completely fitting in, nor being accepted, by the dominant institutions and struggling to cope with misfortune. One addressed peace on Earth, the other an all too human peace of mind (Prins 2020).

In several respects, including a connection between the oneiric and creativity, and an appreciation of the interaction between dream and wakefulness, scholarship has given to Renaissance dream theory a special place in the Western tradition of thought on the subject, and to Cardano a key role in the story (Rupprecht 1993; Maggi 2008). Nor should one forget that his insistence on being the chosen one, reading his own scientific excellence as a divine gift, resulted both from a long cultural tradition of the notion of genius and from the pressure of an academic and book market, in which intellectuals had to be proactive in promoting competitive representations of themselves in order to emerge and survive (Bobory 2003).

In fact, Cardano's self-affirmed exceptionality offered itself easily to feed a tradition of reflection on the nature of genius and its proximity to mental disorder, which ended in the positivistic era with the attention paid to him by Cesare Lombroso, who, as well as formulating general theories postulating such proximity, wrote an essay specifically dedicated to the case of Cardano. He had been preceded by observations on the singularity of the Renaissance man that had engaged several prominent European intellectuals over centuries, among them Gabriel Naudé, Pierre Bayle, Gotthold Ephraim Lessing, Johann Gottfried von Herder and Georg Wilhelm Friedrich Hegel – all of them equating Cardano's greatness to that of some of the key philosophers of Antiquity. The article on the madness of Cardano was the first publication of a young Lombroso, at the time still a student of medicine, so that it worked as the starting point for his wider speculations on the matter (it was followed, a year later and on the same journal, by an essay on the "influence of civilization on madness and of madness on civilization"). Dreams play a part in his first article too: Lombroso noticed their dominant role in Cardano's writing and found Cardano's tale of having had entire books oneirically inspired particularly bizarre. In general, he regarded Cardano's belief in predictive dreams as a naive sharing of popular superstition. At the same time, the nineteenth-century writer was fascinated by his Renaissance predecessor's intellectual achievements and followed his footsteps in having an intensive oneiric life and reflecting on it autobiographically. His subsequently developed theory on the man of genius, contradictorily, while understanding it in pathological terms, also regarded it as the true driving force of history and the cradle of art (Lombroso 1855; Gadebusch Bondio 2017).

Another famous Italian autobiographic writer, the artist Benvenuto Cellini, included references to dreams, together with visions and hallucinations, in narrating his own life story. They feature apparitions of his father, who intervened menacingly to offer him career advice, and of a beautiful young man, who he understood to be his guardian angel. The latter allegedly stopped him from committing suicide while he was in prison in Rome under the accusation of theft in 1539 (he had also broken his leg by attempting to escape from Castel Sant'Angelo) and told him off for his attempt to self-destruction, in contempt of the divine gift of life (Cellini 1998: passim). Cellini also wrote dream sonnets and his own interpretation of them.

Notes

1 It is only implicit in the Latin text and English translation, but clearer from the context and French and Italian versions, that he is referring to his own dreams.
2 For the medieval European experience, see Schmitt 1998, esp. 35–58.

7
THE SIXTEENTH-CENTURY TREATISE ON DREAMS

A quasi-genre

Following and elaborating on the ancient and medieval tradition, several treatises (listed in the Appendix) were published during the period to assess the nature and value of dreams from a medical, philosophical or theological perspective, or else from a combination of them. Beyond individual variation, they tend to frequently present some similarity in structure and content, so that a standard look of a typical Renaissance text of this genre can be obtained by comparing and combining details of actual ones. Differences were inevitably due to diversity of genre and context, so a survey on the development of the genre with particular focus on Italy over the century roughly spanning from 1515 to 1615 will follow this attempt to outline an overall sketch.[1]

Dreams attracted intellectual curiosity and polite conversation as, at the same time, a daily experience and an extraordinary one, which defied the wakeful norms of perception and appeared to open a window to other worlds and times. Their exceptional status required an assessment primarily in the tradition of natural philosophy, regarding first of all the identification of the sleeping and dreaming subject, considering that the two experiences tend to go together (do all humans sleep and dream, and is it an activity peculiar, reserved to them or shared with other creatures?). It could also be considered in more explicitly physiological terms in the medical tradition; and similarities and differences between ordinary and oneiric perception would lead to reflections on the operating and the reliability of the senses and human faculties. Ultimately, the relationship between dreamt images and events and daytime factual reality posed the mother of all challenges, and the most delicate questions for debate in an age in which freedom of thought and expression presented evident and dangerous limitations – if we consider the philosophical and theological implications of attributing to a dream, perhaps based on its supposed origin, the capability to work as a means for diagnosis or prophecy.

An early and influential example of sixteenth-century text is represented by the treatise dedicated to the subject of dreams by Ferdinando Ponzetti (1515), a cardinal who died in 1527 during the Sack of Rome, within his wider Latin *Natural Philosophy*.[2] It opens with the statement that sleep and wakefulness are affects (*passiones*) of the body and the soul together, as they do not involve either of them separately; he adds that the wakeful person is asleep *in potentia*, and vice versa. Despite the apparent parallels, plants do not sleep: it is a prerogative of animals only, since it concerns the suspension of their sensitive faculty; however, we cannot tell when fish and some other animals sleep, because they do not have eyelids.[3] His detailed philosophical and medical enquiry continues by assessing causes and nature of sleep in relation to nutrition, heat and humidity, health and age of humans, as well as of other animals. The main exposition of the received wisdom is accompanied by side questions and answers on matter of detail. For instance, of the drinking of wine the author says that in moderation it helps falling asleep, whereas in excess it keeps one awake (Ponzetti 1515: 99r); the effect on sleep of the listening to stories (*fabule*), instead, varies according to one's complexion (ibid. 99v). Moving on more specifically to the subject of dreams, these too find physiological explanations, as is the case with the statement that people of hotter disposition or ingesting hot and vaporous food dream much (ibid. 105v). Ponzetti also assesses the contribution of astrology and the predictive claims of various other more dubious and forbidden forms of divination. He warns against the risk of rushing predictions from insufficient data ("one swallow does not make a summer", ibid. 123r) and offers guidance on inferences from analogies (*similitudines*). In the end, a couple of folios (ibid. 124v–26v) are filled in the form of a short key of dreams, offering interpretation to given oneiric contents. The last tract in which the book is divided deals specifically with prophecy.[4]

The tradition of scholarly expositions and commentaries on the subject – on which specific Renaissance examples will be described within the typology of textual genres offered in the next chapter – continued throughout the period in oral, handwritten and printed form alike. As a sample of what was left in manuscript, though besides that not significantly different from the material that circulated in print, we can look at a *Disputatio de somniis* written in the year of his death (1561) by Sisto Medici and left unpublished together with a miscellaneous collection of other texts of philosophy, theology and poetry. The author had been a Dominican novice at the convent of Santi Giovanni e Paolo (San Zanipolo) in Venice, where he was close to the old Francesco Colonna (aged 16, he wrote a sonnet in praise of the book on the title page of his copy of the *Hypnerotomachia Poliphili* now held at the University Library in Cambridge, incidentally offering further evidence of the authorship of the romance, on which more below – Fumagalli 1992) and grew to be both a lecturer (in Padua, Florence and Venice) and, repeatedly, a prior of the same religious house, a prestigious church where the funeral services of most doges were held and many of them buried. The 16 chapters, which could have functioned as a cycle of lectures, emphasise the role of phantasy in the creation of oneiric images, to the extent that the text has the rather unusual subtitle "or, of the productivity of reason through rest" (*sive, De rationi foecunditate per quietem*).

The discussion of the subject which is offered by later treatises follows on similar paths, with variations adopted to suit particular cultural contexts. We have, among others, Latin, Italian, French and English texts, with a thicker publishing activity between the last quarter of the sixteenth century and the first decade or two of the following one. The vernacular texts evidently aim at a partly different audience; they belong to various literary genres and cultural milieus and, consequently, adopt their respective style, concerns and attitudes. Some are more scholarly, resembling the structure and phrasing of the exegesis of a received text, even when they are not formally commentaries. Others echo more closely the informal atmosphere of the humanist academies, as is the case with their dialogic nature, which does not mean that they have not read their authorities, nor that they are less keen to show it to the reader: the exposition, however, will be more didactic, and attention will be paid to offering the topic as a subject for polite conversation; or else, more explicitly, moral reflection, in which case we may find ourselves entering a yet slightly autonomous sub-genre.

After the precedents offered by Barbaro and Ugoni, the authors of two earlier texts, which I will examine in Chapter 8 as examples of vernacular sources stretching the limits of religious heterodoxy (see below), the production of Italian vernacular texts intensifies around 1575. In the case of Benedetto Dottori (1575*), a Paduan philosopher also member of Reggio Emilia's Accademia degli Elevati, the treatise declares from its title to be an exposition of the doctrine of Aristotle. This rationale was more standard in works like Boccadiferro's Latin lectures (1570), which will serve as source for a populariser like Tommaso Garzoni (also discussed below); to find it in a vernacular text suggests an interesting instance of the philosophical tradition of the University of Padua reaching out to address a wider public. The posthumous publication, which an editor dedicated to the Duke of Mantua Guglielmo Gonzaga, ascribes the doctrine to another deceased authority, Dottori's Paduan tutor Marco Antonio Passeri, an attribution that suggests antedating this university teaching material to some decades earlier. The book opens with a praise of dreams as a, if not the, marvel of nature, so much to have suggested a supernatural aetiology. After a brief description of the physiology of sleep, centred on the role played by the fumes produced by digestion, dreams are reaffirmed as the main theme and introduced via a description of the quality and duration of the images allowed by our sight, if compared with similar natural phenomena. Since during sleep our senses are in standby, one could define the dream as the return of the image, which memory sends back to our senses: this is the reason why animals, like oysters, that only perceive what is present and do not have memory, do not dream (Dottori 1575: 8r). Imaginative similes colour the text, putting at test the author's competence in the exploitation of the communicative power of language. Thus, the operating of images in the production of dreams is compared to the shapes we perceive in the form and disposition of clouds (an example that comes from Aristotle's *On Dreams* and recurs in other texts too), and, while we look at them intensively, we have the impression first to see a lion, which then turns into a bull, a bear or a goat (ibid. 9v); the initial emerging of images, in its fuzziness, to the sensory confusion of ill people who, in their delirium, take a line on a wall for a snake or someone's cane for a sword (ibid. 10v);[5] the deception caused at some points by the wandering fumes to the visual effect of a finger that, close to our eye, makes us see things double (ibid. 11r); the hiding of substance behind apparencies to a snake that jumps out of the grass to attack (ibid. 12v); and excessive humours expanding in the body to the accumulating of water in a sponge (ibid. 13r). This questioning of the reliability of the senses, and in particular of sight, has been powerfully reconstructed by Stuart Clark (2007b) as a cultural trend of the time, as we will see in further detail in Chapter 8 when discussing the context of beliefs in witchcraft.

Following the doctrine of his tutor, Dottori, after discussing the varying clarity of the dreamt images along the physiological processes of sleep and digestion, distinguished dreams in three categories – natural, intentional and casual – each with its own cause and way of relating to the future. The natural originate from the humours, the intentional from the soul; for the casual opinions are divided, whether their origin is external or internal, but the author compromises for a combination of both. Some sensual experiences are halfway between perceptions and dreams because we still marginally receive them directly from present objects, whereas proper dreams only retrieve images previously deposited in our memory. Here some images fade (as the water changes overnight in rivers, to continue with the inflation of similes), some we must keep alive by refreshing them (as a painter does with his brush), and the most recent ones replace others, so that the hunter will be more likely to dream of hounds, the sailor of winds, lovers of their women and artisans of their trades (Dottori 1575: 13rff.). The predictive power of each sort of dream works as follows: natural dreams are signs of future developments, because their content hints at the specific humoral imbalance responsible for them, thus allowing the physician to readdress it; intentional dreams operate as causes, because they provoke appetites that move the dreamer, once awake, to consequent action; following Aristotle, this is not the case for the casual ones, which may represent remote situations and events, subsequently happening independently from the dreamer: they are therefore predictive *per accidens*. A variation on the lack of causal connection of the last type is provided by dreams that could have warned and prevented an event but have been ignored: this is the case of Julius Caesar's wife dreaming of holding the wounded body of her husband, but not being able to convince him the next day not to go to the Senate (as also retold by Shakespeare).

Dottori's examples combine ancient sources with modern literature: among the classical anecdotes, we find that of Consul Publius Decius Mus, who, warned by a dream, stoically sacrificed his own life to ensure the victory of the Romans over the Latins at the battle of Vesuvius (340 BCE) as narrated by Livy (the scene of a cycle of paintings by Rubens now in the Princely Collections of Liechtenstein: Baumstark 1985; see Figure 7.1); that of Simonides of Ceos whose dream saved him from drowning by shipwreck comes from Cicero's *On Divination* and had been retold by Valerius Maximus; while the sixteenth-century reader did not need to be told that the terrible story of Lisabetta da Messina, whose dream of the lover who had been killed by her brothers helped her finding his body, came from such shared reading material as a novella by Boccaccio (IV.5).[6] History and literature here converge without a significant distinction of roles: whether a fact documented "as it really occurred", or just a plausible fictional narrative, exemplification works as argumentative ploy to attest a particular type of relationship between premonition by dream and subsequent course of events.

A Mantuan dedication, though this time an ecclesiastical one, to the bishop in charge of that diocese, accompanies also Cipriano Giambelli's *Il Diamerone* (1589*), a vernacular dialogue, in the style of the conversation that took place in Renaissance humanistic academies, aptly including regular quotations from poetry ancient and modern. The author, a canon regular from Verona, preached and lectured in the cathedral of Treviso, a city in which he was also, appropriately, member of an academy. It develops over two days (this is incidentally the meaning of the Greek-inspired title): the first exposes the received doctrine on sleep and dreams, while the second concerns friendship. The dialogue form was by far the most common literary structure inherited from the classical tradition, and it should not be intended as a distinctively literary option, before the late-Renaissance rediscovery of the treatise and invention of the essay. It could, however, convey cultural connotations or at least allow for them to be implicitly attached: it has been considered in particular as a form that made it possible to explore different points of view without obliging the authors to take sides, or else to permit them to dare

62 The sixteenth-century treatise on dreams

expressing heterodox views, behind the mask of attributing them to one of the dialogue's personae. Inquisitors, however, were hardly fooled, as the story of Galileo shows (Batkin 1990; Cox 1992).

FIGURE 7.1 Peter Paul Rubens, "Decius Mus Relating His Dream" (oil on large canvas, 1616–1617). From the Decius Mus cycle, commissioned by a Genoese patrician and intended as cartoon for the production of tapestries. The cycle was one of the Flemish artist's first adventures into the representation of episodes of ancient history, inspired by his humanist education and by the study of Raphael cartoons for the *Acts of the Apostles* (now at the Victoria and Albert Museum, London). The dream the consul is narrating to his listening troop had warned him that his death would ensure victory. Rubens cites specific details from Roman iconography, depicting a formal *adlocutio*, authoritative act of speaking on a platform, which adopts rhetorically effective posture and gesture and resembles an iconographic formula also attested in the frieze of the Column of Trajan in Rome. LIECHTENSTEIN, The Princely Collections, Vaduz-Vienna/SCALA, Florence. 2024 © Photo Scala, Florence.

Within a traditional incipit that puts man as the climax of creation, the author emphasises the desire for knowledge as the most valuable gift of this creature, the one that brings it closer to the divine. The tale of the origins is corroborated, among other testifying *exempla*, by a scene from daily life in late sixteenth-century Europe:

> Nor should anyone be astonished when in the public squares, among many gentlemen, one reads the reports of the wars of France and Flanders, and the news of Rome, Venice and all the other parts of the world; and all (though busy with their own business) stop, raise their heads, open their eyes and tends their ears: for all are eager to know everything.
> *(Giambelli 1589: 2–3)*

After the setting offered by this prologue, the reported conversation falls on the topics of sleep and dreams, under the guidance of a philosopher and physician, introduced as a competent scholar of Aristotle and Galen. One thus encounters again themes of natural philosophy already exposed in Latin by Ponzetti: sleep is a property of body and soul together; plants, which do not have senses, do not sleep properly speaking. A long simile describes the physiology of sleep via an iatrochemical parallel between the human body and the distillation of herbal products. By reproposing medical wisdom, some standard advice is also included: do not sleep in daytime, nor immediately after a meal. Wine counselling here takes the form of warning against some too strong types (*vini poderosi*: wines from Crete and others), and the recommendation to mix it with water. The variation of the need to sleep for people of different age or complexion also includes deterministic reference to particular body shapes (large heads, small height) that, by reducing the distance between heart and brain, magnify the effect of the vapours produced from food. The remaining advice concerning sleep regards places and positions. The participants then move to dreams, combining Aristotelian knowledge with quotations from poetry, much in the style of conversations in contemporary academies. They share information on the different types of dream and on the origin of each; and when the subject touches on the spiritual dimension, a theologian intervenes to add his expertise.

I have already cited a couple of times the treatise by Segni (1591*), a Bolognese theologian. He explores the different categories of dreamers and sorts of dreams and their causes, adopting Macrobius's classification. Among his specific topics are the question whether the dead visit the living (with the example of the oneiric apparition of the mother Monica to Augustine), and the warning that it may be the demons that deceptively take the looks of the dead.

Meanwhile, the Italian printing houses continued to issue old and new Latin works too: among the latter, texts by Alessandro Cariero (1575*) and

Celso Mancini (1591*). Cariero, a Paduan law graduate and man of letters (he was one of the adversaries of Dante's poetry in the polemics mentioned in Section 4.3), published the text of a speech in the Aristotelean tradition, which he had given in the local Academy of the Spirited (Accademia degli Animosi); the latter was an ambitious circle founded a couple of years earlier with a philosophical and religious, as well as literary, agenda, and attended by members of the aristocracy of Brescia and Venice. The book was published the same year and by the same Paduan publisher as the vernacular one by Dottori. However, while Dottori's more orthodox Aristotelianism drastically limited the predictive power of casual dreams, Cariero's Averroism, well represented at the university of Padua, provides a systematic dialectic argumentation in favour of the conciliation between classical beliefs in divination and Christian doctrine (a goal shared with contemporary Neoplatonism), supporting the possibility that in dreams, and in dreams only, divine forewarning of the future may be communicated to human beings (Gandolfo 1978: 258–9; Paoli 2011: 45–7). As for Mancini, a year after being appointed to the chair of moral philosophy of the University of Ferrara, he dedicated to the Este duke a collection of tracts he had composed in recent years; the first and longer, on dreams and divination through dreams, occupies 100 pages in quarto (the subsequent tracts concern laughter and the Platonic theory of vision). It is an erudite text, engaging in exposition and discussion with much of the philosophical tradition, and concluding in support of the Aristotelean views.

The string of vernacular treatises continued in 1613* with Paolo Grassi's *Ragionamenti domestici*, which returned to questions of definition of dreams with strict reliance on Aristotle's logic, as well as natural philosophy. His initial discussion as to whether "dreaming is natural to humans" makes use of the various senses in which the philosopher's notion of *proprium* can be intended, and their implications when dealing with how much, and in what sense, dreaming is human. The text offered a traditional exposition, in nine *ragionamenti*, of the physiology of dreams based on Aristotle, including the refutation of the theories held by the competing philosophical schools, by a physician and botanist from Correggio (a small lordship in Emilia), member of a local humanist academy, who dedicates it to the rulers of the land. As in Segni, concluding reference is made to the assessment of dreaming in Catholic casuistry.

Also dedicated to a member of the ruling nobility in the small principates of the Po Valley was the following year Cesare Merli's *Lume notturno* [Nocturnal light] (1614*), subsequently reprinted a couple of times. Offering another vernacular survey of received wisdom, the text, which is described in the long title as a manual (*prattica*), aptly ends with "useful recommendations to avoid making unpleasant dreams". These include going to sleep with pleasant and honest thoughts and avoiding bad and illicit ones, observing a moderate diet, avoiding sleeping supine and reciting a prayer, for which a recommended Latin text follows. On the page immediately preceding these *avvertimenti*, this author too, as some of his closest predecessors, had given a very synthetic summary of the assessment of the subject in casuistry, suggesting that all theologians agree that, since people while dreaming are not in command of their will, they are not morally responsible for them. He added, however, that the responsibility is at stake in case dreams had been encouraged by preceding wakeful thoughts, and if one pleases themselves with them afterwards.

The European scene beyond Italy was undoubtedly active. In France, the book market was significantly occupied by reproposals of the material of the medieval keys of dreams, as well as of Achmet's, with new publications in the medical vein surfacing in the new century (Dupleix *1606 – see Bercé 1988; Dandrey 1988). In English, as well as translations of the *Somniale Danielis* (1556) and of Artemidorus (from 1606), two authors who published works, partly drawn on traditional material, were Thomas Hill and Thomas Nashe (Holland 1999: 142–6). Hill produced two different texts, *A Little Treatise* (*1567) and *The Moste Pleasaunte Arte* (*1576), as well as prognostications for the years 1573 and 1574, which testify to the proximity between oneirocritics and astrology. They combine learned and popular traditions of interpretation and rely heavily on Artemidorus and, directly or indirectly, "Daniel" (Rivière 2017: especially 63–7). While voicing the contemporary concern for nightmares, Nashe's *The Terrors of the Night* (*1598) criticised the belief that dreams were of supernatural origin as superstitious and ignorant: neither predictive nor meaningful, in his opinion they were mere delusions of the imagination resulting from humoral imbalances (Levin 2008: 49–53). In the Iberian Peninsula, the circulation of treatises of oneirocritics during the period appears to have remained limited to the manuscript form and to have been significantly influenced by the Arabic tradition (Jordán Arroyo 2017).

Notes

1 A suggestion of the Italian Renaissance treatise on dreams as a "micro-genre" was already advanced by Paoli 2011.
2 See Rivière 2017: 9 for influence on John Dee and Thomas Hill.
3 For discussions on dreaming of and by animals in early seventeenth-century England, see Fudge 2008.
4 A brief discussion of Ponzetti's dream theory can be found in Gandolfo 1978: 106–7.
5 Some of the same examples of sensory deception occur in the Latin text of Ponzetti 1515: 117r–119v, a theme followed by deception in dreams.
6 On the novella of Lisabetta da Messina, see Bonetti 2009.

8
A SELECTION OF SOURCES ON RENAISSANCE DREAM CULTURES

A sample of texts from a variety of different literary genres and cultural milieus – other than more dedicated treatises on dreams and their interpretation – may offer a further glance and testify to different nuances of the way in which the intellectual traditions, inherited and re-elaborated along the sixteenth century, were employed in specific contexts in the understanding and evaluation of the oneiric experience. It is inevitably a selection, and it cannot avoid being unsystematic; any attempt to systematicity would be forced on a set of ideas and cultural practices that was by its own nature multifaceted and entangled with a variety of other concepts and beliefs.

8.1 The linguistic invention and erotic imagination of a learned friar

If the dream as a literary genre to some extent constitutes a world of its own and is commonly studied by specialised literary criticism in dedicated publications, there is at least one Renaissance Italian text whose nature and influence demands to be mentioned within this brief survey. It was published in 1499 by the most characteristic and prestigious of humanist printers, the Venetian Aldo Manuzio, although on the request and funding of someone else, rather than on his own initiative; it was commissioned by a lawyer, Leonardo Crasso, who dedicated the lavish edition to Guidobaldo da Montefeltro, Duke of Urbino. The title is only the first unusual feature a prospective reader must deal with: *Hypnerotomachia Poliphili* is a Latin neologism created out of three Greek terms, standing for "the strife of love in a dream"; and it is the battle of Polifilo, himself a persona Hellenically named

DOI: 10.4324/9781003279709-8

as the "lover of Polia". The text is now well known to scholars, whereas the general, even learned public has had more limited exposure to its complexity, if not mysteries (until, that is, it was popularised as its deciphering became the centrepiece in the plot of a successful novel, *The Rule of Four* by Ian Caldwell and Dustin Thomason, published in 2005).

For a start, it is written in a most idiosyncratic language, a peculiar Italian vernacular making up frequently words out of Latin and ancient Greek terms – and not everyday classical ones either: a good share of them are rare and appear to have been retrieved from the most updated reference books of humanist erudition. In reviewing the first complete modern English translation, Antony Grafton has compared it to the language of François Rabelais and James Joyce (Grafton 2000, on Colonna 1999). Although this is not the place for an extensive presentation of the book, something about its authorship, content, character and legacy may help position it in a well-deserved space inside the coffer of the Western oneiric imagination.

Although the book was published anonymously, few years later a reader detected the acrostic that, barely hidden in the initial letters of each chapter, declared, in Latin: "Brother Francesco Colonna deeply loved Polia". The predominant identification of the writer is with a Dominican friar who taught humanities and lived between Treviso and Venice, where he was also prior of the already-mentioned leading convent of San Zanipolo. The narrative has the protagonist dreaming that he is in a wood where he had many wonderous adventures, including meeting a hungry wolf, terrifying dragons, a giant snake and sensual nymphs, who played with arousing his sexual desire. He then encounters his beloved, and on Cupid's boat they reach a utopian island. In the next section, Polia narrates her dream, which involves having initially turned down the lover's amorous advances, caused his apparent death, from which he recovered only after she had been convinced to change her mind. Then the couple kisses, the nymphs dance and Polia vanishes at dawn as the protagonist is reminded that the whole experience had been oneiric. So, as the subtitle of the partial Elizabethan translation recites, the book "sheweth, that all humaine and worldlie things are but a dreame, and but as vanitie it selfe" (Colonna 1592).

The dream imagery presented by the book offers the reader multisensory and synesthetic experiences that may have inspired Shakespeare's *A Midsummer Night's Dream* (Fretz 2021). The text is also filled with technical architectural references and enigmatic inscriptions in a variety of obscure languages, including Egyptian hieroglyphics. It has therefore lent itself to work as a model for writing in the field of the occult sciences, as is the case with a 1572 treatise of alchemy by Giovan Battista Nazari, which adopts the narrative structure of revealing its doctrine via an oneiric journey (Bolzoni 2013: 41). Furthermore, it is endowed with an extraordinary rich series of woodcuts (also by an unknown artist, despite attempts to attribute them to various contemporary artists including Pinturicchio, Vittore Carpaccio, Andrea Mantegna and Giovanni Bellini; see Figure 8.1) illustrating the story and its imaginary setting. Just to mention one example of its cultural heritage, Polifilo's dreamed gardens, with their statues and fountains, are thought to have influenced the design of the well-known actual ones subsequently set in Florence, Tivoli, Bomarzo and Versailles (Colonna 1999). The early modern learned public – in general also familiar with the reading of Italian texts in their original language – was significantly aware and impressed by the work, and obliviousness has only descended in more recent times.

One could conclude that the intellectual attraction exercised over the years by this unique artefact made use of the dreamworld as a code for a playful search for esoteric meanings and exclusive aesthetic values, only accessible to a cultured elite, which may have particularly enjoyed the restricted character of the game. Within a rich tradition of interpretations, it has been suggested that the peculiar language of the text may be not only its medium but also its message: since paratexts declare that Polia was old and is by the time of writing dead, she may stand for the Latin language, and the book's project

FIGURE 8.1 Here be dragons. Woodcut from the *Hypnerotomachia Poliphili* (Venice 1499), fol. d3v © Volgi archive/Alamy Stock Photo.

envisages a cultural renewal that builds on the acknowledgement that the beloved classical tongues are no longer alive, and can only survive in the offering of material for the building of the new emerging ones (Agamben 1984).

8.2 Dreaming the powerful

Outside Italy, a remarkable case took place in the Iberian Peninsula. In 1590, the Spanish Inquisition arrested 21-year-old Lucrecia de León, from Madrid, under the accusation of having invented a series of dreams of blasphemous and heretical content, as well as seditious and injurious towards King Philip II; her trial lasted over five years. The political content was particularly delicate, as the young woman did not restrain from bald antimonarchical statements and had, among other events, predicted the defeat of the Armada a year before it occurred. Lucrecia had been having her controversial dreams since childhood. What is extraordinary, however, is that the interest and concern her experience attracted brought two friars to alternate and take notes regularly, for the two and half years prior to her arrest, of the content of more than 400 of her dreams. We have seen above how ancient and modern writers have discussed the relationship between dreams and visions. Here, the fact is that Lucrecia's related experiences, with all the similarities they present with the visionary, are consistently described as dreams, that took place ordinarily at night, occasionally during afternoon siestas[1] (Kagan 1990; Jordán Arroyo 2017: 111–47; Bulkeley 2018).

A dreamer who told oneiric experiences unfavourable to those in power could end up executed: this is what happened following the reports of prophetic dreaming by a mid-sixteenth-century Catholic servant, eventually hanged for predicting the death of Henry VIII (Campbell 2016). A parallel could be drawn with the fairly common contemporary circulation, in Italy, of astrological prognostications regarding the illness and death of kings, princes and popes. Sometimes used to legitimise the rule of a political leader, other times to do just the opposite, they have been appreciated as sources for the understanding of the political history of the period (Azzolini 2010).

8.3 Commerce with the classics: Aristotle and Macrobius

As many other texts in the scholastic canon, the *Parva naturalia* were subject to a medieval tradition of commentary, by which Aristotle's critique of predictive dreams offered the opportunity for a shift towards a laicisation of the theological discourse: the interpretative conception of dreams offered by the biblical and oneirocritic traditions was replaced by a psychophysiological approach that transferred the topic to the field of natural science and, while limiting the scope of divination, associated it with the established kind that was practised by medicine and astrology (Grellard 2010). It is against this background that one can properly appreciate the exegetic contributions brought by Renaissance humanism.

Considering their inclusion in university curricula, editions of the *Parva naturalia* were common by the beginning of the sixteenth century, when the received academic practice encountered and exploited the printing press. Five different editions were published between 1618 and 1623: in Paris and Leipzig by François Vatable, in Bologna by Juan Ginés de Sepúlveda and the rest in Venice, the work of Pietro Alcionio, Niccolò Leonico Tomeo and Agostino Nifo. The last is of particular interest: he was a prominent voice in the period as Latin translator of the oeuvre of Aristotle and professor of medicine and philosophy in several Italian universities, including Padua, Naples and Salerno. In exposing Aristotle's treatises on sleep and dreams, Nifo limits the astrologic connections that dominated both the thought of his predecessor and colleague in Padua Pietro Pomponazzi and a treatise dating from about 1300, at the time attributed to the distinguished Catalan physician Arnau de Vilanova, whereas now it is believed to be the work of a William of Aragon. Also departing from the Neoplatonic focus on the supernatural dimension of the dream as revelation, he proposed a complex mediation between philosophy and medicine that included an articulated interpretation of the physiology of sense perception, with emphasis on the connection between the individuals' humoral balance and their oneiric experience: decoding dreams therefore was secularised in a hermeneutics of signs that pointed at the physical and spiritual conditions of the dreamer, observed with attention to circumstances and to the regularity of the manifestations of given images. On the other hand, in a separate *quaestio* concerning prophecy Nifo rejected attempts to reduce its explanation too in natural terms, adhering instead to Aquinas's statement of its divine inspiration (Gandolfo 1978: 102–5; Sorge 2016).

A few years after Nifo, a commentary to Aristotle's texts was offered by Giovanni Crisostomo Javelli, a Dominican theologian and inquisitor (1531, reprinted several times). He departed from the ancient philosopher in denying the casual correspondence of dreams to events by mere accident or coincidence. He regarded as useful for prognostication dreams not only of humoral or celestial origin but also of supernatural provenience, including demons, who may have some insight into future events when they depend on natural causes. His portrait of the ideal interpreter defined him as male, melancholy and solitary, sober in his lifestyle, and inclined to tell the truth (Javellus 1567; Paoli 2011: 47–8).

The *Somnium Scipionis* was turned into Italian by Antonio Brucioli, translator not only of various classical texts, including works of Aristotle, but also of the entire Bible, and prominent figure in the heterodox scene, constantly under the eye of the Inquisition (Brambilla 2008). If, contrary to Cicero's text, Macrobius's commentary was not the subject of a tradition of vulgarisation, it was popularised by vernacular expositions and adaptations. Pompeo Della Barba, a Tuscan physician and philosopher, offers a good example. He had already copied verbatim sections of Macrobius's commentary on Cicero within a 1549 exposition of the theme of Platonic love, depending on Marsilio Ficino's commentary on Plato's *Symposium* and other standard Neoplatonic literature. Four years later, he published "philosophical discourses" – dedicated to the secretary of the then Duke of Florence Cosimo I de' Medici – in which the *Dream of Scipio* is the alleged subject but Macrobius a key source. Together with all the other scientific material, they contained, in a prologue, a discussion on dream theories, which mostly relied on Aristotle's critique of their predictive value, and an exposition of the five Macrobian types. Among other published works of his, a later dialogue on the secrets of nature, questioning their supernatural explanation, was condemned by the Roman Inquisition (Della Barba 1553: 3r–8v; Meschini 1988). Even the academic career of a prominent humanist as Juan Luis Vives began with a university course (at Leuven, later reprised in Paris) on the *Dream of Scipio*. The mode of the Valencian scholar was satirical, ridiculing medieval scholasticism, the style a meta-dream in which a debate on the value of dreams took place in an oneiric context, only to end giving voice to the Aristotelian scepticism about their meaningfulness. In his *De anima* Vives also displayed an unusual awareness of the phenomenon now known as lucid dreams, in which the subject adventures aware of the nature of the experience (Holland 1999: 132–4; Gantet 2021: 89–90).

8.4 Some vernacular texts in odour of heterodoxy

A not particularly elegant short poem in vernacular may appear not the obvious choice to challenge philosophical and religious orthodoxy, and yet it offers the opportunity to make one's positioning less easy to detect, or at least less problematic to tolerate, considering that it does not pose an open threat to the establishment by appealing overtly to potentially large audiences. Therefore, it may not come as a surprise if a text in which these characteristics have been detected comes from the elite environment of a humanist academy. The author in fact openly claims to have chosen verse as a mode of writing that allows to offer his ideas somewhat covertly. The text in question is Daniele Barbaro's *Predica dei sogni* (1542*), published pseudonymously. The author, a member of an important family of the Venetian patriciate, was great-nephew of the humanist Ermolao Barbaro,[2] and published Aristotelian commentaries of his ancestor. His later career took him to various governmental duties and to the ecclesiastical position of Patriarch of Aquileia. His young years were spent at the University of Padua as scholar versed in both the humanities and natural sciences (one of his last assignments there was the supervision of the establishment of the botanic garden).

Barbaro was probably a member of a nearly forgotten, aptly named Venetian Academy of the Doubtful (Accademia dei Dubbiosi), active in the early 1550s under the leadership of Count Fortunato Martinengo (whose remarkable 1542 portrait by Moretto da Brescia is now at the National Gallery, London), active in the Venetian literary environment as well as in touch with the Neapolitan religious circle of evangelism.[3] It has been suggested that their ideas may have inspired some of Paolo Veronese's complex iconography for Barbaro's Villa di Maser (Villa Barbaro) in the Venetian Mainland, where some details would suggest a role given to sleep in showing a path towards truth (Faini 2016).

In dedicating the text to a Venetian lady, Barbaro declares that it has been "composed almost while dreaming" (Parlato 2011: 509). A prologue plays with the imagery of light and darkness and its symbolic meaning, though a too-rushed association between sleep and deceit is tempered by the medical topic of the physiologic need to rest. The following exposition includes philosophical reflections on dreaming, which, as well as depending on Aristotle (dominating the Paduan university landscape), echo the Neoplatonic theme of the soul reaching out, through the sensory experience, to the world beyond. A hierarchy of several types of dreams follows, which disposes them at different degrees of reliability, on a ladder that heads to those more truthful and prophetic. In the last section of the poem, however, an unnamed teacher, towards whom reverence has been shown throughout the text, intervenes and determines a turn in the argumentation. In his exposition, this world is revealed as a dream, what we regard as real nothing but pretence. The original sin is responsible for this: "an apple caused to dream" (*un pomo fe sognare* – Barbaro 1542: C4v). The philosophical theme of the indistinguishability between dream and wakefulness turns into a condemnation of the illusory and worthless nature of the world (Gandolfo 1978: 147; Parlato 2011: 510; Paoli 2011: 34–7). While this conclusion is seasoned with traditional appeals and prayers to God and the Virgin, a liminal section "On doubt" (*Del dubbio* – Barbaro 1542: D3r–4r) expresses a sceptical eulogy of doubting, friend of truth and father of discovery (*inventione*).

Barbaro's publisher, Francesco Marcolini, also printed in 1540, and again in 1550, a book of *Sorti*, a fashionable kind of game of questions and answers for which allegorical images and quotations from ancient philosophers were provided and had to be combined. Here too dreams offered a subject of meditation in connection with truth and illusion (Faini 2016). Marcolini had commissioned the poetical texts, over 2000 oracular tercets, from one of the most successful and multitalented polymaths of the time, Lodovico Dolce (Dolce 2006).

A dialogue that similarly challenges dominant ideas of truth and devotes to the subject of dreams at least an intermezzo was the work of Stefano Maria Ugoni (1562*), a gentleman and jurist from Brescia, who was tried several times for heresy. In the rest of his "Dialogue on vigil and sleep", Ugoni sets the scene with one interlocutor waking up another, urging him to stop wasting time; the latter is aptly named Endymion, after a shepherd of ancient Greek mythology associated with eternal sleep, or elsewhere with the ability to sleep with his eyes opened (he was the object of a nocturnal love of Diana, who possessed him while asleep: on the myth and its iconography, Gandolfo 1978: 43–75; see Figure 8.2). After the abrupt interruption of his rest, he launches himself in an improbably immediate intellectual defence of the rationale of sleeping in philosophical terms. This quickly turns into a general exposition of the principles of nature – the

FIGURE 8.2 Giovanni Battista Cima da Conegliano, "Sleeping Endymion" (oil on panel, 1505–10). A small *tondo*, possibly created for a bridal chest or for a musical instrument. On the literary and artistic fortuna of the mythical character, see Agapiou 2005. © Heritage Image Partnership Ltd/Alamy Stock Photo.

elements, the heavens and the rest. Incidentally, when Endymion replies to questions in his capacity of representative of the meaning of his name, that is, as Sleep, he emphasises its physiological necessity: "as soon as humans stop sleeping, they immediately perish" (Ugoni 1562: 27). Playing on the ambiguity of this persona's status, when the conversation touches upon the senses, it comes to confront the two interlocutors with the interpretation of things people dream or even do while asleep, as in the case of somnambulism. Here again the two represent opposite views – Gregoria, the female kill-sleep (her name, unsurprisingly, etymologically means "watchful, alert"), affirming that dreams are illusions, Endymion in turn stressing that many are truthful and/or give ideas one may not have ever had while awake; Gregoria is sceptical and labels predictions as a different type of experience, offering a classification that is drawn from Macrobius. The representative of Watchfulness has the better hand of the debate, pushing Sleepy to admit that his memory and reasoning capabilities are to some extent obscured: he is sometimes *stordito* and *mentecatto* – two terms that John Florio's 1598 dictionary renders, respectively, as "astonished, dull, giddie, dizy, madde, foolish, frantik, raving in the head" and "ravished of his wits, senselesse, out of his wits, besides himselfe" (Ugoni 1562: 40). This section bridges to a latter part of the conversation where more general spiritual issues are exposed, beginning from the distinction between the human soul (*anima*), whose functions are shared with other animals, and our exclusive mind, the foundation of our life and will (*mente* is used for the rational, more excellent part of it, but the overall term for this higher, divine faculty is *animo*, not to be confused with *anima*). Gregoria also gives away a recipe against nightmares (described as visions of evil spirits): at bedtime, say a prayer, do the sign of the cross and spray the room with holy water (nota bene: the performing of the ritual only works if you have God in your heart – Ugoni 1562: 46). If in the subsequent part of the text the relevance to the topic stated by the book's title appears to fade, we see it re-emerging, and the two characters resuming their conflictual positions, when it comes to be discussed whether a wakeful or asleep person can do more good or harm towards their salvation. Endymion's point is that one at least cannot do any wrong while asleep, whereas Gregoria stresses how many good deeds they omit (ibid. 66ff.). Salomonically, Carteria, a third interlocutor materialising at the end and representing temperance, acknowledges one his right to seven or eight hours of sleep, and the other the rest of the day for her praiseworthy behaviour. Throughout the dialogue, use is made of the imagery of wakeful intellects versus sleepy ones, as a shorthand for their proximity to the truth. In the latter, spiritual part, darkness is additionally connoted as the colour of sin. Nevertheless, doubts concerning the human access to reliable knowledge are pervading the first part, where much is left as a mystery only in god's mind, to the extent that recent scholarship has recruited

Ugoni and his text as further representatives of the academic environment and scepticism that permeates Barbaro's poem (Faini 2016; see also Paoli 2011: 38–9).

8.5 Platonic theology

As well as in dedicated works, the topic had plenty of opportunities to occupy a writer for part of a text on a connected topic, or within miscellaneous compilations of diverse genres. This was the case of Marsilio Ficino, the Florentine champion of Renaissance Neoplatonism, who contributed to the Renaissance circulation of dream theories by translating the Greek text of Synesius into Latin, and approached dreams in his double capacity of philosopher and physician. Within his *Platonic Theology*, his *magnum opus* published in 1482, Book 13 contains a treatment of the subject that is interesting both on the account of the author's position and for the company in which he sets the oneiric experience.

In his Neoplatonic view, the human soul, divine and immortal, is capable of understanding every place and every time, revisiting the past or anticipating the future without exiting from itself. However, this possibility manifests itself especially when the soul unhooks itself from the connection with the body, and this happens in sleep, but also in other conditions such as fainting fits, a melancholy humour, a temperate complexion, solitude, wonder (*admiratio*) and chastity – yet another meaningful list of phenomena to which dreaming is approached, at least from the respect of the visual experience it facilitates. Sleep is however the most significant case in the series and that on which Ficino's analysis is most detailed. There is an inverse proportionality (we have found it among the rules summarised by Guido Giglioni) between the distancing of the external acts from the soul and the strengthening of the internal ones, that is, the visions of the fantasy and the motions of the reason. Vivid images that are residual of wakeful life do not necessarily offer reliable prognostication: they may derive from previous perturbations of the mind, or conflict between humours, and deceive particularly people who are dominated by immoderate senses and devote their life to the pursuit of pleasure. The more moderate and pious have access to a more rewarding and reliable oneiric world. This, however, does not manifest itself plainly, but requires hunting skills, the ability to follow clues from one image to another in the understanding that, as in conversation we tend to move from one subject to another and may lose the plot, so does the mind's progression through images in sleep. Ficino suggests that two distinct skills may rarely be found in the same person, and while some may have a gift of experiencing properly predictive dreams, others may be better equipped at interpreting them. He also mentions historical examples of actual dreams, including one attributed to Alexander the Great, and cites the Orphic hymns we have mentioned in relationship with Michelangelo's iconography (Ficino 2004: esp. 150–61; Vasoli 1999).

8.6 Oneiromancy between market square and menagerie

Dream interpreters, astrologers and all sorts of fortune tellers were also the object of significant mistrust and caricature. A microcosm where some of this critical attitude can be sampled is offered by Tommaso Garzoni's *La piazza universale di tutte le professioni del mondo* (The market square of all world's trades). A compilation by a clergyman from Romagna plagiarising a variety of pre-existing encyclopaedic texts, sandwiched between a discourse (chapter) dedicated to astronomers and astrologers and one on magicians and spellbinders, it included a chapter (number 40, Garzoni 1996: 640–76) "Of soothsayers in the species, that is, prophets, sibyls, seers, haruspices, augurs, with the species of tripudii, omens and superstitious observations, professors of the speculative art, which consists in monstrosities, portents, prodigies and such like, prognosticators, or natural prescient, professors of oracles, sorcery, and especially tricksters,[4] interpreters of dreams, physiognomists, metoposcopes, pyromancers, hydromancers, aeromancers, geomancers, fortune-tellers, and the like".

It has been calculated that *La piazza* owes more than 90 percent of its content to the sources it plagiarises. This may produce in the modern reader a sense of frustration and lack of interest. And yet we should bear in mind that this was not unusual at the time, that compilation was a standard, if not actively encouraged, way of writing, and allowed the production of extremely popular reference books. This was in fact the case for *La piazza*, Garzoni's largest literary undertaking, which has been defined as one of the last Italian Renaissance classics of European success. Published in Venice in 1585, it enjoyed an exceptional circulation over the following 90 years, being translated into German and Latin, adapted in Spanish and imitated multiple times (Cherchi 1996).

The chapter's (as well as the whole book's) main source, victim of Garzoni's piracy, was Agrippa von Nettesheim's *Of the vanity and uncertainty of arts and sciences*, an influential, Erasmian sceptical attack on the value and reliability of all sciences, in favour of reliance in faith. Published in 1530, it was translated into Italian in 1547 (in English in 1569), and that is the text that Garzoni silently copies and pastes verbatim throughout his compilation. The translator was Lodovico Domenichi, a well-known Italian polymath who five years later was to be sentenced by the Inquisition and to have his books burnt for having taken part in the translation of a collection of texts by John Calvin (Faini 2010). The fact that prominent sixteenth-century polymaths were in one way or another unorthodox has suggested to some that this was the case also for Garzoni. This has however been confuted and the appropriation of material taken from Agrippa and others understood as a rebuttal of their potentially subversive character by competing on the same terrain, so that Garzoni's ranting against a variety of dubious social practices should be understood as predominantly intended to corroborate standard Catholic views (Cherchi 1996). In particular, the section in question addresses, following a list of professions, the reliance and exploitation of superstitious beliefs and occult arts by a few types of practitioners.

Agrippa's chapter 39, "On the interpretation of dreames" (1569: 52v–53r), just over a page in length, provides some classical and biblical information, to conclude by agreeing with the opinion of Cicero on "the vanitie and folie of them, that give credite to dreames". Agrippa states that interpreters are more correctly called "conjectours", a term which Domenichi and Garzoni render as *coniettori* (Florio's dictionary of 1598 has *coniettura*, *conietturare*, otherwise spelled as *congettura*, *congetturare*, meaning "to surmise, to conjecture"). In Agrippa, the chapter comes within a series that is opened (chapter 31) by a critique of judiciary astrology – that is, the branch or current of astrology that believed in an inescapable, deterministic influence of the stars on human life – continues with a treatment of divination in general, to then examine in particular physiognomics, metoposcopy, chiromancy, geomancy, haruspicy and speculatory ("which makes interpretations of thunder and lightning, and other airy meteors, as also of monsters and prodigies"). Dreams are then followed by a topic, "fury", or prophetic delirium, which the author declares as related, as the people who engage in it represent a particular type of dreamers. After divination, the book moves on to magic. Agrippa – prominent humanist and physician whose entire oeuvre ended up in the Catholic index of prohibited books (Adorni Braccesi 2010) – also discussed "Of divination by dreams" and "Of prophetical dreams" in his other major and no less controversial work, *De occulta philosophia* (I, 59 and III, 51) – a plan, in line with contemporary Hermeticism, for a comprehensive refoundation of the art of magic, first drafted in the author's youth in 1510 and published in its entirety in 1533. In the former of the two chapters, he cites Synesius and Aristotle as sources and gives astrological advice on the ideal celestial conditions for them to be true; in the latter, such conditions come to comprise dietary recommendations, in the context of a more articulated presentation of the physiology and variety of types of dreams, which includes an acknowledgement of the existence of some that foretell the future, with historical examples. Those, however, do not require the art of interpretation outlined in the previous chapter, as they tend to present their content explicitly.

To the passage copied from the *De incertitudine*, Garzoni adds several classical anecdotes taken from Cicero's *On divination*, a source that he acknowledges. Neither of Garzoni's sources oriented him in the direction of trusting oneiromancy much. He reports, for instance, that the Roman orator laughed at Pythagoras and Plato for their dietary recommendations, supposed to help certain dreams.

The same author returned to the subject much more extensively in a volume that was only published, with his brother's additions, over 20 years after his death, in which he took the opportunity to develop the curiosity for the occult arts that had only found limited space within the scope of the project of *La piazza*, and its emphasis on occupations. Following the architectural imagination that structures all his works and is linked to the key role buildings and spaces played in the art of memory, *Il serraglio degli stupori del mondo* [The Menagerie of World Marvels] (2004: 329–406) is articulated in "apartments", and each of them divided into "rooms". One of the ten subdivisions of the "menagerie" is the "apartment of dreams", which now occupies just over 75 pages in quarto. It is found here in the company of monsters and prodigies, oracles and astrology, as well as all the wonders narrated both in history and in mythology (topics of the other apartments), the overall logic of the volume being, as the title promises, an in-depth survey on marvels (*stupori*). Compared to Garzoni's previous compilations, this posthumous work, more original and ambitious but stylistically less efficacious, while still nearly encyclopaedic, aspires to engage in demonstration rather than mere description and inserts various forms of divination on a scale that begins from monsters and prodigies and arrives at miracles, the highest genre of marvels whose cause is divine (Cherchi 2004).

The argument opens with classical sources on the origin of the interpretation of dreams, and first deals with the question whether such a thing is justifiable and then what can be said about it. Garzoni collects authorities against and in favour of the validity of the art. The secondary literature from which he gathers lists of primary sources to quote and place in one or the opposite group include such erudite material as the Aristotelian commentaries by Lodovico Boccadiferro, professor of philosophy in Rome and Bologna during the first half of the sixteenth century (Boccadiferro 1570: 72r–105r). The sequence of subsequent "rooms" deals, in turn, with the definition of the dream, of his source and matter; of the divine, angelic and demonic origin of dreams and the way they are transmitted to us; on how you can tell them apart from one another, why God and angels make revelations more in sleep than in wakefulness, how many sorts of dreams there are, what differentiates those sent to pious or impious dreamers (*ai buoni e ai cattivi*) and whether it is right to believe in them, and in which ones; on the dreaming by frenzied people and why good spirits sometimes send some rather obscure dreams; on the interpreters, the act of interpreting, observations concerning both practitioners and practice, and a list of authorities who have discussed the subject.

8.7 A theological commonplace

Commonplace books provide a meaningful entry into the cultural practice of early modern people, the way all sorts of texts were (and were supposed to be) ordinarily read, annotated and compiled (Moss 1996). Within the general category, specific disciplines had their own habits; and sixteenth-century theology, with all what happened in the many reformations of Christian spirituality, did not fail to leave its contribution. A work of this genre was produced, among others, by Pietro Martire Vermigli, an outstanding representative of the Continental contribution to the theology of the Edwardian Reformation, invited to England in 1547 by Archbishop Cranmer and becoming the following year the second Regius Professor of Divinity at Oxford. The first part of the collection contains a series of chapters that, by referring each predominantly to a specific scriptural passage, discuss the nature and value of prophecy, visions and dreams. Chapter 5, of dreams, develops from Judges 7.13, narrating the dream of the Medianite soldier (on which see also Husser 1999: 116–18, under symbolic dreams); in fact, it originally appeared in his comment on that book, based on lectures he had given in Strasbourg in the 1550s (Vermigli 1564: 134–9). The biblical narrative had Gideon leading a successful night attack against the enemy's camp after having overheard a soldier referring a dream of his, in which the collapse of a tent was interpreted as a sign of a divine will for the defeat of his army.

Vermigli opens by attributing to the Jews three sort of dreams: natural, divinely inspired and mixed. He then proceeds to expound each sort. His main sources about natural dreams are Aristotle, Hippocrates and Galen. The Florentine theologian trod on more problematic ground when he moved, in the second half of the commonplace, to comment on dreams of divine origin.

The characteristics that supposedly distinguished them were some kind of images impressed on our phantasy, and a judgement that accompanies and allows us to decipher it. God sometimes delivers them together and other times sends images only, for which the dreamer needs to seek interpretation by someone else: that was, proverbially, the role played by Joseph in Egypt. As an example of an image impressed in the mind but detached from its meaning, he gives the forms transmitted by a teacher to his pupils, suggesting evidently a mnemonic teaching method. The existence of divinely inspired dreams is attested by several scriptural examples. To these Vermigli adds some patristic material, including Augustine's distinction between corporeal, spiritual and intellectual images. Some visions however come from the devil, and in order to detect them one needs to exercise the gift of the discerning of spirits.[5] As a proof of their reality, he cites the pagan practice of incubation in dedicated places in search for oracles. Some space is given towards the end of the text to a confutation of the Aristotelian denial of dreams of divine inspiration (Vermigli 1583: 32–9).

8.8 The interpretation of dreams as a form of entertainment

A test of how widespread and taken for granted the activity of interpreting dreams was, not only by entrusting the task to recognised experts but also as a lay practice of variable levels of seriousness, is offered by the fact that we encounter it in texts that mention it, or describe it more extensively, as a practice undertaken within the apparently purposeless context of leisure time and space – somehow ignoring Giovanni Della Casa's indication in his *Galateo*, followed by French moralists in the seventeenth century, that one's dreams (as well as one's children) were subjects to avoid in polite conversation (Burke 1993; Maggi 2008: 261). Suggesting perhaps a comparatively wide geographical diffusion of the cultural practice, the works I will examine come one from Italy, and the other from France.

The Sienese *veglie* (parties) provide one of the most characteristic historical examples of parlour games played routinely by elites in specific cultural contexts, even if their connection with more popular forms of game is undeniable (McClure 2013; Ortalli 2013–14). Girolamo Bargagli's *Dialogo* (1572) offers a valuable enumeration and discussion of a variety of games practised at the local Accademia degli Intronati, the heart of the city's intellectual life. The academy members followed the humanist fashion of choosing nicknames and *imprese* (emblems); beyond the mask of the academic name, some historical members of the Sienese cultural elite can be surmised. Thus, one of the participants in this conversation, Fausto Sozzini (*il Frastagliato*, "the Jagged"), following the path of his uncle Lelio, was going to live abroad for the sake of his religion and turn into a leading figure in the theology and ecclesiology of the radical Reformation in Eastern Europe and beyond. Here, however, religious orthodoxy is not directly in question – although one could make the point that the refined intellectual milieu of Renaissance humanism functioned as one of the growing fields for the development of religious dissent (Marchetti 1982).

The game in question, like many others, is mentioned only briefly, without much description; we can, however, retrieve some information concerning its status from the context, the role its evocation plays in the characters' discussion. It is number 13 (of 130) and simply entitled "game of dreams" (*giuoco de' sogni*). As many other similar entertainments centred on the inventive deciphering of symbols, the rule simply consists in someone narrating the content of one of their dreams, and all the other participants being obliged (the rules of the game accept no excuse) to offer their own interpretation. Can this be properly counted as a game? The conversation tackles this question, or rather, it is while debating such issues of definition that the game is cited as example or piece of evidence (Bargagli 1572: 33–7). Within a discussion of the origin of the type of games practised within the academy, *il Sodo* ("the Firm"), nickname of Marcantonio Piccolomini, one of the founders of the Intronati and a leading figure in orienting that particular academy towards a programmatic study and lively experimentation of vernacular poetic language, plays the guiding role of defining what is meant by game in this context. He distinguishes it from the ancient public *ludi*, as well as from joking. He premises that it is performed in noble company and qualifies it as

> a festive action of a merry and amorous brigade, wherein upon a pleasant and ingenious proposal made by one as the author and leader of such action all the others do or say something differently from one another, and this for the purpose of amusement and entertainment.
>
> *(ibid. 34)*

The definition sounds somewhat solemn and is reported as heard in the past from a member of the academy who was playfully philosophising. Nevertheless, it provides the company with a blueprint against which to test the nature of their social gathering in its varieties, by weighing each term that it includes, and to argue how it is necessary to exclude less relevant forms of practice. For instance, the purpose is, according to Piccolomini, a defining element, since similar activities undertaken for other functions cease for that reason to qualify as *giuochi*. In this respect he finds that the category does not apply properly to all the entertainments proposed at the beginning of Castiglione's *Libro del Cortegiano*, when the brigade that gathers at Urbino must decide how to kill their time; nor that "to form in words a perfect courtier" is really a ludic pursuit. At this point, Sozzini intervenes in defence of the ludicity of both Castiglione's personae's activities and of the storytelling of those put on stage by Boccaccio; and it is in support of this claim that he cites the game of dreams. Whatever the nuances (for *il Sodo* a key requirement is variation, that there is not just storytelling in isolation, but everyone joining and taking part), dream interpretation as entertainment obtains a unique ennoblement by this association with two literary masterpieces and cultural trend makers.

Jacques Yver was a promising writer in mid-sixteenth-century France, to the extent that he was regarded even abroad as a model of literary style; he died in his early 20s, and consequently the work we are considering here was published posthumously. The title *Le printemps* (Spring) puns on the author's surname, which sounds like "winter". Both in the original French and in an English translation, the book had a significant fortune – particularly on the Elizabethan stage, by providing dramatic plots (Fontaine and Maignan 2015). It is therefore interesting to find that, in gathering *à la* Boccaccio to tell each other stories, the members of the brigade entertain one another in other ways too, including, on the fifth evening, via a discussion on the correct interpretation of one's dream. The lady toasts to whoever slept best, and one of the male characters wins the prize, suggesting that the best sleep is the one that both refreshes the body and entertains the spirit, and telling the others a rather enigmatic dream of his involving an aviary: a small bird that flies out and crashes into a tree, a raven that plucks its most beautiful feathers, after which the bird's old friends reject him, and a snake drags him into his cavern. The ensuing eruption of proposals of keys for its interpretation ("more or less as a good chef can cook an egg in many different ways") – where we see the French characters de facto engaged in the Sienese game – leaves the impression that the interpreters were even greater dreamers than the narrator, since they were producing these imaginary worlds while awake and at table (Yver 2015: 422–5).

The difference of genre between the two books, for our purpose, is of limited relevance. If what Yver writes is plainly fiction, this does not stop his text from resonating with social gatherings and activities that took place for real and could be inspired by the reading of literature. Whereas Bargagli may suggest that he is reporting true academic meetings and giving voice to historical personae; that does not prevent his text from being a literary description, and reinvention, of a social practice.

It has been suggested that it was between 1630 and 1660, in particular in France, that oneiromancy moved from being the object of scholarly consideration to become a pleasant object of recreation (Andries 1988: 51), a process that by the eighteenth century had moved keys of dreams far away from the connection with the search of knowledge they still presented in the sixteenth (Gantet 2021). It is likely that there is truth in such a shift. Nevertheless, as we have seen, interpreting dreams as a form of entertainment had been practised long before, somewhat preparing the terrain for that cultural shift. Even more baldly and intriguingly, it has been proposed that abandoning the idea that dreams are a source of truth to derive from them a form of secularised pleasure may have played a significant role in the genesis of modern subjectivity (Cavaillé 1995) – a theme on which we will return, in Chapter 10.

8.9 A dictionary of gesture

The relations between gesture and dreams may not appear so obvious (unless one thinks of the dreamer's potential physical agitation), and yet a reference book for the former, *L'arte de' cenni*, published in Vicenza in 1616 but written about 20 years earlier, offers some interesting insights into the latter. First, it may prove useful to mention that a dictionary of gesture is a very unusual type of book; it did not benefit from any classical precedent. The author, Giovanni Bonifacio, a jurist from the Venetian Mainland who wrote on legal matters as well as on history and for the theatre, dedicated it to the Accademia Filarmonica of Verona, a city where he had been holding public office and had the opportunity to enter the cultured elite. Even though, for its uniqueness, the book is nothing like the representative of an existing literary genre, Bonifacio's remarkable phrase collecting provides us with an intriguing stock of motives, with which his predecessors and contemporaries were familiar in a variety of discursive contexts.

Reference to dreams appear in both parts of the book. The shorter Part Two is a slightly odd addendum to the main purpose of the volume, as it extends the notion of sign beyond human action and proposes to decipher the semiotics of nature as well as of human artefacts and disciplines. The most relevant chapter here is the one the author devotes to "how medicine makes use of gestures" (II, 17; Gazzola 2018: II, 568–70), which includes the following passage:

> It is also from the dreams of the sick person that the learned physicians understand the quality of the infirmity, and according to those dreams they apply the appropriate medicaments; and Hippocrates, in his Book of Dreams, holds them in such high esteem that he explains the nature of the infirmity according to this or that image, which it seems to the sick person to have seen, and teaches various medicines to cure it. And in this way, the dreams of the sick give the wise man matter to philosophise about.
>
> *(Gazzola 2018: II, 569)*

The first part responds more closely to reader expectations, by running through the parts of the body, from head to toes, and registering the literary references to gesture and their respective meanings, from the Bible and the classics to the literary production of Bonifacio's own time. It should be added, however, that even here his notion of gesture is somewhat wider than one may expect and includes such features as clothing and hairstyles; in a way, the extension is made legitimate by the fact that these are forms of self-presentation that an individual controls and has the opportunity to use as a form of communication; on the other hand, they would communicate to the onlooker regardless the fact that the subject is aware of it and has made deliberate choices. So, a chapter where we find reference to dreams is dedicated to the beard (I, 10; Gazzola 2018: II, 92–96). Bonifacio's source here is the key one inherited from Antiquity:

> Nature gave a man a beard, so that he would be recognised as a male even in the face, and to make him respectable and worthy of reverence ... Artemidorus said that sons were as ornamental to their fathers as the beard was to their faces. And the dream, which one has about his beard, is interpreted as concerning his sons.
>
> *(Gazzola 2018: II, 92)*

Biblical references appear too, though the Pharaoh's dream interpreted by Joseph is registered under having a ring on one's finger, which is what happened to the Jewish interpreter as a gift from the Egyptian king (I, 28, 26;

Gazzola 2018: II, 350). The chapter on shoulders includes a section on being a hunchback, where we can read: "The aruspices interpreted Domitian's dream that he had become a hunchback as a good wish for the future, but in fact it was a prophecy that he died violently and his name was disgraced" (I, 44, 6; Gazzola 2018: II, 434). Here, however, Bonifacio's reading departs from tradition (Suetonius VIII, 59), deleting from the narrative the detail that the dreamt growth was golden, and the precious material was the reason for its interpretation as a good omen. The modern reinterpreter, instead, concentrates on the deformity itself, which is also in contradiction with his distrust of physiognomics: in his opinion, as expressed at the end of the chapter devoted to astrology, something that is someone's permanent feature for that precise fact does not communicate (II, 3; Gazzola 2018: II, 508). Domitian appears again in the chapter on clothing, under the headline "being deprived of the belt, or weapons", a sign of vituperation, and of depriving someone of honour: "Suetonius [VIII, 51] writes that Domitian dreamt, shortly before he was slaughtered, that Minerva departed from her temple, saying that she could no longer defend him, since she had been disarmed by Jupiter" (I, 49, 14; Gazzola 2018: II, 488). While here it is the goddess who suffers the dreamt degrading, the presage is definitely negative and close to the emperor's assassination; the reader is left with the doubt as to whether Bonifacio has mixed the two up (or assumed that the goddess was the oneiric alter ego of the dreaming emperor).

Overall, the dream itself does not play a specific role in *L'arte de' cenni* – nor one would expect it to. The examples provided by the literary tradition and the interpretation they were taken to convey – whether in classical, biblical or oneirocritical context – are freely used as confirmation of standard associations between gestures and meanings, which in a way takes for granted that dreams have a meaning, and this assumption has something to tell us.

8.10 Popular interpretation

If much of the above may leave one with the impression that cultured elites were the heirs of a rich, complex and long tradition, from which the illiterate were more or less excluded, this may be worth reconsidering. As well as oral transmission, the written publication of ready practical material became a profitable business in the early modern period, providing pedlars with aids for one of the most common form of divination. Keys of dreams, in which people could look up the main objects and topics of their nocturnal experience and learn something about their immediate future, were the easiest type of reference book. But if we look at what circulated as late as the French seventeenth century in printed publications of this genre, we realise that the list and decodification derived directly from the early medieval sources, with few predictable adaptations, such as the elimination of topics pertaining to ancient myths and cults, past forms of practice (like the games of the circus) and problematic nature – chiefly the world of sexuality, troubling the morality of the Christian reader, or at least of his censor; while, conversely, adding a few objects and cultural practices of recent introduction. The same can be said for guides for interpretation in other format, ultimately drawn from Artemidorus – a text whose survival through millennia and across changing cultural contexts is truly remarkable (Andries 1988).

Other social dimensions of the interpretation of dreams that could be found in popular prints and at the end of the day derived from Artemidorus include a distinction of the meaning of a given symbol according to the rank of the dreamer, and also the descending reliability of the testimony of a dreamt figure depending on their role on a hierarchy, starting from the divine and coming down the various echelons of the human (Andries 1988). A family of vernacular keys of dreams consisting in variations and adaptations of the *Somniale Danielis* circulated in France, between the late fifteenth and the early seventeenth century, both in print and in manuscript form. Their explicits were clear advertisements, and they were sold by either pedlars or booksellers. Following the characteristic of many European popular prints and manuscripts of the time, they tended to mix easily accessible oneiromancy with other lore in the style of almanacs, like monthly prognostications and recipes. The oneiric imagery they purposed to decipher was dominated by the body, food, clothing, gesture and human activities, all ordinarily explained via a simple symbolism that associated each dream subject to either gain or loss (Berriot 1990). In England, throughout the early modern period almanacs included even increasingly a section devoted to popular dream interpretation, to the extent that it has been observed that the fact is in contrast with Keith Thomas's well-known thesis of the decline of magic (Rivière 2017: 58–61).

A cultural form that also testifies to the nature and diffusion of popular oneiromancy is offered by folk stories, where a few recurring narratives appear to be particularly common; their parallels can be found in indexes of folk literature, as is the case for magic knowledge from dream (Thompson 1955–57: D1810.8), future revealed in dream (D1812.3.3), bad dream as evil omen (D1812.5.1.2), dream showing events in distant places (D1813.1), realistic dream (F1068), knowledge from dream (J157), treasure discovered through dream (N531), or love through dream (T11.3). Although literary short stories can be a sophisticated cultural product that could not simply be identified with a popular and oral tradition, the relationships between the two are as obvious, so that a reference to the dream in the Renaissance novella would not be out of place here.

Some of these narratives show, in an expanded form, close resemblance to the tradition of medieval moral exempla. This is the case for a vernacular tale from a Sienese collection dating from the late thirteenth century, in which the fate of parents is revealed to their daughter in a dream: the mother is shown in hell, the father in heaven. The two had conducted morally opposed lives, but the circumstances of their death, the bad weather having postponed for days a proper burial for her father, make the girl think that it does not matter how you behave, a reward may wait for you in the next life in any case. This is the point when God intervenes to correct her misjudgement: her spirit is taken to visit the otherworld while her body remains in bed and can eyewitness the harsh and ceaseless torments of her mother, the glory of her father; repented, she gives everything to the poor and devotes herself to God (Zambrini 1862: 101–17; Thompson 1955–57: J157).

As for popular medicine, Laurent Joubert's very successful *Popular Errors* (1578) only included the subject of dreams in a liminal, miscellaneous list of popular sayings, which are not discussed specifically in his work ("Whether it is true that sleeping with the head low causes dreaming; and whether eating cabbage causes it also", sandwiched between two sayings on snoring and one on "Why common people say he who hasn't a hard tummy won't sleep very soundly": Joubert 1989: 17).

Somewhere in-between cultures of different social milieus we can find the work of the storyteller Giulio Cesare Croce. In the year 1600, he published a booklet entitled *Sogni fantastichi della notte* (Fantastic dreams of the night) and dedicated to the Bolognese painter Annibale Carracci, containing an extraordinary flux of dreamlike imagery. Most of the text has the form of a poem and has its own merits in documenting a certain popular vein of literary writing. Even more striking, however, are the two prose pages that, after the dedicatory letter, precede the verses, in the form of an address to the reader (*Sogno bizarro*, bizarre dream): it is worth translating this section in its entirety as it provides a telling example of a folkloric imagery with which the learned cultural production, both textual and visual, must constantly have had to interact and negotiate:

Bizarre dream
The other evening after supper, having touched the jug a little, I took off the table much more cooked than raw, by courtesy of Sir Bacchus, who with his good liqueur had clouded my memory a little; and thus, having the head fullof other stuff than lye, I was attacked by a sleep so heavy that the bombards would not have woken me up. So that, not having time to go to bed, I fell asleep on a bench in the antechamber of my study. And thus, sleeping deeply, it seemed to me I had become a goose, and that the Jews wanted to cut my throat; at that point to escape from them I fluttered so much, that in the end I left my head in their hands, and ran away. And I arrived in a beautiful meadow, and suddenly I was a shepherd, and wanting to kiss a nymph, a wolf with his mouth open comes and eats me, then he goes to evacuate me to another mountain; sliding all down from which

it seemed that I turned into a barrel of Trebbiano wine. And here came a company of Germans, and they drank me up, then it seemed to me that they were going to urinate me in a well. As soon as I reached the bottom I became a frog, and when a maid came to get some water, she pulled me out with a bucket, whereupon I soon jumped into the grass. And then I became a baboon, and immediately it seemed that I was caught by a mountebank, who led me to somersault in the square. And while I was jumping up, I seemed to turn into a jug, and an innkeeper took me, and filled me with vinegar; and there comes the wife to season the salad, and she puts me on the top of a sideboard: a cat jumps up on the sideboard, and he threw me into fifty pieces. Then I began to cry as much as I could, whereupon the innkeeper, his wife, and all the customers rushed, and they had me sewn together. And it seemed that I became a pair of cowhide boots, and a courier puts them on his feet, and runs fifty post stations without ever stopping, so that both my soles fell off. And when I was detached I jumped out of his legs, and soon I was a doctor's mule, and while he was going on a visit, I could hear him reason, and so I began to learn grammar, and to make concordances for all cases, numbers and figures, so that I beat all the other cattle; and it seemed to me that I entered in the master's study, and I ate all his books, both on medicine, and philosophy, as well as mathematics and poetry. And I had made such a big feed of them that I looked really pregnant, so the patron, realizing this, took a stick, and straightened my hair, in a way, that made me come back to my senses again. So that when I woke up with that impression on my head, I found myself filled with poetic fury, because while sleeping I had digested all the other sciences, and because I became a poet in dreams, it seemed to me I should write the present chapter on dreams, which occur while sleeping, showing how many chimeras pass through our brain, finally concluding with the opinion I hold about this. And this will serve as a preface to the work: read and stay healthy.

(Croce 1600: A2r–v)

While serving as a justification for the poetic form chosen for the rest of the booklet, the preface represents a distillate of early modern Bakhtinian imagination, including a rich palette of comic commonplaces: from the ethnic stereotypes (the Jews, the drunken Germans), to the parody dominance of the lower body and the satisfaction of its needs. Despite its obvious nature of invention, it exemplifies vividly a key form of the oneiric experience such as the metamorphosis. Piero Camporesi, the late scholar of the minor literature of early modern Italy who paid most attention to the oeuvre of Giulio Cesare Croce, by placing him in the context of a largely shared imagery of the body and daily life in hard times, remarked that Croce's interest in dreams developed in a Bolognese milieu that, around 1600, showed significant attention to the oneiric experience, by publishing a few academic treatises – the ones by Mancini, Segni, Merli and Grassi mentioned in Chapter 7 – together with the Carracci painters' workshop, fascinated by the Ovidian imagery of metamorphoses (Camporesi 1994: 112–13).

8.11 Dreaming the witches' sabbath?

In his already-mentioned seminal article of 1973, Peter Burke (1997a) also raised the question of the statute and existence of collective dreams. This was presented as the case for the *benandanti* from Friuli, whose belief of souls leaving and entering the body corresponds to an entry in the *Motif-Index of Folk Literature* (Thompson 1955–57: E720; Ginzburg 1983). Further reflection and debate on that Italian case has engaged in telling comparisons with the world traditions of shamanism.

In general, the whole experience of early modern witchcraft, which aroused contemporary polemics about its nature and credibility, poses the question of how much of it and in which terms could be understood as oneiric. In fact, while reviewing sleep and dream pathologies, we have already encountered Burton's subsection "Of the force of the imagination", where imagination caused some people to be "troubled with *Incubus*, or Witch ridden ... if they lie on their backes, they suppose an old woman rides, and sits so hard upon them" – though the Oxford don offered a physiological reduction of the experience as the effect of bad humours. For seventeenth-century Basque and Swedish cases of alleged abductions to the Sabbath, reference has been made to dream-epidemics, as that was the condition in which the phenomenon was believed to have occurred (Sörlin 2008: 118–19).

The problem was known at the time and can be found in the literature that debates witchcraft and the culpability of suspects. The point is interestingly dramatised in the second of the dialogues by which the Swiss physician and Calvinist theologian Thomas Erastus contrasted his Dutch colleague's Johan Wier's famous critique of the culpability of witches (they were published as an appendix to the French translation of Wier's *De praestigiis daemonum* in 1567). Furnius, Erastus's fictional interlocutor, proposes the dream argument to clear the suspects from the reality and danger of a pact with the devil; but in his rebuttal, Erastus finds precisely the fact that many people allege to experience the same dream as implausible, and on this basis convinces his counterpart that witchcraft narratives must have some real ground. Diverging opinions on the reality of witch narratives could be expressed either by writers of different cultural allegiance (as members of competing religious orders) or by exponents of diverse disciplines, with conflicting epistemologies, such as theology versus law. The latter case (with a reprise of the former) was in question in the early contrast expressed in print in the 1520s between the Florentine jurist Gianfrancesco Ponzinibio, who, silently reusing sceptical arguments from a Franciscan writer, found such narratives as unbelievable, even if corroborated by untrustworthy confessions, and the Dominican Bartolomeo Spina from Pisa, who attacked him by supporting the reality of the preternatural (Max 1993).

Wier's interpretation of the witches' flight and sabbath as a dream also adopted – and helped the circulation of – the hypothesis that it was a pharmaceutically induced illusion. Both Girolamo Cardano and Giovan Battista Della Porta ascribed such power to anointments that included herbs and children's fat, a mixture of somniferous substances to which Francis Bacon's *Sylva Sylvarum* added tobacco. The development of natural sciences, with sixteenth-century botanists exploring the mountains of Northern Italy to identify and collect different varieties of such drugs of dreaming as aconite or belladonna, further strengthened the thesis that the sabbath was only a dream. In the cultural history of this topos, the value sign of the witches' pharmacopeia was reversed from negative to positive in the archaeology of drug cults that can be found in the Romantic imagination of Jules Michelet's *La sorcière* (1862): the sabbath there was thought as real, a peasant revolt that used popular herbal medicine to induce a hallucinogen escape from the misery of daily life (Meurget 1993; for its representation in seventeenth-century Dutch art, Davidson 1993). Somehow on the footsteps of Michelet, the controversial thesis advanced by Hans Peter Dürr (1985), who also searched for early modern hallucinogen recipes, generalised the alternative dimension which shamanic cults reached via altered states of consciousness as a desirable "world we have lost".

The common representation of Wier as a defender of the witches tends to exaggerate his novelty by portraying him as a champion of modern science when not a precursor of nineteenth-century psychiatry. To be more accurate, if he offered a medical explanation of some of the visions of the alleged witches, partly in terms of humoral balance and diet producing vapours affecting the brain, he was also a Christian believing in the reality and power of the devil, and this played a part in the story. He in fact shared the conviction that, as a master of disguise and deceit, the devil, having been allowed by God to do so, produced illusory images by which the witches believed they joined the nocturnal flight and participated into the sabbath: but in reality they lay still in their beds and were simply assisting to a show that was demonically induced in their vision (Maus de Rolley 2007; Giglioni 2013). Before its shift to the witch craze, the medieval Church had already held a similar position. In decrees such as the *Canon Episcopi*, included in the mid-twelfth century in Gratian's *Decretum*, the suggestion was that the night flight was all a dream, specifically experienced by women, and a cleric had solved the problem of how several people could possibly participate into one and the same dream, by sentencing that every woman dreamt individually, and all the other women that appeared in her vision were just disguised devils (Stephens 2011).

Overall, however, it may be concluded that the hypothesis that it was only a dream did not play a remarkable role on either side of the discussion (Préaud 1988). Nevertheless, British historian Stuart Clark, who has proposed one of the most systematic attempts to frame the belief in the reality and danger of witchcraft in the shared, dualist worldview of premodern Europe (Clark 1997), offered a more wide-ranging and thought-provoking consideration of the impact that Renaissance demonological literature had on contemporary dream theory. Clark noticed that, since at least late Antiquity, and in particular the second-century CE writings of Sextus Empiricus, the philosophical questioning of the oneiric experience had followed a different path from oneirocritics. The problems discussed by dream interpreters and writers who belonged in that tradition concerned the origin of dreams, their premonitory value and their moral statute; on the contrary, Sextus's scepticism expressed in the most radical and striking form the clearly separate paradox according to which our visual perception cannot really distinguish between images dreamt and images perceived while awake, and each of them could reasonably claim to be true in its own dominion. Clark finds a reprise of the latter type of questioning in two key thinkers of the period, Montaigne and Descartes, and suggests that it was precisely the first printed edition, in Paris in 1562, of the Latin text of Sextus's *Outlines of Pyrrhonism* that triggered their and others' reflection (Clark 2007a). It will not come as a surprise, therefore, if this line of thought of Clark's was inserted in an overall reconsideration of the historical anthropology of the senses, which framed witchcraft and dreams as two episodes of a general cultural shift, between the sixteenth and the seventeenth century, towards a more sceptical doubt on the reliability of senses, and of sight in particular (Clark 2007b). That Montaigne's scepticism extended to question the belief in the meaningfulness of dreams, which he regarded as laughable, suggesting that he would find more sensible to make his life decisions by casting dice, rather tells us another story, one of a distance between some rationalist learned elites and the mindset and behaviour of most of their contemporaries – thus anticipating the modern Western attitude that confines related sets of superstitious beliefs and ritual practices to the minds and bodies of primitive or illiterate people (Holland 1999: 132–4; Plane and Tuttle 2013b: 11).

8.12 The other half of the oneiric world

Gender is a factor in the differentiation among historical oneiric experiences that surely deserves further investigation. Among others, the case of women's dreams in early modern England has been explored with telling results. The study examined how men and women read women's dreams. Women often dreamt of their childbearing and relationship with their children including, for instance, lactation. One effective way of judging what we can make of this source is formulated by the author towards the end of her essay, as a way of summing up her findings, by asking, "What would we have if dreams were our only source about women's lives?", a question to which she replies:

> At the most basic level, we could take recorded dreams as fragments of evidence about lives and thoughts, reflecting women's concerns and preoccupations. Dream narratives demonstrate that religious belief and language were at the core of women's being, and that women were preoccupied with life, death, sickness, salvation, and wholeness. We could say that dreams gave a woman access to her own knowledge which had not yet emerged into her waking consciousness, although we know that she would speak of this in terms of divine guidance. Because of gendered social prohibitions, such knowledge could not easily emerge in other ways.
> *(Crawford 2000: 138–39)*

In the end, they "provided women with an opportunity to experience their wishes and fears", thus working "as an avenue to self-knowledge" (ibid.).[6]

8.13 *Pour (en) finir avec Descartes*

It is traditional to conclude chronologically and logically a survey of a Renaissance intellectual tradition with the philosophy of René Descartes. The Parisian house Vrin has published since 1911 a book series entitled "De Pétrarque à Descartes", which in the choice of the two names summarises the timespan of a significant development, the collection being "devoted to Renaissance authors, philosophers and erudite writers, to debates on ideas, literary style and the history of the transmission of knowledge characteristic of Renaissance humanism at the dawn of modernity" (from the publisher's website). Our topic has special reasons to pay a debt to the experience and reflections of this particular thinker.

In the autumn of 1619, the 23-year-old René Descartes, then quartered in Bavaria, had the leisure to entertain himself in his thoughts, and came to the decision to re-elaborate the entire system of human knowledge by conceiving his new method. So he tells us, retrospectively, nearly 20 years later in his *Discourse on Method*. What the *Discourse* does not mention, however, is that among the experiences that marked his reorientation on that occasion were three dreams, all experienced in a single night. In the first one, the dreamer is assaulted initially by ghosts and then by raging winds. Hampered by the elements, he seeks refuge in the courtyard of a college, sees an acquaintance, and a stranger who tells him that a friend has a present for him – which Descartes imagines may be a melon. When he wakes up, he invokes God's help and meditates for two hours. In the second dream, whose description at least is shorter, he hears a deafening sound that he interprets as thunder and wakes him up, to see the room full of fire sparks. Once fallen asleep again (after further philosophical meditations), he dreams of a dictionary and an anthology of Latin poetry and of reading poems and discussing them with another stranger. Then the books disappear and reappear modified, the anthology enriched with portraits of the poets. His interpretation starts already during the dream and continues when he opens his eyes: he finds the last one pleasant and a premonition of his future life of study (the detail of the added portraits has an explanation the next day, when an Italian painter pays a visit to the author), and the first perhaps a reference to some events from his past. He prays again for divine help, promises a pilgrimage and projects a treatise (Kennington 1961; Browne 1977; Hallyn 1995; Holland 1999).

We no longer have the Latin notebooks in which the French philosopher wrote down his memories of that night. We only have fragments that, variously reported, translated and commented, were included by later biographers: they are known as *Olympica*. The fact that he had not prepared (nor probably intended) those notes for publication makes the reader feel like an intruder. Nevertheless, precisely this nature of the documentation may add to it an aura of sincerity. Specialists have duly discussed whether they should be intended as a literary invention, following a tradition of precedents and respecting some rules of the genre, or else the report of a "real" experience: overall, this has been judged as an ill-posed question, while, if anywhere, the balance has tended to lean towards recognising in them the narration of actual dreams (Hallyn 1995). Unsurprisingly, modern psychoanalysis did not miss the chance to retrospectively enquire into the meaning of the experience of such an exceptional dreamer: in 1929, Sigmund Freud was asked by a correspondent to comment on the *Olympica*; however, the father of the psychoanalysis exercised restraint and claimed that the available information only allowed to accept the interpretations offered by the philosopher himself: after all, the impossibility to interact with the dreamer impeded the dialogic process intrinsic in the analytic method. Freud did, however, understand the 1619 oneiric experience as a type of dream "from above" (*Träume von oben*), a psychological rather than mystic category, intended to distinguish some thoughts and intentions that could also have been expressed while awake, but which during sleep may partly mix with unconscious desires (Quakelbeen 1995).

For a philosopher who aimed at re-establishing from scratch the epistemological and ontological foundations of Western thought and based a crucial part of his *pars destruens* on the methodological doubt whether one is awake or asleep and dreaming, it is quite appropriate that some juvenile experience had significantly involved the oneiric. And yet between the fragmentary testimony of Descartes's earlier dreams and the use he makes of the dream argument in his mature reflection there is a substantial gap. It has been observed that the *Olympica* are still fully immersed in the oneirocritic tradition. The interpretation of dreams following received rules and keys to their symbolism is so much taken for granted by the young Descartes that it begins already during his dreams. It has been observed that his attitude towards dreams, as documented by this material, implied that: the dream may have a sense, and one that deserves interpretation; it can put the dreamer in contact with higher powers, given its external origin, which needs to be properly determined; despite its superhuman origin, under certain circumstances it can be interpreted; and finally, in a literal passage of his testimony of the day Descartes portrays himself as "full of enthusiasm", and this condition would have allowed him to think metaphorically, like poets, spiritual things starting from physical ones. This mode of thought, characteristic of the Renaissance intellectual milieu, still depending on the categories and elements of ancient natural philosophy, was structured on the base of the similarities of all things, as brilliantly portrayed by Michel Foucault (Simon 1995; Foucault 2002). To pick one example, that of the melon, Descartes thinks it signified the attractions of solitude, presented via purely human (rather than spiritual, à la Petrarch) solicitations. (The choice of the gift may surprise the postmodern palate, but one should perhaps consider that at the time the melon was regarded as a hybrid fruit, seductive but dangerous, since proverbially feasting excessively on it was believed to be responsible for deaths – Giannetti 2022: 107–22). On the contrary, in his later argumentation leading to the *cogito*, both in the *Discours* and in the *Meditations*, the dream appears as a paradigm for illusion, the doubt whether one is asleep serves to put provisionally in question the reliability of all that we appear to feel and think: the dream loses any sense because it does no longer put us in contact with anything other than our own consciousness. To close the case once and for all, his *Passions de l'âme* state that our dreams' illusions are imaginations that have no other cause than our body (Simon 1995).

This survey has inevitably pointed the attention to a selected range of source material, which hopefully was worth reviving and may help retrieving part of the historical interpretation and evaluation of the oneiric experience. Much more research is needed before further comparisons between cultural contexts and historical generalisation can be safely made. The idea was partly to aim at raising the status of the subject as one that, given the importance people from the past gave to their dreamt life, deserves a special place in any convincing project of historical anthropology (as advocated, among others, by Richter 2014). The research that has already taken place over the past few generations promises the success of such an enterprise, particularly considering the theoretical awareness and systematic approach it has by now reached. Chapter 11 of this volume will offer a short summary of this scholarly tradition.

Notes

1 The tradition of short afternoon naps has been connected to the need for agricultural workers to have a break during the hottest hours of the day. For as rooted as the custom may be in the Iberian tradition, the name of the *siesta* comes from the ancient Roman numbering for the time of day, and we have seen how in sixteenth-century Italy too, despite medical and moral resistance, naps were becoming increasingly tolerated.
2 Ermolao Barbaro had been instrumental to the late fifteenth-century circulation of influential texts and relevant themes, for example via his Latin translation of the paraphrasis on Aristotle written in the fourth century CE by Themistius (Gandolfo 1978).
3 The term defines in particular a group of Catholic reformers inspired by the Spanish theologian Juan de Valdés, whose spirituality included a doctrine of justification by faith not so distant from the Lutheran.
4 Garzoni's term here is *lottatori*, but without reference to wrestling; rather, to the organizing of raffles in public places, with emphasis on the fact that in many ways participants will be tricked.
5 On the charismatic grace of discernment in medieval and early modern Catholicism, see Caciola 2003; Sluhovsky 2007.
6 A gender perspective is also present in Milne 2011, briefly described in the iconographic section of the present book.

9
A LOOK AT IMAGES

Dreams are experiences that are later verbalised, but we first encounter them with our senses and retrieve them with our memory. Images may play a predominant part in what we sense, but the Aristotelian doctrine of dreams as appearances allowed for them to be the result of the lingering of perceptions of any of the five senses. In fact, the synesthetic nature of the oneiric experience is obvious, and the sources examined do not lack reflection on at least the aural dimension (in fact, we have found Cardano expressing a preference for it). The rendition of multisensory dimension has in particular been identified in the literary recreation of dreamworlds in the *Hypnerotomachia Poliphili* and, a century later, in Shakespeare's *A Midsummer Night's Dream*, not without the suggestion of a possible direct influence of the former over the latter.

Ancient Greek culture associated the divine apparitions that could visit dreaming humans with a special brilliant whiteness, which Homer calls *enargeia*. Late antique rhetoric attributed similar vividness to *ekphrasis*, a descriptive speech that brings the subject to be shown before the eyes. *Ekphrasis* – a concept that in recent visual studies has developed a wider meaning (Mitchell 1994: 151–81) – was to be deployed to provoke *enargeia* in the audience: Quintilian specified that it was not the plausibility of the described images that mattered, but rather the ability of the orator to provoke emotions. Both the process and a list of recommended topics regarded as effective for the scope resembled the images experienced in a dream and their effect. It is as if the most successful orator was the one able to play effectively with the oneiric repertoire and experience of his audience – a connection with which Synesius was well aware. During the Renaissance, these concepts were principally

DOI: 10.4324/9781003279709-9

present within the discourse on poetics (Galand-Hallyn 1990; Mack 2004; Stavru 2018).

Another classical and Renaissance field that presented a close relationship with the oneiric imagery was the art of memory, which also enjoyed a major attention within the practice of rhetoric, as a means for memorising a speech, or any other useful data. The way memory was believed to operate suggested that it employed techniques of associating thoughts – by similarity, contrariety and contiguity – which coincide with those of the oneiric work and resemble poetic and artistic creativity, thus positioning the art of memory somewhere between nature and artifice. At the heart of the discipline was the disposition, within a memorable architectural setting, of unusual, "acting images" (*imagines agentes*), which would have the power of arousing emotions and remaining impressed in one's memory. In the rich tradition of Renaissance manuscript and printed treatises transmitting that art, in fact, it is frequent to find extremely inventive images, resorting to metamorphosis and hybridisation, which aimed at striking the reader-viewer's attention (Bolzoni 2013).

Not unrelated to mnemotechnics was a habit to compare dreams to picture-writing.[1] It has been suggested as a parallel to the role played today by cinema, not only with dream narratives exposed following the blueprint of film scenes and plots but also with the experience of viewing moving pictures actively feeding and affecting the dreamer's oneiric imagination. Similarly, early modern people were familiar with a few codes relating symbolic images to hidden meanings, from hieroglyphs to heraldry and alchemy; and acquaintance with such pictorial languages could feed back into the imagery appearing at night time. A telling example is offered by the famous Bolognese naturalist Ulisse Aldrovandi, who in his treatise of ornithology gave the meaning of the appearance of some birds in dreams, as if it was an intrinsic property of each species. However, the model of all such associations could be found nowhere else than in the Bible, where the logic of Joseph's and Daniel's dream interpretation is based on simple correspondences between symbolic images and their reputedly fixed meaning (Browne 1981). That it was the religious imagery, anyway, that inspired much of the nocturnal imagery of premodern Europeans is testified, among indefinite possible other examples, by the case of Andreas Ryff, a late-sixteenth-century Swiss merchant who, while suffering of plague and undergoing medical treatment, dreamt to be climbing Jacob's ladder (Ulbricht 2001; a Renaissance illustration of Jacob's dream can be seen on this book's cover).

Besides this interplay between words and visual experiences, it would be a serious limitation if a revisitation of a past culture in a field of human experience tightly intertwined with the role of imagination did not offer some room to consider actual images. The figurative representation of what artists may have intended as a vision offered in a dream, either their own or someone else's, forms an obvious part of this area of enquiry, but it does not exhaust it. The visual culture within which the textual sources examined in this book should be considered also includes, for instance, the representation of sleeping figures and the production of a whole set of fantastic imagery that may suggest in various ways to be in contact with the world of dreams and nightmares (Milne 2011). Furthermore, the visual culture of the Renaissance did not only find expression and nourishment in artworks in various media, some of which we can still admire in museums and galleries; but it also consisted of an extremely lively, rich and various tradition of performing arts and related ephemeral artefacts, which people of all social statuses would have encountered frequently and found very familiar. Here again fantastic imagery was well represented, also in such forms – as hybrid and metamorphic bodies – that connect with dreamlike vision. These performing traditions prominently included Carnival (Milne 2011).

The Renaissance figurative rendering of the dream has been explored, for instance, on the occasion of dedicated exhibitions (Rabbi Bernard, Cecchi and Hersant 2013). On the other hand, the pictorial representation of sleep, including the deep sleep in which we do not experience dreaming, witnesses interesting developments during the period. Among the elements of its cultural framework is a general tendency at stigmatising sleep as wasteful, as paradoxically expressed by the extreme monastic ideal of a night spent awake in prayer. Thus, according to their specific contexts, sleeping figures may act as metaphors of sloth or melancholy, their horizonal position contradicting the natural, erect one that defines being human. But the epoch also produced a variety of images of sleeping beauties, both female and male, each inspiring either sexual desire or different reactions and meanings. The image of the sleeping body could also evidently resemble the corpse, and sleep has often served and been commented as synonym of death. The connotations of this proximity, however, could also vary, as is the case with Lutheran theology, which, by understanding the interval between the individual's death and the Last Judgment as a total sleep, wiped away the traditional Catholic room for interaction between the living and the dead (Seretti 2021). Not unrelated is the issue of the representation of night and darkness, which according to some interpreters was conceptually precluded to Renaissance painting, before light and shadow were reinvented by Caravaggio (Corrain 1991b).[2]

In her *Carnivals and Dreams*, Louise Milne (2011) has examined the oneiric imagery of Pieter Bruegel the Elder and his primary source, the art of Hieronymus Bosch, by relating them to a medieval tradition of imagination of hybridity and metamorphosis of bodies, which was further emphasised by trends of Renaissance thought, as the revival of Neoplatonism and Hermeticism. She observed that the distorted figuration of things out of their ordinary proportions resembled standard learned descriptions of the oneiric work. Under the pressure of the sixteenth-century religious reforms, the performative genres of nonsense characteristic of the carnivalesque folk fantasy tended to migrate from ritual to the oneiric life and particularly into bad dreams. The latter, a disordered economy of vision shifting towards nocturnal representations, were interpreted in terms of melancholia, witchcraft and gynophobia, adding a gender perspective depending on views about the instability of the female mind and a fear of women's desire.

It is in general not so easy to tell if (part of) an image is supposed to represent the content of a dream or a vision, and contextual information may be required to confirm it. After all, the markers – a halo, stars, some masking or a special colouring, as gold – that should help distinguishing an apparition as not "real" – pose an epistemological conundrum: when I dream, no marker is necessarily there, and I tend to take the situation and event I witness for real; they are only justifiable as mere pictorial conventions (Freedberg 1999). Jean-Claude Schmitt (2002c) has carefully examined the conventions and the evolution of the illustrations that, in the central Middle Ages, offered the readers a visualisation of dreams in illuminated manuscripts of the Bible. They were accompanying the text (whether or not this openly referred to sleep or dreams, as they could work as pictorial commentaries suggesting an oneiric experience even where it was not explicit); consisted of a representation of the dreamer and of the dreamt scene, with various possibility in the position of the former – lying, with the head up or down, with their eyes closed or open (not undermining the fact that they intended to be shown asleep), facing or not the apparition, if not even in contact with it. The makers of such images had to negotiate manifold problems, from how to suggest that an image had supernatural origins to ways to display synchronically the diachronic development of a dream narrative.

It took a highly innovative artist's personal dreaming experience to abandon similar conventions. The uniqueness of Dürer's innovation, and its position as marker of a cultural shift in visual conventions and experiences, has been stated in relationship with the practices of representation that had preceded it. From the Middle Ages to the early Renaissance, the reproduction of dreamt scenes, whether biblical, mythological or historical, in a variety of media – from book illumination to fresco – had surely not been lacking. However, it presented, beyond individual stylistic nuances, some common features: the dreamt image tended to appear within a narrative context, rather than in isolation; in its appearance, as we said, there was no formal distinction marking the different reality status between the dreamer and the dreamt scene.

What Dürer's watercolour – now at the Kunsthistorisches Museum in Vienna (see Figure 9.1) – recorded, in painting and in a handwritten inscription, is a dream, held on a night of June 1525, of enormous masses of water descending from the sky, and pouring down on earth with devastating force, some closer and some further away from him, an experience from which he

FIGURE 9.1   Albrecht Dürer, "Dream landscape with text" (pen and ink and watercolour on paper, 1525). The German writing includes: "I saw in a dream what this sketch displays: a number of waterspouts falling from the sky. The first struck the earth some four leagues off: the blow and its noise were terrifying, and the entire region was inundated. I was so frightened I woke up. Then other waterspouts fell in appalling violence and number, some striking the earth farther off, some nearer. And they fell from such a height that they all seemed to fall in slow motion. But when the first waterspout was close to the earth, its fall became so rapid and was accompanied by such a noise and such a roaring wind that I woke up, trembling in every limb, and took a long time to get over it". © Bridgeman Images.

awoke frightened and trembling (in our own times, climate anxiety has been found to hit particularly children and young people: Hickman et al. 2021). With its particular choice of colouring, the image evokes an emotional state – the anxiety dream. The historical context, with the Peasants' War approaching its tragic climax, and floods having always featured in the apocalyptic imagery, may have helped to give the document some of its flavour. But this is not a public image of the sort that the artist used to do with his engravings: it is the record of a personal traumatic experience, an exercise of introspection; the represented scene has been labelled as an inner landscape. We also know that Dürer used to share the content of his dreams with friends, so that private interpersonal dimension might have been one he was considering in making this leaf (Wirth 1976, including a review of early twentieth-century criticism; Poesche 1994; Bournet-Bacot 2016; Besson and Schmitt 2017: 461–6); verbal and visual records also show the impact that the familiarity with classical literature and the Bible had on the oneiric imagery of his circle (Massing 1986).

An insightful reading of the watercolour was offered in 1977 by Marguerite Yourcenar. She sets Dürer apart from other artists and writers who reported some of their oneiric life. She finds that Dante, Leonardo da Vinci or Cardano in one way or another exposed an experience that had occurred somewhere between proper dreaming and wakefulness. None of this, instead, in the image and text that appear on the page from Dürer's diary. The dream strikes her for its complete lack of symbols. While a psychoanalyst could suggest that the artist was obsessed with water, his oeuvre does not support such a claim: there is a limited appearance of it, and never as dramatic as in this nightmare. Even in his woodcut prints of the *Apocalypse*, the only water featuring are large drops of rain falling from a cloud in which there appears a dragon with a lamb's head, and that is a minor detail. The artist at work here instead is a realist, careful in recording the varying speed of the falling water and the loud sound it makes. The terror he experiences is perceivable, and Yourcenar cannot stop noticing how the shape of the extraordinary atmospheric phenomenon reminds us of an atomic mushroom. More significantly, the twentieth-century writer notes that "there is no religious symbol in the margin, no avenging angels signifying God's wrath, no alchemical symbol" nor humanistic meditation (Yourcenar 1992: 68). Apart from a final pious formula, which helps us remember that the man who left us this record was a Christian who lived through the Age of Reformation.

Although this does not yet appear to have been the question with Dürer, by 1601 it was possible for a Netherlandish painter, Karel van Mander, the author of the first comprehensive book of history and theory of northern art, to draw in the ancient god of dreams Morpheus, child of Somnus, an embodiment of the working of the artistic imagination, thus situating the creative process in a border zone with dreamt worlds (Göttler 2018). Besides, dreams have been suggested, together with sex and sleep, as telling metaphors of the Renaissance notion of inspiration (Ruvoldt 2004). On the other hand, two millennia of intellectual tradition have associated in particular the melancholic, more prone to dreaming, with a special creative gift, due to a liberation of the spirit from reason and a lively imagination (Pigeaud 1995; Seretti 2021).

Theatre and spectacle, including the ephemeral world of public and private displays in festivals and civic or religious rituals, offered multiple opportunities to display oneiric experiences and exploit their potential within plots. The specific case of Shakespeare has been seen to attest his use of scenes of dream and sleep to subvert traditional genre conventions, and in particular the opposition between comedy and tragedy, a use made possible, together with other conditions, by the cultural ambiguity of dreams (Fretz 2020). In general, the experience of the theatre was associated to the practice of forming mental images, including the ones belonging to mnemotechnics (Lochert and De Guardia 2012). One should also not miss the connection that the contemporary viewer could make between the illusions created on the theatrical scene and the deceiving imagery that, as we have seen discussing witchcraft, were believed to be the working of the devil.

Dance is a performing art which had the capability to represent and evoke dreamworlds through a combination of media. For a start, as attested, among others, by sixteenth-century French poets, it was acknowledged that "the power to change the way in which we view the world ... lifted the observer on to another plane of being, transferring him to a marvellous and transfigured realm" (McGowan 2008: 209). Various genres of sixteenth- and seventeenth-century ballet showed, among others, the possibility to explore hybridity and metamorphosis, almost making the viewers believe that they were assisting at transformations of the performers into animals or monstrous creatures. This was due to the skills of the performers and the care for detail of costumes, in the context of a taste for the exotic, the strange and the grotesque (McGowan 2012: esp. 62–7).

The relationship between music and sleep was known and explored since Antiquity, with particular forms and sounds believed and employed to have relaxing and enchanting effects (Boccadoro 2019). Music clearly contributed to the creation of the atmosphere of the just-mentioned performative experiments; nevertheless, identifying what musical forms and techniques may be particularly prone and effective at suggesting the world of dreams is no simple matter. Sixteenth-century instrumental music, becoming progressively independent from the vocal, developed a new attention for timbre and orchestration, allowing *intermedi* and early operas to evoke mythical worlds in a multisensory experience. Conversely, both dance and music could help a literary text such as the *Hypnerotomachia Poliphili* to produce in the reader a dreamlike adventure (Gallo 1987; Gabriele 2007).

A musical form that developed a noticeable capability to express and provoke emotions was the madrigal, which set into polyphonic chamber music poetry from Petrarch as well as from contemporary authors. A master of the genre was Cipriano de Rore, one of the many Flemish composers who fled to Italy to exploit the many professional opportunities offered there by the dynamic music life of courts and chapels. He was *maestro di cappella* of the Duke of Ferrara Ercole II d'Este around 1550 and became later the object of a cult, acknowledged by Claudio Monteverdi and others to have shown a special sensitivity to the text and thus anticipated the musical reforms that followed at the turn of the century. It is therefore interesting to find, in

Cipriano's second book of four-part madrigals (1557), *O sonno* (Oh, sleep), on lyrics by Giovanni Della Casa, an invocation for sleep, "quiet child of peaceful, fresh and shadowy night", to come and offer oblivion of ills and relief to weary limbs. Unfortunately, the call appears to be sung in vain. The repetition of the invocation dominates the text, which, as for other madrigals in his later production, is rendered in a tendentially homophonic, declamatory style, which also attracted the enthusiastic praise of the Florentine *Camerata*, the circle that advocated the shift from polyphony to monody and led the way to the birth of the baroque opera. In fact, a prominent member of the group, Vincenzo Galilei, the father of Galileo, composed a madrigal resembling (and possibly inspired by) *O sonno*, *Dolcissimo riposo* (Sweetest rest), from a poem by Giovanni Battista Strozzi (1587). Defining again sleep as the son of the night and the father of dream, it describes it as shadowy and adopts the image of the wings of darkness spread over the sleeper (La Via 1997; Schick 2016).

Anguishing over insomnia is found again in the first book of madrigals by Luca Marenzio, published in Venice in 1588, which included a setting to music of "Fuggito è 'l sonno a le mie crude notti", a stanza extracted from Petrarch's "Mia benigna fortuna e 'l viver lieto" ("My kindly fate, and a life made happy", *Canzoniere* 332), a double sestina from which Cipriano instead had put into music the first two stanzas. The general theme – in the Urtext that inspired its sixteenth-century epigones – is the poet's leitmotiv sighing and crying for love, down to the desire of death over life: alas, here too "Escaped is sleep from my cruel nights". Although it would look as if we have stepped away from dream proper, the way contemporary artistic invention expressed and elaborated the grey zone between night and day, sleep and wakefulness, with all its connotations, may not be insignificant for the scope of this survey.

Notes

1 On Freud's use of this imagery, see Derrida 2001: 246–91.
2 Nevertheless, on this field too there have been exhibitions (*Italia al chiaro di luna* 1990; for a critique, Corrain 1991a).

10
FRAGMENTS TOWARDS A GRAND NARRATIVE

Historical research on dreams could offer a significant contribution to the building of a history of experience – which has been recommended, in a recent manifesto, as a merging of the kind of perspectives the histories of emotions and of senses have developed over the past generation of scholarship (Boddice and Smith 2020). The challenges are obvious but may work as a factor of intellectual stimulation and encouragement, rather than dissuasion. In the initial, "Basics" section of his essay "Towards a Transmedial Poetics of the Dream", Manfred Engel (on whom more in Chapter 11) defines the dream as a "fictional mental event, created and experienced by the sleeping mind", one which "introduces us to a world which is different from that of our waking mind" (Engel 2020: 33, 36). Although any definition is to some extent subjective and culturally situated, this seems a reasonable starting point to pin down on a map of the spectrum of human experience what sort of phenomenon we are talking about here. It is a slice of experience that may have, and have had in the past, a considerable impact on people's life. Girolamo Cardano has offered a very particular observation point, considering that he was arguably the sixteenth-century man mostly attentive to the value of dreams and knowledgeable about the tradition of their interpretation. In this sense, he may be positioned at one end of the spectrum of critical awareness of the oneiric world. But this does not mean that his contemporaries were totally ignorant or dismissive of that experience. Everyone to their own extent and in their own way, men and women of the past have dreamt, forgotten, remembered, told and retold dreams; and the meaning they gave to that night-time world – or, for that matter, to dreamlike visions experienced in daytime – is likely to have affected significantly the way they went about in their daily life, if we only think how belief in the prophetic value of visions can guide in choosing one or another course of action. In this sense, an aetiology and psychology of agency would be all the poorer if it failed to consider the historical subject also as a dreaming subject.

Coming to some concluding remarks, it may be worth saying something more on the matter of chronology and paradigm shifts. French medievalist Jean-Claude Schmitt (more on that in Chapter 11) has worked on the subject repeatedly; and the issue of the journal *Sensibilités: Histoire, critique & sciences sociales* dedicated, in 2018, to "The society of dreams", as well republishing, from the *Annales*, Peter Burke's 1973 seminal essay on "The social history of dreams", included a lively round table on the collection of medieval autobiographical dreams, coedited by Schmitt together with Gisèle Besson (Besson and Schmitt 2017). The conversation on the book hosted by *Sensibilités* presents the additional point of interest of being particularly transdisciplinary, considering that the authors' two interlocutors are a historian of psychoanalysis and an anthropologist expert of the kanak culture of New Caledonia, whose practice of divinatory dreaming on wooden boards is described elsewhere in the same issue of the journal, and here compared with Mediterranean incubation (Schmitt et al. 2018). This anthropological perspective is particularly present in Schmitt and Besson's take on medieval dream narratives, as their way of understanding them is based on a clear distinction between the Western modern dream culture and those they characterise as typical of "traditional societies". The latter label is broad and eclectic, as it includes not only the societies ordinarily studied by Western anthropologists in other parts of the world but also distant past cultures, as the Western ones from Antiquity to the Middle Ages, as well as significant fringes of today's Western culture, where oneiromancy and popular astrology remain alive and attract ethnologic interest (Besson and Schmitt 2017: 8–9). One of the key contrasts between the two so defined dream cultures is the emphasis the modern one puts on the single individual, whose experience is postulated as emerging from the depths of their own personality. On the contrary, in the traditional understanding the dream comes from elsewhere, the individual receives it from outside and is visited by it (Besson and Schmitt 2017: 9–10).

> Through dreams, it is the external world of the spirits, of the dead, of the demonic and of the divine that enters a relationship with the individual, to reveal them by means of some images and voices more or less explicit what is going to happen to them and to the group to which they belong.
> *(ibid. 10)*

The autonomous subject, particularly based on the influence of psychoanalysis, is what we tend to evoke as key for the interpretation of our dreams.

Nothing of the sort in traditional views, where on the contrary the dream means the external powers' domination over the world, humans and their destiny, and therefore the dreamer. The dreamer does not stand as an autonomous subject; (he or she) rather, actually, thinks as an *alienated* subject, dependent on an Other.

(ibid. 11)

The notion of *subject* is thus contextualized, as Schmitt and Besson point out that the medieval meaning of the word was ambivalent, also referring to the condition of being *subject* to invisible powers, and above all the Creator. Medieval autobiographic dream narratives, where the use of the first person is not unknown, thus reflect such ambiguity, expressing people's fears and remorse, as well as perhaps aspirations and ambitions. With their frequent display of demonic temptation, they document the moral culpability that found expression in the sacrament of confession and testify to the psychological processes contemporary Christians underwent (for the devil as subject of dreams in early modern Spain, see Amelang 2012). Although not unusual, dreaming of the devil could be such a traumatic experience to be regarded as responsible for someone's death. In one of Giorgio Vasari's rare references to an artist's dream, he relates a story of the late-fourteenth-century painter Spinello Aretino, concerning his frescoing of the principal scene behind the altar of the now destroyed church of the Confraternity of Saint Michael in Arezzo, which depicted the fall of the rebel angels and the archangel combating them, while Lucifer has already turned into a horrible beast. It is particularly the latter figure that the painter was apparently proud to have represented in its full ugliness. But he claimed that afterwards the figure appeared to him in a dream, confronting him because it had been represented so badly. And the scene terrified him, woke him up, trembling and unable to scream. His wife offered him help; but the heart attack left him scarred and with bulging eyes, and he did not survive for long (Acidini 2013: 20).

One could conclude that such a portrait of the distance between our modern experience and that of past or other cultures may offer further grounds to identify the Renaissance as a turning point. Nevertheless, we should not rush to enrol that period of transition under the flag of modernity. Reconsidering Jacob Burckhardt's idea of the Renaissance has to a significant extent required, for subsequent historiography, nuancing the supposed break from the Middle Ages and the degree of novelty, particularly on the front of the birth of individualism and of the overcoming of community ties. Besides, the whole grand narrative of an evolution from an understanding of the dream as source of truth to an interiorisation of the experience has been questioned, both in the sense that the oneiric as path of self-knowledge pre-existed in the Middle Ages and in the opposite direction, of a survival of its recognition as a fount of knowledge (Plane and Tuttle 2013a). Special caution needs to be exercised in identifying and examining the forms that self-knowledge and self-expression took in a transitional period. There surely were a multiplicity of them, writing of self as well as portraiture were the arena in which more than one conception of personal identity was rehearsed in various styles of self-fashioning and self-presentation (Burke 1997b).

Along with the literary tradition of humanist autobiographical writing, a distinct line has been observed in the Tuscan merchant writers, whose take on identity put (still) less emphasis on individuals and more on their role within their families and on community ties. At the beginning of the fifteenth century, the Florentine Giovanni di Pagolo Morelli has been seen as a case in which a search for personal identity through writing is already more distinguishable. His memory book contains visions experienced while remembering, in touching prose, the death of his son on its anniversary. The well-known episode includes a traditional moment of prayer and sorrow, followed by the experience of demonic temptation dragging him towards the sin of despair, and finally what he describes as a divinely inspired dream, not a wakeful ecstatic vision (although it has been assimilated to the medieval hybrid genre of dream visions). In it, mindful of many details of Dante's literary journey, Giovanni sees a bird, copulating pigs symbolising the sin he must overcome, saint Catherine of Alexandria and eventually the soul of his son, who reassures him about his state of grace while also guiding the father towards the achieving of his own (Morelli 2019: 280–92; Bartuschat 1997; Besson and Schmitt 2017: 433–59). In the words of a late medieval merchant, the narrative shows, among other facts, how a dream could intervene to help self-understanding and the reassuring discovery of a path to salvation, in difficult personal circumstances as well as in a problematic era. Early modern middle class and popular autobiographers, as their elite counterparts, continued to write their dreams frequently (Greyerz 1984: 230; Amelang 1998: 235).

Over the following centuries, Christian churches will hesitate between encouraging such deep personal experiences and warning against their spiritual dangers. In the new world of the Reformation, while Melanchthon took dreams, including his own temptation dreams, still rather seriously, Luther refused to take their supernatural origin as reason to take religious guidance from them (Grafton 2006; Roper 2021: 42–63). All churches, old and new, had ultimately something to fear from faithful's claims of direct communication to God via dreams and visions. In the 1530s, there was even the case of a German Anabaptist sect, known as the Dreamers, who justified their unorthodox sexual behaviour by entering in new relationships in obedience to revelations by the Spirit; they were persecuted by Lutheran authorities. In general, divine guidance via oneiric experiences continued to be claimed by dissenting groups, as it occurred in the following century with the Quakers – as well as constituting a very common path to conversion, in whatever direction (Roper 1994: 80–105; Gerona 2004; Plane and Tuttle

2013b: 12–13). Despite this aura of suspicion, the belief in prophetic dreams was so rooted that it could be exploited also in the context of confessional polemic and propaganda. In the late sixteenth century, a text began to circulate which claimed to describe a dream by which the Elector of Saxony Frederick the Wise, the protector of Martin Luther, had received an oneiric anticipation of the gesture of the Reformer affixing the 95 Theses. By the centenary of the event in 1617, the circulation of the fictional narrative was accompanied by a woodcut representing the scene in the style of contemporary pictorial controversies, with Luther writing directly on the door of the Wittenberg chapel with a quilt so long that it pierced the pope's tiara (Gantet 2021: 104–7).

With the Enlightenment usually identified as the key age of paradigm shift, witnessing a loss of belief in "supernatural" dreams (prophetic and admonitory: see Pigman 2019), the preceding centuries may be perceived as lacking originality, and marked by a continuity in beliefs and practice. However, many developments in related fields contributed to reorientate that experience: texts documenting classical oneirocritics were rediscovered and appreciated – with Artemidorus above them all, fairly incongruously, serving as major key to decipher oneiric symbols in widely different cultural contexts; the questioning of the authenticity of visions became a delicate battleground at a time of hard theological conflicts and frequent, controversial prophetic admonitions; the functioning and reliability of human senses and faculties were further scrutinized due to the developments in natural philosophy; travels and cultural encounters saw the arrival of alien dream cultures in the Western intellectual debate; the printing press ensured a wider circulation also of the material that concerned this range of phenomena. Significant developments have been identified already as having occurred towards the end of the Middle Ages. Thirteenth-century scholasticism, with its recovery of Aristotle, had the effect of scaling down the weight of the supernatural in the understanding of dreams, consigning it predominantly to human physiology and consequently to the territory of medicine (Le Goff 1980b; Abbruzzetti 1997).

Despite the continuing and versatile manuscript transmission and re-elaboration of texts, the active role of printing needs to be fully acknowledged for its place in the story; and it did not play it in a spaceless dimension, but with important contributions situated in specific areas. It should be obvious that a prominent one was Venice, the sixteenth-century European capital of publishing, and the city where, just to give the most remarkable example, the printing life of Artemidorus and of the Greek text of Synesius began – and in the house of the heirs of Aldo Manuzio, the inventor of portable classics. Venice also offered itself as the printing hub for the University of Padua that, together with others but most systematically than all, during the decades around 1500 was the centre that consistently studied other key ancient Greek works such as those of Hippocrates and Aristoteles and put them in circulation in Latin translations with commentaries. Nevertheless, other places did not miss their chance to participate in the business offered by an audience eager to consult dream books: so did Lyon, where, for instance, from the late 1530s, the public benefitted from the publication of Scaliger's commentary on Hippocrates, of a number of editions of Macrobius, of Latin and French translations of Artemidorus, as well as of new dedicated oneirocritic material; and all this was the result of a fertile encounter of book entrepreneurship with humanist philology (Cooper 1990: 57–8). However, we have also registered an interested sub-culture emerging around Bologna in the early seventeenth century.

While all this occurred, different discourses endeavoured to define nature and meaning of dreams; European vernaculars struggled to invent an adequate terminology; literature, drama and the visual arts explored and represented that area of human experience, which a contemporary adage had taken to signify life itself, its deepest nature; and individuals from different social and cultural groups developed strategies for narrating and analysing their own dreamlife, with the aim to better understand themselves and consequently operate in the world. In attempts to summarise the historical developments in this area, it has been suggested that, while medieval literary dreaming included the visitation of the otherworld, Renaissance writers switch, preferably, to explore the human cosmos (Joukovsky 1991: 44–5); and, while notions of the self were evolving during the early modern period, by the seventeenth century it was a shared tenet that dreams offered a window towards self-knowledge (Levin 2008: 45–9). Self-knowledge is a perspective that we have encountered also in an attempt to assess the specific early modern oneiric experience of women. Furthermore, it has been observed that dreaming was at the same time a sociocultural phenomenon and an individual experience that offered opportunities for self-assertion and for the building of specific forms of connection with others: a dreamer who decides to reveal their visions to others constructs, and, by so doing, a persona and, if a dream is believed to have supernatural origins, may qualify as a distinctive form of agency, challenging the established order (Plane and Tuttle 2013b: 7–8).

The evolution which occurred has been described as a psychologization of the dream, a process that unfolded all along the early modern period but made significant inroads in the second half of the sixteenth century (Gantet 2001). Besides, Claire Gantet has identified and summarised in the sixteenth century a period in which the interpretation of dreams played a very specific and intriguing role in the sphere of knowledge:

> In the sixteenth century, dreams belonged to fields of knowledge alternative to those debated by the established sciences. By promising a form of

knowledge that laid below or above the discursive one produced by the mediation of the five senses and the clerical or scholastic hierarchy, they served as vehicle for various individuals or groups in search of self-knowledge. The dream, however, held more of a tangential place to institutionalised science than a marginal one. Its humanist valorisation following the rereading of the ancient texts made it the concretion par excellence of a way of knowing based on the conjecture of correspondences, a secret path between microcosm and macrocosm. If a science of dreams did not exist, the dream held by the divinatory arts, therefore by the foundations of knowledge.

(Gantet 2021: 217)

A place in this story was played by texts that today are neither well known nor regarded as historically significant. In this group we may classify Achmet's text. Even before circulating in the vernaculars or in the sixteenth-century translation known to Robert Burton, Leo Tuscus's version attracted a remarkable number of prominent readers. It has been suggested that it also unusually appealed to a female readership because, while most dream books tended to interpret women's dreams in relation to their husbands, this work registered several objects and activities understood specifically in connection to women (Camozzi Pistoja 2014). It also offered itself to interpretations of dreaming leaning towards secularisation and individualism. With Tuscus misunderstood as the author of the text, a manuscript copy dedicated to Lorenzo di Pierfrancesco de' Medici, cousin of Lorenzo the Magnificent, was accompanied by an original preface by the humanist Filippo Buonaccorsi (a member of the Accademia Romana of Junius Pomponius Laetus who moved to Poland after being accused of conspiracy and sodomy). He denied that sleep offered the opportunity for external intervention in the human body and mind and suggested that the variety of the oneiric experience rather depended on the nature of the dreamers, on their existential or psychological condition (Gandolfo 1978: 100–2).

Over the past few decades, the Renaissance as historical paradigm has been contested or abandoned under a cluster of charges centred on that of ethnocentrism, and its survival and renewal owes much to its revisitation through the perspective of the growing general interest for cultural diversity and cultural exchange, in particular by emphasising how much the richness of the West owed to its interaction with the East (Mediterranean and beyond): overall, the case of dream cultures appears to confirm and strengthen such an interpretative shift. Sixteenth-century Europeans tended to frame their oneiric experience in categories, and read them against precedents, that had significantly been shaped in the schools, courts and market squares of ancient and medieval Greece and Near East. An intensive circulation of texts renewed acquaintance with that tradition, and this body of knowledge came to incorporate the merging of the actual encounter of exotic oneiric cultures with the previous imaginary representation of the other.

In the Codex Arundel now at the British Library, Leonardo da Vinci noted: "The eye sees a thing more clearly in dreams than with the imagination awake" (*vede più certa la cosa l'occhio ne' sogni che colla immaginazione stando desto*). Given the fact that the Italian universal man owned copies of three Italian vernacular incunable editions of the *Somniale Danielis*, the aphorism has been read in connection with the old belief system, which medieval epistemology had inherited from Antiquity, according to which, in order to better understand reality, it is necessary to leave the material plane and reach a level of abstraction that allows to grasp the nature of things more deeply. In this respect, dreams had long been considered a privileged dimension in which truth reveals itself (Cappozzo 1918: 1). However, if we consider the work of Cardano and the rest of Renaissance oneirocritics, to consign the meaning of the phrase to a vanishing past may be a rushed interpretative choice. In an epoch in which the foundations of knowledge were put at test, observation was given renewed importance, but at the same time the evidence of perception was put under critical scrutiny, the oneiric "second world" could offer uncharted paths to the understanding of self and the world. We now fully appreciate how much, from Copernicus to Newton, the new natural philosophy owed to old beliefs and forms of practice: the early modern interpretation of dreams may deserve to be acknowledged its place beside alchemy and its sister disciplines.

11
THE DEVELOPMENT OF THE STUDIES IN HISTORICAL DREAM CULTURES

Considering the nature of the topic, its intrinsic pervasiveness and the multiplicity of the approaches it allows, a survey on what has been said about it can only aim at gathering a sample of studies. And yet, some appear to have left a significant mark (or might in the foreseeable future, in respect of recent or ongoing developments) on the way we see and investigate that human experience.

A trans-disciplinary approach to the study of dreams was promoted, perhaps without much subsequent continuity, by the Near Eastern Center of the University of California at Los Angeles, with an international colloquium held at the Abbaye de Royaumont, whose proceedings were edited by G.E. von Grunebaum and Roger Caillois (1966). It devoted a significant space to psychology (including psychoanalysis) and the Islamic tradition, and hosted prominent contributors in a variety of fields, among them Roger Bastide for sociology (and Brazil) and Mircea Eliade for shamanism. Caillois's own contribution, on logical and philosophical problems of the dream, was extracted by his introduction (Caillois 1963b) to an anthology of stories, selections from novels and other literature dealing with dreams, published few years before (Caillois 1963a). Others noted that the selection of world religions that had been considered oddly excluded Christianity (Dulaey 1973: 9).

Caillois's interest and approach is testified by his 1963 literary selection (also in English), as well as by a previous (French) essay of reflections on "the uncertainty that comes from dreams", in which the social theorist, rejecting all traditions attributing meanings to dreams, found that they had for him "barely more sense than the shapes of clouds or the patterns on butterfly wings" (Caillois 1956, perhaps unaware of the presence of the parallel to clouds in the Aristotelian tradition of dream criticism). The literary selection

DOI: 10.4324/9781003279709-11

itself is interesting and motivated by the editor, as it devotes a specific section to "Chinese dialectics" and then, after a couple of ancient and medieval examples, heads directly to nineteenth-century fiction. The reason Caillois gave for the choice and omissions is that, according to him,

> recorded dreams and interpreted dreams are both old and plentiful; invented dreams are relatively recent. Narratives in which one discovers at the end that the events recounted were dreams and not real, or which contain dreams told so as to give the reader the same feeling of reality that the dream gives to the dreamer, are rare and date from only yesterday, if not from today. It is works such as these that I have preferred to use in this collection. Only they can make me experience the impression of dreaming, that is to say, when I close a volume of such stories or otherwise interrupt my reading, I experience an impression analogous to that which I feel on waking from a dream. Most of the other stories of dreams have the serious fault of being presented as such at the outset, thereby spoiling everything.
> *(1963b: XXXII)*

While not every literary scholar or fiction reader may agree with him, Caillois's criterion and claim that the dream has been used only recently in the literary process is certainly clear. It makes his anthology jump from Marco Polo to Mérimée; some early modern references, from Calderón's play to thought experiments by Descartes, only appear within the argumentation of his Introduction.

Although many streams of research had preceded and followed in the study of civilisations of many times and latitudes, the role ancient dream culture played in Eric Dodds's *The Greeks and the Irrational* (Dodds 1951: 102–34) requires to be singled out, in particular since, by challenging the traditional view of Greek knowledge as a moment of triumph of rationalism, it also opened the path to a more nuanced view of the Renaissance case. With the relevance that an anthropological approach has maintained over the subsequent generations of classicists, studies of the ancient oneiric cultures have thrived since.

In 1973, Peter Burke published, in the *Annales*, a pioneering essay entitled "The social history of dreams" (Burke 1997a). The French historiographical scene was significantly receptive to the experiment, if one considers that, during the previous three years, Jacques Le Goff had published two contributions that touched upon the subject – first one on the Indian Ocean seen from the medieval West as an "oneiric horizon", thus exploring the mythical dimension of the European visions of alterity, mixed as they were with a variety of topoi, including images of Earthly Paradise, and then a brief more general introduction to "Dreams in the culture and collective psychology of the medieval West", the description of a research project – carried out in the context of an introductory course for young historians at the École Normale Supérieure – which was explicitly inspired by psychoanalysis (Le Goff 1980a and 1980b).[1] From the same Parisian circle of medievalists, Jean Claude Schmitt's research has subsequently provided crucial contributions to the field, partly thanks to his attention for imagery, including ghosts and *revenants* (though see also Schmitt 1985, 1999, 2007, 2016).

Burke's article – which was subsequently included in a collection of essays of his on the *Varieties of Cultural History* (1997), and from there translated in many other languages – remained a landmark also within the French historiographical memory, to such an extent that, when the journal *Sensibilités: Histoire, critique & sciences sociales* planned, in 2018, an issue on "The society of dreams", they republished it, with a selected bibliographical update and short revisitation by the author, who recollects how at the time the subject had come, almost by chance, to his attention. While studying in Oxford, his supervisor, Keith Thomas, suggested that he worked on archbishop Laud, who before taking the leading office in the Anglican Church had been president of Peter's college, St John's: the library held the manuscript of his diary, and this contained several descriptions of Laud's dreams. In fact, the experiment Burke offers in that article is precisely a tentative parallel analysis of the reported dreams of four seventeenth-century Englishmen. What is even more interesting for us here, though, is its methodological premise. Half a century later, it may come to us as a slight surprise that Burke qualified his approach as "social" rather than "cultural". One must consider, however, both the language of the historiography of the time and the fact that Burke has subsequently claimed a relative interchangeability between the two adjectives, suggesting that "social" may be a more significant definition of an approach to a subject that belongs uncontroversially to culture – as it may well be the case for dreams.

But this qualification is also part of the question. Burke claimed that it was possible, indeed exciting, to explore a social history of dreams, since both their manifest and latent content, in a given society and period, revealed the evolution of its myths and taboos. As I mentioned in the Introduction, the possibility for such a history to be written was stated in explicit opposition to "classic" psychoanalytic dream theory as, both in its Freudian and Jungian formulations, Burke found that it postulated a universality of symbols and their meanings that left no room for cultural and historical variation.[2] A similar way of formulating the justification for the historical perspective that takes into account recent scholarly developments would be to say that, as other fields of enquiry, the historical study of dreams needs to defend its legitimacy by rejecting any attempt to deny, perhaps on the basis of alleged scientific discoveries, as is the case with all the research driven by the neurosciences, that not just the interpretation, but the human experience of dreaming per se is cultural, and not simply a biological phenomenon. Burke specified that his interest was in reconstructing the history of actual dreams, rather than the comparatively distinct one of their interpretation (Burke 1997a).

In his reappraisal, Peter Burke signalled the important contributions that dream studies have received from the social sciences. History too, as he noticed, has seen a major development over the past few decades, and it may be worth surveying a selection of some of the most significant research paths if we want to assess the state of the art and appreciate where we stand in the development of critical awareness of the subject in all its aspects and implications; beyond the invaluable contribution of some individuals' scholarship – as Steven Kruger's reconstruction of the medieval experience (1992), Patricia Cox Miller's work on Late Antiquity (1994) or Jesse Keskiaho's on the Early Middle Ages (2015) – it is the orientations and findings of some groups and networks, sometime developed around provincial university centres rather than capitals, that proved particularly promising and may recommend mention. Conferences have continued to provide ad hoc opportunities to gather scholars whose complementing specialities combine to develop fuller and richer pictures. One held in Cannes in 1987, while intending to go interdisciplinary, registered at the publication of the proceedings a predominance of literary scholars and a limited attraction, among others, of art historians, among the fields of expertise the organisers had in mind (Charpentier 1990).

Over the past two decades, a series of French studies of the medieval, Renaissance and seventeenth-century scene have focused on the fictional dream as a literary construction (both within larger creative works and as an emerging specific genre), but avoided to consider it in isolation and rather contextualised it in the dream cultures of each period. Mireille Demaules (2010) has examined fictional literature of the twelfth and the thirteenth century, registering, among other things, a continuity of the image that she uses as title: Penelope's two gates, taken as a shortcut reference to a distinction between truthful and untrustworthy nocturnal narratives and images. Sylviane Bokdam (2012) has worked on the dream as poetic genre of the French Renaissance, by connecting it with the philosophical and theological framework that affected the contemporary understanding and evaluation of the working of the imagination and of the dangers of illusion. Florence Dumora (2005) studied the French "classic age" again by framing the literary representation of dreams within a tradition of dream discourse that crossed a variety of disciplinary fields (medicine, philosophy and demonology, among others), exploited the baroque commonplace according to which "life is but a dream" and explored – with Descartes and others – the sceptical argument offered by the oneiric experience.

Building on this critical tradition, a team of scholars led by Demaules opened the horizon of enquiry to an area wider than dream in a narrower sense and explored, within a project based for two years at the University of Artois, oneiric experiences in literature and the arts from the Middle Ages to the seventeenth century (the final conference was held in 2013 and the ensuing volume published three years later: Demaules 2016a). In her preface, the editor emphasised the diversity and vastity of the subject area and, to encourage reflection, questioned standard modern French dictionary definitions of *rêve*, which appear to take for granted that the experience in question is a psychic phenomenon that occurs during sleep and includes a visual element. There are plenty of examples that would not fit the description: starting from dream narratives in the Bible, where God may talk in dreams to his chosen people, and such experience could not properly be defined as psychological, as it is understood to come from elsewhere, rather than being interior; nor does it involve vision, being aural.

Ten years before the conference in Arras, a collective volume had been published in Québec as the result of another two-year research project, in this case developed in Toulouse (Dauvois and Grosperrin 2003). Its subject was dreams and dreamers from the thirteenth to the seventeenth century. While again primarily surveying a literary experience, it unfolds a variety of reflections, including theoretical. In the opening essay, "Faire l'histoire du rêve", Dumora-Mabille (2003) again reminds us that what we have at our disposal as historical document testifying dreams from the past are dream discourses, both in the form of narratives and theoretical texts concerning this human experience. However, we do not know anything of the night-time experience beyond what has been turned into a narrative and/or a series of images; and there exists a critical tradition questioning the very existence of a dreaming experience before the construction of a narrative at the time of awakening that, for what we know, could be the actual moment when pictures and stories are created. The connected research topics of the cultural histories of the night and of sleep have also attracted attention (Bertrand 2003; Leroux, Palmieri and Pigné 2015).

Scholarship in English has been no less active. A comparative, cross-cultural perspective was explored in a workshop promoted by the Einstein Forum in Potsdam and the Institute of Advanced Studies of the Hebrew University of Jerusalem 100 years after the completion of Freud's *Interpretation of Dreams*, issuing the publication that arguably, with its title, contributed most to the diffusion of the expression "dream cultures" (Shulman and Stroumsa 1999). *Dreams and History* (Pick and Roper 2004) collected a thought-provoking series of essays, most of which had originally been published, between the years 1999 and 2000, on the *History Workshop Journal*. More ground-breaking work has been done on literary sources (Brown 1999), on the English court culture (Levin 2008) and on subjectivity (Mageo 2003), also in relationship to sleep (Simpson-Younger and Simon 2020), not to mention the perspective of early modern cultural encounters, where "reported dreams and visions often played a critical role in struggles for power and influence" (Plane and Tuttle 2013b: 26; see in general Plane and

Tuttle 2013a). Work on other aspects and moments on the history of dream cultures has been cited here and there throughout this book. Studies, sometimes again prompted by the centenary of Freud's work, have also appeared in other languages, including German (Gerok-Reiter and Walde 2012), with surveys on the history of the philosophical distinction between dream and reality (Gehring 2008), or again also with a focus on the literary tradition (Alt 2002; Scholler and Xuan 2020).

Overall, it would appear safe to say that the study of dream cultures has developed over the last quarter of a century with increasing methodological sophistication. Within the types of source material with which historians can work, we may roughly distinguish between an epoch's and context's dream discourse, the narrative of real dreams and the dream narrative as a fictional literary genre. Various scholars (among them Kruger and Dumora) have emphasised the need to make more than one of these groups of documents interact with one another, even when their authors explicitly excluded their reciprocal connection, if we want to get closer to an understanding of that culture.

Moving a step forward, over the past ten years a dedicated network, coordinated by Bernard Dieterle and Manfred Engel, has emerged with the aim "to promote research on all cultural aspects of the dream". They organised a series of conferences promoted within the institutional framework of the International Comparative Literature Association and edited their proceedings in five volumes, which consequently stand out as the most systematic project in the field to date (Dieterle and Engel 2017, 2018, 2019, 2020 and 2022). While the background in literary studies is detectable, an attention for the historical perspective is clearly stated, for instance, by reference to the history of dream theories as one of the major planned areas of research. The expression "dream theory" has been in use for decades to refer to a variety of cultural understandings of the oneiric experience from different historical milieus. In his essay opening the second volume, *Theorizing the Dream* (2018), "Towards a Theory of Dream Theories", Engel proposes fruitful material for a meta-reflection, articulated in a descriptive matrix for dream theories and suggestions for a typology of dream theories. The matrix is intended as a checklist of basic elements of dream theories, which should be used in order to establish comparisons between them. It features:

1 Explanations of the origin of dreams;
2 Evaluations of dreams;
3 Techniques for the deciphering of dreams;
4 Dream types;
5 Associated rituals and practices;
6 Neighbouring phenomena;
7 Place and status in the system of knowledge of a cultural period.

Engel's typology – also intended to allow to relate one theory to another genetically – embraces:

a Supernatural Theories;
b Epistemological/Ontological Theories;
c Rational Theories;
d Natural Supernaturalism/Romanticist Theories (Engel 2018).

I believe that all these reflections and suggested classifications may prove of significant interest as frameworks and tools for research.

Engel's opening essay to the fourth volume, *Mediating the Dream* (2020), "Towards a Transmedial Poetics of the Dream", is also thought-provoking and helpful in its systematicity. Before proposing differentiations by genres and media (factual dream reports, fictional dream representations in literature, dreams in the visual arts, in films and in music), it addresses dream representations by offering another, descriptive matrix, which includes the following:

1 Marking the dream – by inserting it into a frame, or by recurring to paratextual markers or by content or formal markers (such as "techniques of creating incoherence to equate the non-sequentiality of dreams");
2 Oneirising it, according to a poetic of deviation from waking reality;
3 Narrating it, which requires the adoption of a mode, of focalisation and of plots;
4 Embedding it, either as an insert or autonomously;
5 Contextualising it, by offering information and reflection on its meaning or function;
6 Semiotising it, explicitly or implicitly/symbolically; and
7 Functionalising it, either in relation to a supernatural realm or, for instance, to fulfil rhetorical or compositional functions (Engel 2020).

At the time of writing, the study I feel closer to the scope of the present book is the monograph by Claire Gantet (2021, in French; see also 2007, 2010a and 2010b, the last in German). The geographic scope and relevance of it goes well beyond its stated concern for Germany. Its dimension and the authorship by a scholar who has been working in the field for a while ensure an in-depth analysis of cultural aspects of the story that are engaging, carefully contextualised in the developments of the early modern history of knowledge, while paying special attention to the religious dimension of the story, and allow some generalisations. To sum up, as such publications confirm, the field is yielding and promising further rewarding harvests, particularly as further cultural contexts are studied in depth and the results contribute to forming a wider and articulated picture. I hope this survey too, with its own specificities, may help to encourage it.

Yet another collective work allows me to bring in a type of questioning that I had not explicitly mentioned so far, if not with reference to some historical sources. Under a project on "Literature as an Object of Knowledge" based at St John's College, Oxford, from 2010 to 2013, a group of researchers has explored the "cognitive confusions" that are revealed in the way early modern culture negotiated dreams, delusions and illusions. The question posed would be valid for the twenty-first century:

> How do humans distinguish between factual and counterfactual scenarios? When do rational thoughts and beliefs become delusions and illusions and why do we often fail to monitor the boundaries between different forms of cognitive activity? Where do dreams fit into our lived experience of the world and what role do they have, if any, in our strategies and procedures for thinking about it?
> *(Mac Carthy, Sellevold and Smith 2016: ix)*

But so they were in the premodern and early modern period. It is particularly intriguing to explore how they were discussed and settled, since they are key problems that may bring us closer to appreciate both the importance and value men and women from the past gave to their oneiric life and the ways they distinguished it, or else blurred it or mixed it up, with the world as we know and live it while awake.

Notes

1 A subsequent contribution by Le Goff was included in Gregory 1985 (Le Goff 1985).
2 Burke (1997a: 24) however acknowledged that for neither Freud nor Jung symbols were intended as fixed and distinguished their two perspectives, for instance by noting that Jung was more interested than Freud in the manifest content of dreams. He was also a passionate bibliophile who owned a large library and had direct knowledge of early modern oneirology (Gantet 2021: 287–8).

12
A CODA ON THE ONEIRIC PRESENT*

During the recent – or rather ongoing – covid pandemic, a network, intended to run from 2022 to 2024, was set to study sleep and the rhythms of life. Its rationale is the acknowledgement that "sleep is highly dynamic and very little about sleep is unchangeable", and "changed social conditions over the past 100 years appear to have had a marked impact upon key elements of sleep":

> Recent studies on circadian rhythms and sleep, along with historical insights, have shown that such changed societal conditions have resulted in a detachment of these key biological rhythms from the geophysical cycle of light and dark, with major deleterious effects upon human functioning, wellbeing, and creativity.
> *(https://www.torch.ox.ac.uk/sleep-and-the-rhythms-of-life)*

In particular, the network aims at studying the impact such changes may have on the humanities.

In various instances during the exceptional global health crisis, sleeping and dreaming patterns have come under observation. There have been dedicated blogs and internet surveys on what people dreamt during the pandemic (Robb 2020), partly inspired by the work done by psychoanalyst Charlotte Beradt on what people dreamt in the first years of Nazi Germany (Beradt 1985). Attested patterns include oneiric experiences affected by worries as well as by the unusually long sleeps allowed by the suspension of ordinary tasks. Also, during the lockdown of spring 2020, Hervé Mazurel, whom we

---

* Although I directly cite their sources, I owe some of the references used in this section to anonymous articles that appeared on the Italian online newspaper *Il Post*.

DOI: 10.4324/9781003279709-12

have already encountered as historian of the unconscious, and Élizabeth Serin, a psychoanalyst, with a "nomadic laboratory of psychoanalysis", collected 400 dreams told by people of all ages and all walks of life, relying in particular on associations of ideas and interpretations. As well as recording an unprecedented moment in history, their idea was that the collection of dream narratives could serve to encourage dialogue between the social sciences and psychoanalysis (Carroy, Mazurel and Serin 2021).

On a wider timespan, albeit still with increased intensity over the past few years, attention has been paid to the case of lucid dreaming. Lucid dreams are dream experiences one embarks in deliberately. Their existence has been debated since Antiquity. Research conducted over the last 50 years has concluded that half of the world population has experienced them at least once (Saunders et al. 2016). In recent times, it has become some sort of sport; there are social network groups exchanging experiences, experts teaching how to do it and research conducted on volunteers, with claims that the practice may promise therapeutic benefit, such as helping to control nightmares (Chevlen 2021). In collecting and publishing his own, French writer Georges Perec noted: "I thought I was recording the dreams I was having; I have realized that it was not long before I began having dreams only in order to write them" (Perec 2012: Preface).

If the Renaissance is regularly considered as a period of paramount transition, and some historiography has emphasised the psychological impact of change and labelled it as an age of anxiety (Rabb 2006), to compare the role dreams play in the negotiation with reality in our time and in the past may not prove a wasteful exercise.

APPENDIX

A selection of dedicated printed sources, in chronological order of first edition

Date	Language	Description
From 1472	Latin	Macrobius, *Commentary* on Cicero's *Dream of Scipio* (first edition: Venice). Manuscripts were among the commonest from the early Middle Ages: 6 incunable editions were all printed in Italy; over 20 followed in the sixteenth century and included among the printing places, Paris, Cologne, Lyon, Leiden and Geneva. A thirteenth-century Byzantine translation became a tool for the teaching of the Greek language (Macrobius 1952: 59–64; 2007: 165–77).
Latin edns 1475–	Italian from 1487, French [1500?], English 1556	*Somniale Danielis*. The most popular medieval dreambook. Composed in Greek around the fourth century CE and translated into Latin in the ninth. Three Italian vernacular incunable editions (*De alcuni insonii de Daniel et li insonii de Joseph*, trans. by Simon Pasquali, Bologna and Florence) and several in the early sixteenth century (Schutte 1983: 155–6). Modern English translation in Oberhelman 2008: 59–115.

(*Continued*)

Date	Language	Description
1497	Latin (Greek 1518)	First edition of the ancient treatise *De insomniis* by Synesius, translated into Latin by Marsilio Ficino, and published after Iamblichus's *On the Mysteris of the Egyptians, Chaldeans and Assyrians* (Venice: Aldo Manuzio); reprinted also by Auger Ferrier (see below, ca 1540). The original Greek text was first published together with Artemidorus (Venice 1518) and subsequently included, together with a commentary by Nicephorus Gregoras (ca 1325), in a selection of works by Synesius published in Paris in 1553 by the royal printer Adrien Turnèbe, the teacher of Joseph Justus Scaliger (a copy of a 1555 reprint at the Bibliothèque nationale de France has Montaigne's signature and manuscript notes by Theodore Beza). The same selection was published in 1560 by Froben in Basel in a Latin translation by Janus Cornarius in an edition that was preceded by George Pachymeres' compendium of Aristotle's philosophy. In 1586, Greek text and Latin translation of the *De insomniis* were published again in Paris, together with the first Latin translation, by Antoine Pichon, of Gregoras' commentary. Finally, in 1612 (and subsequent reeditions) Claude Morel in Paris published the complete Greek and Latin works of Synesius, once again inclusive of Gregoras' commentary on the book on dreams (Synesius 2004: LXXVIII–LXXX). Modern editions of Gregoras' *Explicatio* in Gregoras 1999 and Monticini 2023.
1499	"Italian", partial English trans. 1592	[Francesco Colonna], *Hypnerotomachia Poliphili* (see Section 8.1 above).
ca 1515	Hebrew (trans. Yiddish 1694)	Solomon Almoli, *Pitron ḥalomot* (Thessaloniki; republished several times).
1515	Latin	Ferdinando Ponzetti (d. 1526), *Tertia pars Naturalis phylosophie* (Rome). Book 3 (and last), occupying 40 folios (92v–133r), is entirely dedicated to dreams and the scholarship on them. Besides Aristotle, *opiniones* exposed in dedicated chapters include Plato, Avicenna, Averroes and Albert the Great.

(Continued)

Date	Language	Description
1518	Greek (later in the century also Latin 1539–, Italian 1558?, French, English 1606– and German)	First edition of the Artemidorus's *Oneirocritica* (together with Synesius). Printed by the house of Aldus Manutius the Elder (after his death) from a manuscript (still held today at the Marciana National Library in Venice) copied on behalf of Cardinal Bessarion by the Byzantine copyist Michael Apostolius, who fled Constantinople after the Ottoman conquest of 1453. Latin translation, first published in 1539, by the medical humanist Janus Cornarius; reprinted (Paris 1603) with notes by Nicolas Rigault and additional oneirocritic material by Achmet (see 1525 below), Astrampsychus (see 1600) and Nicephorus.
1525	Italian (later Latin, Frankfurt 1577; French, 1581)	*Expositione de gli insomnii secondo la interpretatione de Indy, Persy, et Egyptii* (Venice; reprinted 1534, 1546, 1551 – *Short-title Catalogue* 1958: Indians). Cf. *Apomazar des significations et evenemens des songes, selon la doctrine des Indiens, Perses et Egyptiens* (Paris 1581). The French version was preceded by the edition mentioned by Robert Burton: [Biblion oneirokritikon. Latin.] *Apomasaris apotelesmata, sive De significatis et eventis insomniorum, ex Indorum, Persarum, Agyptiorumque disciplina*, ed. by János Zsámbok, Latin trans. by Johannes Leunclavius (Frankfurt 1577). The same Latin translation was also included, together with Astrampsychus (see below: 1600), in Nicolas Rigault's 1603 edition of Artemidorus, the edition that two years later could be found also, listed among the "libri artium", in *The First Printed Catalogue of the Bodleian Library* (*First Printed Catalogue* 1986: 278). Zsámbok (Sambucus), instead, is listed there for his own paraphrasis of the *Somnium Scipionis* (ibid.: 631). Modern English translation in Oberhelman 1991.
[1530s]	French (possibly trans. Flemish 1542)	Jehan Thibault, *La Phisionomie des songes et visions fantastiques des personnes* (Lyon s.d.). A publication plagiarising much content of *Somniale Danielis*, with initial additional material by the author, *médecin ordinaire* of François I. Subsequently incorporated in Anselme Julian, *De l'art de jugement des songes et visions nocturnes* (see 1567 French); and, anonymously, in *Exposition des songes avec la prognostication sur la nativité d'un chacun et de l'interprétation des esternuëmens* [ie, of sneezing] (Paris 1610; cf. Cooper 1990).

(*Continued*)

Date	Language	Description
1539	Latin	*Hippocratis liber De somniis cum Iulii Caesarus Scaligeri commentariis* (Lyon). Third known Latin translation and first modern commentary to the Hippocratic text. Others followed, and several reprints, at times with other works. Posthumous enlarged reprints of Scaliger's commentary: Lyon 1561, Amsterdam 1649, Giessen 1610 – the last edition also including the Greek text of Aristotle's three treatises (Roselli 1995).
ca 1540	Latin	Auger Ferrier, *Liber de somniis* (Toulouse); repr. Lyon 1549 in enlarged edition complete with Latin version of the dream works of Hippocrates, Galen and Synesius (Cooper 1990).
1542	Italian	Daniele Barbaro (under the pseudonym, borrowed from Ovid, of Hypneo da Schio; a dedication signed by the author with the real name appears only in one of the known copies), *Predica dei sogni*. Entitled as a "sermon", though in fact is a short poem.
1559	English	Thomas Hill, *The moste pleasaunte arte of the interpretacion of dreames* (London – only extant in a 1576 edition). Essentially a translation of books 1 and 4 of Artemidorus (Rivière 2017: 55). See also his 1567 *Little treatise*.
1562	Latin	Girolamo Cardano, *Somniorum Synesiorum omnis generis insomnia explicantes libri quatuor* (Basel; reprinted in his posthumous *Opera omnia*, Lyon 1663).
1562	Italian	Stefano Maria Ugoni, *Dialogo della vigilia, et del sonno* (Brescia).
1567	English	Thomas Hill, *A little treatise of the interpretation of dreams* (London). "Published by William Copland and at only 48 pages (8vo), this simplified dreambook was designed by Hill as a quick, easily referenced, dictionary of dream interpretation. Within this handbook, 161 dreams are interpreted, including everything from dreaming of one's teeth falling out, to animals and the dead, to eating fish. The first section of the dreambook briefly discusses the kinds of dreams, the qualities of the ideal 'expounder of dreams' and summarizes Aristotle's views of dreams. Following this shorter section is a longer one that includes brief summaries of dreams with their interpretations and predictive outcomes. In this dreambook, the interpretations of dreams are taken from another dreambook circulating at the time, which was ascribed to Joseph" (Rivière 2017: 72).

(Continued)

Date	Language	Description
1567	French	Anselme Julian, *L'art et jugement des songes et visions nocturnes* (Lyon); composed around 1550 and reprinted also during the following century. Re-elaboration, with additions, of material from the medieval keys plus Artemidorus and Thibault (see [1530s]; Berriot 1990; Bach 2007).
1575	Latin	Alessandro Cariero, *De somnijs deque divinatione per somnia brevis consideratio* (Padua). 16 cc. in quarto.
1575	Italian	Benedetto Dottori, *Trattato de sogni secondo l'opinione d'Aristotile* (Padua; 2nd edition, 1578, following orations to the Venetian Doge). Posthumous, dedicated by Antonino Compagna to the Duke of Mantua Guglielmo Gonzaga, includes references to the private Paduan teaching of Marco Antonio Passeri (ca 1491–1563) author of a commentary on the *De anima* (also posthumous, 1576).
1589	Italian	Cipriano Giambelli, *Il Diamerone ove si ragiona della natura, e qualità de' sogni, e della perfettione, et eccellenza dell'amicitia humana* [D., where the nature and quality of dreams, as well as the perfection and excellence of human friendship, are debated] (Venice). Dedicated to the Bishop of Mantua (with ref. to his aristocratic lineage rather than pastoral office). A vernacular dialogue: day one (1–66) on sleep and dreams; day two, twice as long, on friendship. Presented as conversations held the previous Lent, when the author was preaching in Mantua Cathedral, in the house of a local aristocrat.
1591	Latin	Mancini, *De somniis ac synesi per somnia* [About dreams and visions through dreams] (Ferrara). A year after being appointed to the chair of moral philosophy of the University of Ferrara, he dedicated to the duke a collection of tracts he had previously composed while in Ravenna. The first and longest, on dreams and divination through dreams, occupies 100 pages in quarto.
1591	Italian	Giovanni Battista Segni, *Trattato de' sogni*. Published in Urbino, where the author was lector in the cathedral.
1594	English	Thomas Nashe, *The Terrors of the Night* (London).

(Continued)

Date	Language	Description
1600	Greek, Latin	Astrampsychus, *Onirocriticon*; edited by Joseph Justus Scaliger together with the *Stromateus prouerbiorum graecorum versibus conceptorum* (Leiden). In 101 verses. Latin translation by Johannes Opsopäus included, together with Achmet and Nicephorus, in Nicolas Rigault's 1603 edition of Artemidorus. Modern English translation in Oberhelman 2008: 149–52. As other texts in various disciplines, spuriously attributed to a magus who lived in Persia before the conquest of Alexander the Great; it appears (according to Guidorizzi in Nicephorus 1980) to be derived from the one by Nicephorus (see below, 1603).
1600	Italian	Giulio Cesare Croce, *Sogni fantastichi della notte* [Fantastical dreams of the night] (Bologna). Eight-leaf booklet dedicated to the Bolognese painter Annibale Carracci. Extraordinary flux of dreamlike imagery, in verse, preceded by a prose preface on similar, if not more openly satirical, mode.
1603	Latin	The already-mentioned Paris edition of Artemidorus, Achmet and Astrampsychus also included a text in verses by Nicephorus, translated from Greek by Nicolas Rigault – presumably Nicephorus I, Patriarch of Costantinople 806–15 CE, a defender of the value of images against iconoclasm, a stand consistent with taking dream interpretation seriously. Modern English translation of different variants in Oberhelman 2008: 117–48; see also Nicephorus 1980, where the attribution is assessed as apocryphal, as it was standard that Byzantine dream books circulated as the work of great men.
1606	French	Scipion Dupleix, *Les causes de la veille et du sommeil, des songes et de la vie et de la mort* (Paris); subsequently reprinted.
1613	Italian	Paolo Grassi, *Ragionamenti domestici intorno alla natura de' sogni* [Domestic arguments on the nature of dreams] (Bologna).

(*Continued*)

Date	Language	Description
1614	Italian	Cesare Merli, *Lume notturno overo Prattica di sogni ove si discorre della natura, delle cagioni, e delle differenze di essi; e si mostra se a quelli sia lecito dar fede* [Nocturnal light or else Dream manual where their nature, causes and differences are exposed, and is demonstrated whether it is legitimate to trust them] (Bologna; reprinted Bologna 1634 and Venice 1568 [rectius 1668]). C. 180 pp. in octavo, dedicated to the Princess of Mirandola. Preface acknowledges the recent local precedent of Grassi, while regretting its limited distribution.

TABLE OF MOST NOTABLE TOPICS

The sixteenth century was the zenith of the enrichment of printed books with subject indexes, each publisher competing with the rest in providing the potential readership with an attractive bonus service. Rhapsodic in style and not infrequently erratic in the alphabetic order, they still offer a very rich access to topics covered by the book that could otherwise be overlooked. Here follows an exercise to signal some topics cursorily mentioned in the present book in a way in which they could have been publicised at the time:

Adam and Eve dreamt already before the Fall (*Dreams as divine communication*: Intro; cf. also Vermigli)
Age influences the appropriate amount of sleep: children need more, the elderly less, and why (Giambelli 1589: 25–9), 17–18, 63
Angels (Segni 1591: 23–4; Giambelli 1589: 56), 32, 56, 78, 100, 105
Animals, whether they all dream (Merli 1614: 42 et al.), 58, 60
Better men have better dreams, says Aristotle (Grassi 1613: 39)
Body and soul compared, 25, 35, 39, 43, 58, 60, 63, 72, 74–5
Children, at what age they begin to dream (Merli 1614: 43; Segni: *fanciulli non sognano* [children do not sleep], 7 – cf. putti)
Clouds, the transformation of images we see in them similar to what happens in dreams (Dottori 1575: 9v; Grassi 1613: 52), 60
Daytime sleep harmful (Giambelli 1589: 23), 18–19, 63
Death, dreaming one's own (Levin 2008: 56, 58)
Devil, how they can send dreams (Giambelli 1589: 61)
Digestion determines the appropriate length of sleep and the time when it should finish (Giambelli 1589: 30; Cavallo and Storey 2013: 115–19), 18, 60

Table of most notable topics

Eyelids, lack of, impediment to verify if some animals sleep (Ponzetti 1515), 58
Frights in dream (Segni 1591: 33)
Great men turned into stars (Segni 1591: 21)
Imagination (*fantasia*) is the source of dreams (Giambelli 1589: 37)
Liars rarely have truthful dreams, says Avicenna (Giambelli 1589: 63–4)
Lions never sleep, theory disputed (1591, Intro)
Lion (stone) biting hand in dream, and how the dream became true (Grassi 1613: 79)
Meals, sleep should not follow them immediately (Giambelli 1589: 25), 63
Melancholics have many dreams, and this endows them with a higher chance to receive premonitions (Dottori 1575: 28v), 36
Memory a requirement – animals that do not have one do not dream (Dottori 1575: 8r)
Mirrors, dreams as (Kruger 1992: 136–9)
Murderer discovered through a dream (Levin 2008: 19–)
Nape scratching customary to help memory recover (Grassi 1613: 30)
Night the right time to sleep, daytime sleep unwise – although it also depends on the season (Giambelli 1589: 21–5), 63
Paintbrush reviving fading images resembles some form of operating of our memory (Dottori 1575: 15v)
Place and position in which one should sleep (Giambelli 1589: 31–2), 19, 38, 63
Plants only sleep as a manner of speaking (Giambelli 1589: 13), 58, 63
Scholars dreaming of loss of books (Dee in Levin 2008: 56), 54
Scratching one's head and position recommended for remembering dreams (Michael Scot in Cappozzo 2018: 30)
Snakes hiding in the grass, evoked to suggest how perceived images sneak through to impress our faculties (Dottori 1575: 12v), 60
Snow whiteness remains impressed on one's sight for some time (Giambelli 1589: 34)
Storytelling helps some falling asleep but keeps others awake (Ponzetti 1515: 99v), 58
Wine, effect on sleep (Ponzetti 1515: 99r), 58, 63
Worms cause fright in dream (Segni 1591: 34)

BIBLIOGRAPHY

Abbruzzetti, Véronique. 1997. "À propos du *Trattato dei sogni* de Jacopo Passavanti." In *Arzanà 4, 1997. Rêves et récits de rêves, sous la direction de Claude Perrus*, 73–88.
Acidini, Cristina. 2013. "Finestre, nebbie, bolle: la materia e lo spazio del sogno." In *Il sogno nel Rinascimento*, edited by Rabbi Bernard, Cecchi and Hersant, 20–9.
Adorni Braccesi, Simonetta. 2010. "Agrippa von Nettesheim." In *Dizionario storico dell'Inquisizione*, edited by Prosperi, vol. 1, p. 25.
Agamben, Giorgio. 1984. "Il sogno della lingua. Per una lettura del Polifilo." In *I linguaggi del sogno*, edited by Vittore Branca, Carlo Ossola and Salomon Resnik, 417–30. Florence: Sansoni.
Agapiou, Natalia. 2005. *Endymion au carrefour: la fortune littéraire et artistique du mythe d'Endymion à l'aube de l'ère moderne*. Berlin: Gebr. Mann.
Agrippa von Nettesheim, Heinrich Cornelius. 1992. *De occulta philosophia libri tres*, edited by Vittoria Perrone Compagni. St Paul, MN: Llewellyn.
Agrippa von Nettesheim, Heinrich Cornelius 1993. *Three Books of Occult Philosophy*. Translated by James Freake, edited by Donald Tyson. Leiden: Brill.
Almoli, Shelomo. 1998. *Dream interpretation from classical Jewish sources [c. 1515]*. Translated by Yaakov Elman. Hoboken, NJ: KTAV.
Alt, Peter-André. 2002. *Der Schlaf der Vernunft: Literatur und Traum in der Kulturgeschichte der Neuzeit*. Munich: C.H. Beck.
Amelang, James S. 1998. *The Flight of Icarus: Artisan Autobiography in Early Modern Europe*. Stanford: Stanford University Press.
Amelang, James S. 2012. "Sleeping with the Enemy: The Devil in Dreams in Early Modern Spain." *American Imago* 69: 319–52.
Andò, Valeria. 2009. "Sogni etorici e seme femminile nella antica medicina greca." *Medicina nei secoli* 21: 663–30.
Andries, Lise. 1988. "L'interprétation populaire des songes." In *Revue des Sciences Humaines*, edited by Gautier, 49–64.
Arcangeli, Alessandro. 2012. *Cultural History: A Concise Introduction*. London and New York: Routledge.

Bibliography 131

Arcangeli, Alessandro 2024. "Dream Cultures of the Italian Cinquecento." In *Redreaming the Renaissance: Essays on History and Literature in Honor of Guido Ruggiero*, edited by Mary Lindemann and Deanna Shemek, 48–66. Newark: University of Delaware Press.

Argenterio, Giovanni. 2018. 1556. De somno et vigila. Florence: L. Torrentinus.

Aristotle. 2018. *On the Soul and Other Psychological Works*. Translated by Fred D. Miller, Jr Oxford: Oxford University Press.

Artemidorus. 2020. *The Interpretation of Dreams*. Translated by Martin Hammond. Oxford: Oxford University Press.

Auger, Danièle. 2021. "Les portes de corne et d'ivoire de l'*Odyssée*." *Communications* [Paris] 108: 13–24.

Azoulai, Martine. 1993. *Les péchés du Nouveau Monde: Les manuels pour la confession des Indiens, XVIe–XVIIe siècle*. Paris: A. Michel.

Azzolini, Monica. 2010. "The political uses of astrology: predicting the illness and death of princes, kings and popes in the Italian Renaissance." *Studies in History and Philosophy of Biological and Biomedical Sciences* 41: 135–45.

Bach, Valérie. 2007. *Les clefs des songes médiévales, XIIIe–XVe siècles*. Stasbourg: Presses universitaires de Strasbourg (OpenEditions 2019).

Bar, Shaul. 2001. *A Letter That Has Not Been Read: Dreams in the Hebrew Bible*. Translated by Lenn J. Schramm. Cincinnati: Hebrew Union College Press.

Barbaro, Daniele. 1542. *Predica dei sogni*. Venice: F. Marcolini.

Barbierato, Federico. 2002. *Nella stanza dei circoli*: Clavicula Salomonis *e libri di magia a Venezia nei secoli XVII e XVIII*. Milan: Edizioni Sylvestre Bonnard.

Bargagli, Girolamo. 1572. *Dialogo de' giuochi che nelle vegghie sanesi si usano di fare*. Siena: Bonetti.

Barras, Vincent. 2016. "Le rêve des médecins antiques." In *Clés des songes et sciences des rêves de l'Antiquité à Freud*, edited by Carroy and Lancel, 21–31.

Bartuschat, Johannes. 1997. "Le rêve de Giovanni di Pagolo Morelli: observations sur l'autobiographie et l'écriture au XVe siècle." In *Rêves et récits de rêve (Arzanà 4)*, edited by Perrus, 147–77.

Batkin, Leonid M. 1990. *Gli umanisti italiani: stile di vita e di pensiero*. Rome: Laterza.

Baumstark, Reinhold. 1985. *Peter Paul Rubens: The Decius Mus Cycle*. New York: Metropolitan Museum of Art.

Beradt, Charlotte. 1985. *The Third Reich of Dreams*. Translated by Adriane Gottwald. Wellingborough: Aquarian Press.

Bercé, Yves-Marie. 1988. "La raison des songes, chez Scipion Dupleix (1606)." In *Revue des Sciences Humaines*, edited by Gautier, 123–31.

Bernardi, Anne-Marie. 2011. "L'*Oneirocriticon* d'Achmet e la christianisation de la tradition grecque d'interprétation des rêves." *Kentron* 27: 81–98.

Berriot, François, ed. 1989. *Exposicions et significacions des songes et Le songes Daniel*. Geneva: Droz.

Berriot, François 1990. "Clés des songes françaises à la Renaissance." In *Le songe à la Renaissance*, edited by Charpentier, 21–31.

Bertrand, Dominique, ed. 2003. *Penser la nuit (XVe–XVIIe siècle)*. Paris: Champion.

Besson, Gisèle and Jean-Claude Schmitt, eds. 2017. *Rêver de soi. Les songes autobiographiques au Moyen Âge*. Toulouse: Anacharsis.

Blum, Claes. 1941. "Manuscript Studies in Artemidorus." *Eranos* 39: 56–63.

Blum, Paul Richard. 2007. "'Cognitio falsitatis vera est'. Benedictus Pererius critico della magia e della Cabala." In *La magia nell'Europa moderna. Tra antica sapienza e filosofia naturale*, edited by Fabrizio Meroi, 345–62. Florence: Olschki.

Bobory, Dóra. 2003. "Being a chosen one: self-consciousness and self-fashioning in the works of Gerolamo Cardano." *Annual of medieval studies at Central European University Budapest* 9: 69–92.

Boccadiferro, Lodovico. 1570. *Lectiones in Aristotelis Stagiritae libros, quos vocant Parva naturalia*. Venice: G. Scoto.

Boccadoro, Brenno. 2019. "La musique et le someneil." In *Éveil*, edited by Jackie Pigeaud and Baldine Saint Girons, 107–30. Rennes: Presses Universitaires de Rennes.

Boddice, Rob and Mark Smith. 2020. *Emotion, Sense, Experience*. Cambridge: Cambridge University Press.

Bokdam, Sylviane. 2012. *Metamorphoses de Morphée. Théories du rêve et songes poétiques à la Renaissance, en France*. Paris: Champion.

Bokdam, Sylviane 2016. "Faire parler les morts: nature et surnaturel dans les songes de l'au-delà, chez Cardan." In *Expériences oniriques dans la littérature et les arts du Moyen Age au XVIIe siècle*, edited by Demaules, 181–204.

Bolzoni, Lina. 2013. "Sogni e arte della memoria." In *Il sogno nel Rinascimento*, edited by Rabbi Bernard, Cecchi and Hersant, 36–41.

Bonetti, Fabio. 2009. "Somnium and visio in the Decameron." *Medicina nei secoli* 21: 611–29.

Boriaud, Jean-Yves. 1999. "La place du *Traité des songes* dans la tradition onirocritique. Le problème de l'image onirique: l'*idolum* et la *uisio*." In *Girolamo Cardano. Le opere, le fonti, la vita*, ed. by Marialuisa Baldi and Guido Canziani, 215–25. Milan: FrancoAngeli.

Boriaud, Jean-Yves 2008. "De quelques rêves de Cardan...." In *Une traversée des savoirs. Mélanges offerts à Jackie Pigeaud*, edited by Philippe Heuzé and Yves Hersant, 313–28. Québec: Presses de l'Université Laval.

Boriaud, Jean-Yves 2010. "Jung analyste de Girolamo Cardano." *Bruniana & Campanelliana* 16: 407–28.

Boriaud, Jean-Yves 2012. "Cardan et le songe." In *La pensée scientifique de Cardan*, edited by Jean-Yves Boriaud, 23–44. Paris: Belles Lettres.

Boulet-Sautel, Marguerite. 1988. "Le rêve et le droit." In Boulet-Sautel, Marguerite. 1988. "*Le rêve et le droit* edited by Gautier, 115–9.

Bournet-Bacot, Marianne. 2016. "Un rêve de Dürer." In *Expériences oniriques dans la littérature et les arts du Moyen Age au XVIIe siècle*, edited by Demaules, 163–80.

Brambilla, Simona. 2008. "Antonio Brucioli traduttore del *Somnium Scipionis*: origini e fortuna di un volgarizzamento ciceroniano nel Cinquecento e oltre." In *Antonio Brucioli. Humanisme et évangélisme entre Réforme et Contre-Réforme*, edited by Élise Boillet, 99–129. Paris: Champion.

Brotton, Jerry. 2006. *The Renaissance: A Very Short Introduction*. Oxford: Oxford University Press.

Brown, Peter, ed. 1999. *Reading Dreams: The Interpretation of Dreams from Chaucer to Shakespeare*. Oxford: Oxford University Press.

Browne, Alice. 1977. "Descartes's Dreams." *Journal of the Warburg and Courtauld Institutes* 40: 256–73.

Browne, Alice 1979. "Girolamo Cardano's *Somniorum Synesiorum Libri IIII*." *Bibliothèque d'Humanisme et Renaissance* 41, no. 1: 123–35.

Browne, Alice 1981. "Dreams and Picture-Writing: Some Examples of this Comparison from the Sixteenth to the Eighteenth Century." *Journal of the Warburg and Courtauld Institutes* 44: 90–100.

Bulkeley, Kelly. 2018. *Lucrecia the Dreamer: Prophecy, Cognitive Science, and the Spanish Inquisition*. Stanford: Stanford University Press.
Bulkeley, Kelly 2020. "A midsummer night's dream: Shakespeare's play of dreaming." *Dreaming* 30: 297–316.
Burke, Peter. 1993. *The Art of Conversation*. Cambridge: Polity.
Burke, Peter 1997a. "The Cultural History of Dreams." In *Varieties of Cultural History*, 23–42. Ithaca, NY: Cornell University Press. Originally published in French as "L'histoire sociale des rêves," *Annales* 28, 1973: 329–42; reprint with a new introduction as "Une histoire sociale des rêves revisitée," *Sensibilités* 4, "La société des rêves", 2018: 44–57.
Burke, Peter 1997b. "Representations of the Self from Petrarch to Descartes." In *Rewriting the Self: Histories from the Renaissance to the Present*, edited by Roy Porter, 17–28. London: Routledge.
Burke, Peter 1998. *The European Renaissance: Centres and Peripheries*. Oxford: Blackwell.
Burke, Peter 2020. *The Polymath. A Cultural History from Leonardo da Vinci to Susan Sontag*. New Haven and London: Yale University Press.
Burke, Peter 2021. *Play in Renaissance Italy*. Cambridge: Polity.
Burton, Robert. 1989-2000. *The Anatomy of Melancholy*. 6 vols. Oxford: Clarendon.
Caciola, Nancy. 2003. *Discerning Spirits: Divine and Demonic Possession in the Middle Ages*. Ithaca and London: Cornell University Press.
Caelius Aurelianus. 1950. *On Acute Diseases and On Chronic Diseases*. Edited and Translated by I. E. Drabkin. Chicago: University of Chicago Press.
Caffiero, Marina. 2012. *Legami pericolosi: ebrei e cristiani tra eresia, libri proibiti e stregoneria*. Turin: Einaudi.
Caillois, Roger. 1956. *L'incertitude qui vient des rêves*. Paris. Gallimard.
Caillois, Roger, ed. 1963a. *The Dream Adventure*. New York: Orion.
Caillois, Roger 1963b. "Introduction." In *The Dream Adventure*, edited by Caillois, IX–XXXIII.
Cairns, Douglas. 2022. "Introduction A: Emotions through Time?" In *Emotions through Time: From Antiquity to Byzantium*, edited by Douglas Cairns, Martin Hinterberger, Aglae Pizzone and Matteo Zaccarini, 3–33. Tübingen: Mohr Siebeck.
Cameron, Euan. 2010. *Enchanted Europe: Superstition, Reason, and Religion, 1250–1750*. Oxford: Oxford University Press.
Camozzi Pistoja, Ambrogio. 2014. "The *Oneirocriticon of Achmet* in the West. A Contribution towards an Edition of Leo Tuscus' Translation." *Studi Medievali* s. III, 55.2: 720–58.
Campbell, Mary Baine. 2016. "Imputed Dreams: Dreaming and Knowing in Tudor England." *Études Épistémè* [Online] 30.
Camporesi, Piero. 1989. *Bread of Dreams: Food and Fantasy in Early Modern Europe*. Translated by David Gentilcore. Cambridge: Polity.
Camporesi, Piero 1994. *Il Palazzo e il cantimbanco: Giulio Cesare Croce*. Milan: Garzanti.
Canetti, Luigi. 2010. "L'incubazione cristiana tra Antichità e Medioevo." *Rivista di storia del cristianesimo* 7: 149–80.
Canetti, Luigi 2011. "Sogno e terapia nel medioevo latino." In *Terapie e guarigioni*, edited by Agostino Paravicini Bagliani, 25–54. Florence: SISMEL-Edizioni del Galluzzo.
Cappozzo, Valerio. 2018. *Dizionario dei sogni nel Medioevo. Il Somniale Danielis in manoscritti letterari*. Florence: Olschki.

Cardano, Girolamo. 2002. *The Book of My Life (De Vita Propria Liber)*. Translated by Jean Stoner (originally published in 1930), reprinted with introduction by Anthony Grafton. New York: New York Review Books.

Cardano, Girolamo 2008. *Somniorum Synesiorum libri quatuor. Les quatre livres des songes de Synesios*. Edited and Translated by Jean-Yves Boriaud. 2 vols. Florence: Olschki (reprinted 2021 with additional notes, Paris: Belles Lettres).

Carroy, Jacqueline and Juliette Lancel, eds. 2016. *Clés des songes et sciences des rêves de l'Antiquité à Freud*. Paris: Belles Lettres.

Carroy, Jacqueline, Hervé Mazurel and Élizabeth Serin. 2021. "Rêves de confins. Esquisses sur la vie onirique au temps du Covid-19 et du confinement (entretien avec Jacqueline Carroy)." *Communications* [Paris] 108: 227–43.

Cavaillé, Jean-Pierre. 1995. "L'itinéraire onirique de Decartes: de l'âge des songes aux temps du rêve." In *Les Olympiques de Descartes*, edited by Hallyn, 73–89.

Cavaillé, Jean-Pierre 2003. "'Veillé-je ou si je dors?' Une question sceptique, entre théâtre et philosophie." In *Songes et songeurs (XIIIe-XVIIIe siècle)*, edited by Dauvois and Grosperrin, 113–28.

Cavallo, Sandra. 2021. "Invisible Beds: Health and the Material Culture of Sleep." In *Writing Material Culture History* [2015], edited by Anne Gerritsen and Giorgio Riello, 2nd edn, 181–7. London: Bloomsbury.

Cavallo, Sandra and Tessa Storey. 2013. *Healthy Living in Renaissance Italy*. Oxford: Oxford University Press.

Cellini, Benvenuto. 1998. *The Autobiography*. Translated by George Bull, revised edn. London: Penguin.

Charpentier, Françoise, ed. 1990. *Le songe à la Renaissance*. Saint-Étienne: Université de Saint-Étienne.

Cherchi, Paolo. 1996. "Invito alla lettura della *Piazza*." In *Il serraglio de gli stupori del mondo* [1613], Garzoni, XXI–LXVI.

Cherchi, Paolo 2004. "Introduzione." In *Il serraglio de gli stupori del mondo* [1613], Garzoni, ix–xxxvii.

Chevlen, Dorie. 2021. "So You Want to Have a Lucid Dream?", *The New York Times*, 24 March.

Ciruelo, Pedro. 1977. *A Treatise Reproving all Superstitions and Forms of Witchcraft* [1538]. Translated by Eugene A. Maio and D'Orsay W. Pearson. Rutherford: Fairleigh Dickinson University Press.

Clark, Stuart. 1997. *Thinking with Demons: The Idea of Witchcraft in Early Modern Europe*. Oxford: Oxford University Press.

Clark, Stuart 2007a. "Songes diaboliques et paradoxes visuels." In *Fictions du diable*, edited by Françoise Lavocat, Pierre Kapitaniak and Marianne Closson, 167–96. Geneva: Droz.

Clark, Stuart 2007b. *Vanities of the Eye: Vision in Early Modern European Culture*. Oxford: Oxford University Press.

Closson, Marianne. 2016. "Le 'cauchemar': quand le démon habite nos rêves." In *Expériences oniriques dans la littérature et les arts du Moyen Age au XVIIe siècle*, edited by Demaules, 239–53.

Colonna, Francesco. 1592. *Hypnerotomachia. The Strife of Love in a Dream*. Translated by R. D. London: for S. Waterson.

Colonna, Francesco 1999. *Hypnerotomachia Poliphili. The Strife of Love in a Dream* [1499]. Translated by Joscelyn Godwin. London: Thames & Hudson.

Cooper, Richard. 1990. "Deux médecins royaux onirocritiques: Jehan Thibault et Auger Ferrier." In *Le songe à la Renaissance*, edited by Charpentier, 53–60.

Corrain, Lucia. 1991a. "Chiari di luna e pittura di luce." In *La notte. Ordine, sicurezza e disciplinamento in età moderna*, edited by Sbriccoli, 165–72.
Corrain, Lucia 1991b. "Raffigurare la notte." In *La notte. Ordine, sicurezza e disciplinamento in età moderna*, edited by Sbriccoli, 141–62.
Corrias, Anna. 2018. "When the Eyes Are Shut: The Strange Case of Girolamo Cardano's Idolum in *Somniorum Synesiorum Libri IIII* (1562)." *Journal of the History of Ideas* 79.2: 179–97.
Cox, Virginia. 1992. *The Renaissance Dialogue: Literary Dialogue in Its Social and Political Contexts, Castiglione to Galileo*. Cambridge: Cambridge University Press.
Crawford, Patricia. 2000. "Women's dreams in early modern England." *History Workshop Journal* 49: 129–41 (edited by Pick and Roper 2004, 91–103).
Croce, Giulio Cesare. 1600. *Sogni fantastichi della notte*. Bologna: V. Benacci.
Dandrey, Patrick. 1988. "La médecine du songe au XVIIe siècle." In *Revue des Sciences Humaines*, edited by Gautier 1988, 67–101.
Dannenfeldt, Karl H. 1986. "Sleep: Theory and Practice in the Late Renaissance." *Journal of the History of Medicine* 41: 415–41.
Dauvois, Nathalie and Jean-Philippe Grosperrin, eds. 2003. *Songes et songeurs (XIIIe-XVIIIe siècle)*. Quebec City: Presses de l'Université Laval.
Davidson, Jane P. 1993. "Plantes médicinales et vénéneuses: le sabbat des sorcières dans la peinture néerlandaise du XVIIe siècle." In *Le sabbat des sorciers (XVe-XVIIIe siècles)*, edited by Jacques-Chaquin and Préaud, 419–26.
de Azpilcueta, Martín. 1573. *Manuale confessorum pœnitentiumque*. Venice: Bindoni.
Della Barba, Pompeo. 1553. *I discorsi filosofici sopra il platonico, et divin Sogno di Scipione, di Marco Tullio*. Venice: G. M. Bonelli.
Della Porta, Giovan Battista 1560. *De i miracoli et maravigliosi effetti dalla natura prodotti, Libri IIII*. Venice: L. Avanzi.
Della Porta, Giovan Battista. 1589. *Magiae naturalis libri XX*. Naples: O. Salviani.
Delumeau, Jean. 1990. *Sin and Fear: The Emergence of a Western Guilt Culture, 13th–18th centuries*. Translated by Eric Nicholson. New York: St Martin's Press.
Demaules, Mireille. 2010. *La corne et l'ivoire: étude sur le récit de rêve dans la littérature romanesque des XIIe et XIIIe siècles*. Paris: Champion.
Demaules, Mireille, ed. 2016a. *Expériences oniriques dans la littérature et les arts du Moyen Age au XVIIe siècle*. Paris: Champion.
Demaules, Mireille 2016b. "Avant-propos." In *Expériences oniriques dans la littérature et les arts du Moyen Age au XVIIe siècle*, edited by Demaules, 7–23.
Derrida, Jacques. 2001. *Writing and Difference*. Translated by Alan Bass. London: Routledge.
Desrosiers-Bonin, Diane. 2020. "Le *Songe de Scipion* et le commentaire de Macrobe à la Renaissance." In *Le songe à la Renaissance*, edited by Charpentier, 71–81.
Dieterle, Bernard and Manfred Engel, eds. 2017. *Writing the Dream / Écrire le rêve*. (Cultural Dream Studies, 1). Würzburg: Königshausen & Neumann.
Dieterle, Bernard and Manfred Engel 2018. *Theorizing the Dream/Savoir et théories du rêve*. (Cultural Dream Studies, 2). Würzburg: Königshausen & Neumann.
Dieterle, Bernard and Manfred Engel 2019. *Historizing the Dream / Le rêve du point de vue historique*. (Cultural Dream Studies, 3.). Würzburg: Königshausen & Neumann.
Dieterle, Bernard and Manfred Engel 2020. *Mediating the Dream / Les genres et médias du rêve*. (Cultural Dream Studies, 4). Würzburg: Königshausen & Neumann.
Dieterle, Bernard and Manfred Engel 2022. *Typologizing the Dream / Le rêve du point de vue typologique*. (Cultural Dream Studies, 5.). Würzburg: Königshausen & Neumann.

Dodds, E.R. 1951. *The Greeks and the Irrational*. Berkeley and Los Angeles: University of California Press.

Dolce, Lodovico. 2006. *Terzetti per le "Sorti". Poesia oracolare nell'officina di Francesco Marcolini*, edited by Paolo Procaccioli. Treviso and Rome: Fondazione Benetton Studi Ricerche-Viella.

Domínguez Leiva, Antonio. 2007. *La vie comme songe? Une tentation de l'Occident*. Dijon: Editions Universitaires de Dijon.

Dottori, Benedetto. 1575. *Trattato de sogni secondo l'opinione d'Aristotile*. Padua: L. Pasquati.

Dulaey, Martine. 1973. *Le rêve dans la vie et la pensée de Saint Augustin*. Paris: Études augustiniennes.

Dumora, Florence. 2005. *L'œuvre nocturne: songe et représentation au XVIIe siècle*. Paris: Champion.

Dumora-Mabille, Florence. 2003. "Faire l'histoire du rêve." In *Songes et songeurs (XIIIe-XVIIIe siècle)*, edited by Dauvois and Grosperrin, 15–32.

Dürr, Hans Peter. 1985. *Dreamtime: Concerning the Boundary Between Wilderness and Civilazation*. Translated by Felicitas Goodman. Oxford: Blackwell.

Edwards, Nina. 2018. *Darkness: A Cultural History*. London: Reaktion.

Ekirch, A. Roger. 2001. "Sleep We Have Lost. Pre-Industrial Slumber in the British Isles." *American Historical Review* 106: 343–86.

Ekirch, A. Roger 2005. *At Day's Close: Night in Times Past*. New York: Norton.

Engel, Manfred. 2003. "The Dream in Eighteenth-Century Encyclopaedias." In *The Dream and the Enlightenment/Le Rêve et les Lumières*, edited by Bernard Dieterle and Manfred Engel, 21–51. Paris: Champion (International 18th Century Studies 7).

Engel, Manfred 2018. "Towards a Theory of Dream Theories." In *Theorizing the Dream/Savoir et théories du rêve*, edited by Dieterle and Engel, 19–42.

Engel, Manfred 2020. "Towards a Transmedial Poetics of the Dream." In *Mediating the Dream / Les genres et médias du rêve*, edited by Dieterle and Engel, 31–64.

Engel, Manfred 2022. "The Precarious Status of Erotic Dreams in Western Literature and Film." In *Typologizing the Dream / Le rêve du point de vue typologique*, edited by Dieterle and Engel, 277–346.

Faini, Marco. 2010. "Domenichi, Lodovico." In *Dizionario storico dell'Inquisizione*, edited by Prosperi 1, 505–6.

Faini, Marco 2016. "A ghost Academy between Venice and Brescia: philosophical scepticism and religious heterodoxy in the Accademia dei Dubbiosi." In *The Italian Academies 1525-1700. Networks of Culture, Innovation and Dissent*, edited by J. E. Everson, D. V. Reidy and L. M. Sampson, 102–15. Oxford: Legenda.

Farinelli, Arturo. 1916. *La vita è un sogno*, 2 vols. Turin: Bocca.

Farr, James R. 2020. "The Self: Representations and practices." In *The Routledge Companion to Cultural History in the Western World*, edited by Alessandro Arcangeli, Jörg Rogge and Hannu Salmi, 269–90. London: Routledge.

Fattori, Marta. 1985. "Sogni e temperamenti." In *I sogni nel Medioevo*, edited by Gregory, 97–109.

Fattori, Marta and Massimo Bianchi, eds. 1988. *Phantasia-imaginatio*. Rome: Edizioni dell'Ateneo.

Febvre, Lucien and Henri-Jean Martin. 1976. *The Coming of the Book: The Impact of Printing, 1450–1800*. Translated by David Gerard. London: N.L.B.

Ficino, Marsilio. 2004. *Platonic Theology*, vol. 4: books XII–XIV, edited by James Hankins. Translated by Michael J.B. Allen. Cambridge, MA: Harvard University Press.
Fine, Gary Alan and Laura Fischer Leighton. 1993. "Nocturnal Omissions: Steps Toward a Sociology of Dreams." *Symbolic Interaction* 16.2: 95–104.
First Printed Catalogue. 1986. *The First Printed Catalogue of the Bodleian Library (1605)*, a facsimile. Oxford: Clarendon.
Florio, John. 1598. *A Worlde of Wordes*. London.
Florio, John. 1611. *Queen Anna's New World of Words*. London.
Fontaine, Marie Madeleine and Marie-Ange Maignan. 2015. "Introduction." In *Le Printemps d'Yver* [1572], Yver, VII–CLI.
Foucault, Michel. 1986. *The Care of the Self (The History of Sexuality*, 3). Translated by Robert Hurley. New York: Pantheon Books.
Foucault, Michel 2002. *The Order of Things: An Archaeology of the Human Sciences* [1966]. London: Routledge.
Fragonard, Marie-Madeleine. 1990. "'Vos jeunes gens auront des visions et vos vieillards des songes'. Les commentaires de Joël, II-28 au XVIᵉ siècle." In *Le songe a la Renaissance*, edited by Charpentier, 209–20.
Freedberg, David. 1999. "Images dans les rêves." In *Crises de l'image religieuse/Krisen religiöser Kunst*, edited by Olivier Christin and Dario Gamboni, 33–53. Paris: Éditions de la Maison des Sciences de l'Homme.
Fretz, Claude. 2020. *Dreams, Sleep, and Shakespeare's Genres*. Cham: Palgrave Macmillan.
Fretz, Claude 2021. "'The eye of man hath not heard, the ear of man hath not seen': Multisensory Dreams in Shakespeare's *A Midsummer Night's Dream* and Colonna's *Hypnerotomachia Poliphili*." In *Träumen mit allen Sinnen*, edited by Stephanie Catani and Sophia Mehrbrey, 159–77. Boston: Brill.
Freud, Sigmund. 1957. *Leonardo da Vinci and a Memory of his Childhood (2010)*. London: Routledge and Kegan Paul.
Fudge, Erica. 2008. "'Onely Proper Unto Man': Dreaming and Being Human." In *Reading the Early Modern Dream*, edited by Hodgkin, O'Callaghan and Wiseman, 31–43.
Fumagalli, Edoardo. 1992. "Due esemplari dell'*Hypnerotomachia Poliphili* di Francesco Colonna." *Aevum* 66: 419–32.
Fumi, Bartolomeo. 1561. *Summa, sive Aurea Armilla*. Paris: M. Iuvenis.
Fumi, Bartolomeo 1588. *Somma Armilla*. Venice: D. Nicolini.
Gabriele, Mino. 2007. "Armonie ineffabili nell'*Hypnerotomachia Poliphili*." *Musica e Storia* 15: 57–66.
Gadebusch Bondio, Mariacarla. 2017. "Il genio si racconta: Il *De vita propria* di Cardano e alcuni suoi celebri interpreti." In *Summa doctrina et certa experientia. Studi su medicina e filosofia per Chiara Crisciani*, edited by Gabriella Zuccolin, 375–96. Florence: SISMEL-Edizioni del Galluzzo.
Galand-Hallyn, Perrine. 1990. "Le songe et la rhétorique de l'enargeia.'" In *Le songe à la Renaissance*, edited by Charpentier, 125–35.
Gallo, Alberto. 1987. "La 'chorea o vero ballo' dell'*Hypnerotomachia Poliphili*." In *La letteratura, la rappresentazione, la musica al tempo e nei luoghi di Giorgione*, edited by Michelangelo Muraro, 239–44. Rome: Jouvence.
Gandolfo, Francesco. 1978. *Il "dolce tempo". Mistica, ermetismo e sogno nel Cinquecento*. Rome: Bulzoni.

Gantet, Claire. 2007. "Dreams, standards of knowledge and orthodoxy in Germany in the sixteenth century." In *Orthodoxies and Heterodoxies in Early Modern German Culture: Order and Creativity 1500-1750*, edited by Randolph C. Head and Daniel Christensen, 69–87. Leiden: Brill.

Gantet, Claire 2010a. "Le rêve dans l'Allemagne du XVIe siècle. Appropriations médicales et recouvrements confessionels." *Annales HSS* 65, 1: 39–62.

Gantet, Claire 2010b. *Der Traum in der frühen Neuzeit*. Berlin and New York: De Gruyter.

Gantet, Claire 2021. *Une histoire du rêve. Les faces nocturnes de l'âme (Allemagne, 1500-1800)*. Rennes: Presses universitaires de Rennes.

Garzoni, Tommaso. 1996. *La piazza universale di tutte le professioni del mondo* [1585], edited by Paolo Cherchi and Beatrice Collina. Turin: Einaudi.

Garzoni, Tommaso 2004. *Il serraglio de gli stupori del mondo* [1613]. Russi (Ravenna): VACA.

Gautier, Jean-Luc, ed. 1988a. "Rêver en France au XVIIe siècle." *Revue des Sciences Humaines* 82: 211.

Gautier, Jean-Luc, ed. 1988b. "Rêver en France au XVIIe siècle: une introduction." In *Revue des Sciences Humaines*, edited by Gautier, 7–24.

Gazzola, Silvia. 2018. *L'Arte de' cenni di Giovanni Bonifacio*. 2 vols. Treviso: ZeL.

Gehring, Vera. 2008. *Traum und Wirklichkeit: zur Geschichte einer Unterscheidung*. Frankfurt: Campus.

Gerok-Reiter, Annette and Christine Walde, eds. 2012. *Traum und Vision in der Vormoderne*. Berlin: Akademie Verlag.

Gerona, Carla. 2004. *Night Journeys: The Power of Dreams in Transatlantic Quaker Culture*. Charlottesville: University of Virginia Press.

Giannetti, Laura. 2022. *Food Culture and Literary Imagination in Early Modern Italy*. Amsterdam: Amsterdam University Press.

Giglioni, Guido. 2010a. "Fazio and his Demons. Girolamo Cardano on the art of storytelling and the science of witnessing." *Bruniana & Campanelliana* 16.2: 463–72.

Giglioni, Guido 2010b. "Synesian Dreams. Girolamo Cardano on dreams as means of prophetic communication." *Bruniana & Campanelliana* 16.2: 575–84.

Giglioni, Guido 2011. "Coping with Inner and Outer Demons: Marsilio Ficino's Theory of the Imagination." In *Diseases of the Imagination and Imaginary Disease in the Early Modern Period*, edited by Haskell, 19–51.

Giglioni, Guido 2013. "Phantasmatica Mutatio: Johann Weyer's Critique of the Imagination as a Principle of Natural Metamorphosis." In *Transformative Change in Western Thought: A History of Metamorphosis from Homer to Hollywood*, edited by Ingo Gildenhard and Andrew Zissos, 307–30. London: Legenda.

Giglioni, Guido 2016. "Delusion, Drowsiness and Discernment: Degrees of Awareness in Renaissance Dream Activity." In *Cognitive Confusions: Dreams, Delusions and Illusions in Early Modern Culture*, edited by Mac Carthy, Sellevold and Smith, 89–109. Cambridge: Legenda.

Giglioni, Guido 2022. "The Human Self." In *A Cultural History of Ideas in the Renaissance*, edited by Jill Kraye, 33–50. London: Bloomsbury Academic.

Ginzburg, Carlo. 1980. *The Cheese and the Worms: The Cosmos of a Sixteenth-Century Miller*. Translated by John and Anne Tedeschi. Baltimore: Johns Hopkins University Press.

Ginzburg, Carlo 1983. *The Night Battles: Witchcraft and agrarian cults in the sixteenth and seventeenth centuries*. Translated by John and Anne Tedeschi. London: Routledge & Kegan Paul.
Goffen, Rona. 1987. "Renaissance Dreams." *Renaissance Quarterly* 40: 682–706.
Goris, Harm. 2012. "Thomas Aquinas on Dreams." In *Dreams as Divine Communication in Christianity: From Hermas to Aquinas*, edited by Bart J. Koet, 255–76. Leuven: Peeters.
Göttler, Christine. 2018. "Imagination in the Chamber of Sleep: Karel van Mander on Somnus and Morpheus." In *Image, Imagination, and Cognition: Medieval and Early Modern Theory and Practice*, edited by Christoph Lüthy, Claudia Swan, Paul Bakker and Claus Zittel, 147–76. Leiden: Brill.
Gowland, Agnus. 2011. "Melancholy, Imagination, and Dreaming in Renaissance Learning." In *Diseases of the Imagination and Imaginary Disease in the Early Modern Period*, edited by Haskell 2011, 53–102.
Grafton, Anthony. 1999. *Cardano's Cosmos: The Worlds and Works of a Renaissance Astrologer*. Cambridge, MA: Harvard University Press.
Grafton, Anthony 2000. "The Bright Book of Strife." *The New Republic* 22 May: 31–6.
Grafton, Anthony 2006. "Reforming the Dream." In *Humanism and Creativity in the Italian Renaissance. Essays in Honor of Ronald G. Witt*, edited by Christopher S. Celenza and Kenneth Gouwens, 271–92. Leiden: Brill.
Gregoras, Nicephorus. 1999. *Explicatio in librum Synesii* De insomniis: *scholia cum glossis*, edited by Paolo Pietrosanti. Bari: Levante.
Gregoric, Pavel and Jakob Leth Fink. 2022. "Introduction: Sleeping and Dreaming in Aristotle and the Aristotelian Tradition." In *Forms of Representation in the Aristotelian Tradition*, vol. 2: *Dreaming*, edited by Christina Thomsen Thörnqvist and Juhana Toivanen, 1–27. Leiden: Brill.
Gregory, Tullio, ed. 1985. *I sogni nel Medioevo*. Rome: Edizioni dell'Ateneo.
Grellard, Christophe. 2010. "La reception médiévale du *De somno et vigilia*. Approche anthropologique et épistémologique du rêve." In *Les* Parva naturalia *d'Aristote. Fortune antique et médiévale, d'Albert le Grand à Jean Buridan*, edited by Christophe Grellard and Pierre-Marie Morel, 221–37. Paris: Éditions de la Sorbonne.
Greyerz, Kaspar von. 1984. "Religion in the Life of German and Swiss Autobiographers (Sixteenth and Seventeenth Centuries)." In *Religion and Society in Early Modern Europe, 1500–1800*, edited by Kaspar von Greyerz, 223–41. London: German Historical Institute-G. Allen & Unwin.
Groebner, Valentin. 2004. *Der Schein der Person*. Munich: Beck.
Grottanelli, Cristiano. 1999. "On the Mantic Meaning of Incestuous Dreams." In *Dream cultures: explorations in the comparative history of dreaming*, edited by Shulman and Stroumsa, 143–68.
Grunebaum, G. E. von and Roger Caillois, eds. 1966. *The Dream and Human Societies*. Berkeley and Los Angeles: University of California Press.
Haller, Benjamin. 2009. "The Gates of Horn and Ivory in Odyssey 19: Penelope's Call for Deeds, Not Words." *Classical Philology* 1044: 397–417.
Hallyn, Fernand, ed. 1995. *Les* Olympiques *de Descartes*. Geneva: Droz.
Handley, Sasha. 2016. *Sleep in Early Modern England*. New Haven: Yale University Press.
Haskell, Yasmin, ed. 2011a. *Diseases of the Imagination and Imaginary Disease in the Early Modern Period*. Turnhout: Brepols.

Haskell, Yasmin. 2011b. "The Anatomy of Hypochondria: Malachias Geiger's *Microcosmus hypochondriacus* (Munich, 1652)." In *Diseases of the Imagination and Imaginary Disease in the Early Modern Period*, edited by Haskell, 275–99.

Hickman, Caroline, Elizabeth Marks, Panu Pihkala, Susan Clayton, Eric Lewandowski, Elouise E. Mayall et al. 2021. "Climate anxiety in children and young people and their beliefs about government responses to climate change: a global survey." *The Lancet. Planetary Health* 5.12: e863–e873.

Hippocrates of Cos. 1931. "Regimen 4, or Dreams." In Id., *Nature of Man. Regimen in Health. Humours. Aphorisms. Regimen 1-3. Dreams. Heracleitus: On the Universe*, 220–47. Translated by W. H. S. Jones (Loeb Classical Library, 150.) Cambridge, MA: Harvard University Press.

Hodgkin, Katharine. 2008. "Dreaming Meanings: Some Early Modern Dream Thoughts." In *Reading the Early Modern Dream*, edited by Hodgkin, O'Callaghan and Wiseman, 109–24.

Hodgkin, Katharine, Michelle O'Callaghan and S.J. Wiseman, eds. 2008. *Reading the Early Modern Dream*. New York: Routledge.

Holland, Peter. 1999. "'The interpretation of dreams' in the Renaissance", inedited by Brown, 125–46.

Holton, Stephanie. 2022. *Sleep and Dreams in Early Greek Thought: Presocratic and Hippocratic Approaches*. London: Routledge.

Hsia, R. Po-Chia. 2005. "Dreams and Conversions: A Comparative Analysis of Catholic and Buddhist Dreams in Ming and Qing China. Part One." *Journal of Religious History* 29: 223–40.

Hsia, R. Po-Chia 2010. "Dreams and Conversions: A Comparative Analysis of Catholic and Buddhist Dreams in Ming and Qing China. Part Two." *Journal of Religious History* 34: 111–41.

Huizinga, Johan. 1996. *The Autumn of the Middle Ages* (1919; 2nd edn, 1921). Translated by Rodney J. Payton and Ulrich Mammitzsch. Chicago: University of Chicago Press.

Huizinga, Johan 2020. *Autumntide of the Middle Ages* (1919; 1941 edn). Translated by Diane Webb. Leiden: Leiden University Press.

Husser, Jean-Marie. 1999. *Dreams and Dream Narratives in the Biblical World*. Sheffield: Sheffield Academic Press.

Italia al chiaro di luna. 1990. *Italia al chiaro di luna/Italy by Moonlight. The Night in Italian Painting 1550-1850*. Rome: Il Cigno Galileo Galilei.

Jacques-Chaquin, Nicole and Maxime Préaud, eds. 1993. *Le sabbat des sorciers (XVe-XVIIIe siècles)*. Grenoble: J. Millon.

Javellus, Chrysostomus. 1567. *Epitome in universam Aristotelis philosophiam*. Venice: H. Scotus.

Jordán Arroyo, María V. 2017. *Entre la vigilia y el sueño: soñar en el Siglo de Oro*. Madrid and Frankfurt: Iberoamericana-Veruert.

Jouanna, Jacques. 1998. "L'interprétation des rêve et la théorie micro-macrocosmique dans le traité hippocratique *Du régime*: sémiotique et mimesis." In *Text and Tradition: Studies in Ancient Medicine and its Transmission, Presented to Jutta Kollesch*, edited by Klaus Dietrich Fischer, Diethard Nickel and Paul Potter, 161–74. Leiden: Brill.

Joubert, Laurent. 1989. *Popular Errors*. Translated by Gregory David de Rocher. Tuscaloosa: University of Alabama Press.

Joukovsky, Françoise, ed. 1991. *Songes de la Renaissance*. Paris: C. Bourgois.

Jung, Carl Gustav. 2014. *Dream Interpretation Ancient and Modern: Notes from the Seminar Given in 1936-1941*, edited by John Peck, Lorenz Jung and Maria Meyer-Grass. Princeton: Princeton University Press.
Kagan, Richard L. 1990. *Lucrecia's Dreams. Politics and Prophecy in Sixteenth-Century Spain*. Berkeley: University of California Press.
Kennington, Richard. 1961. "Descartes' *Olympica*." *Social Research* 28: 171–204.
Kepler, Johannes. 1967. *Kepler's Somnium*. Translated by Edward Rosen. Madison and London: University of Wisconsin Press.
Keskiaho, Jesse. 2015. *Dreams and Visions in the Early Middle Ages: The Reception and Use of Patristic Ideas, 400-900*. Cambridge: Cambridge University Press.
Knox, Dilwyn. 1990. "Ideas on gesture and universal languages, *c.* 1550-1650." In *New Perspectives on Renaissance Thought: Essays in the History of Science, Education and Philosophy, in Memory of Charles B. Schmitt*, edited by John Henry and Sarah Hutton, 101–36. London: Duckworth.
Koselleck, Reinhart. 1985. *Futures Past: On the Semantics of Historical Time*. Translated by Keith Tribe. Cambridge, MA: MIT Press.
Koslofsky, Craig. 2011. *Evening's Empire*. Cambridge: Cambridge University Press.
Kottek, Samuel S. 2009. "Les rêves dans les sources juives anciennes." *Medicina nei secoli* 21: 503–30.
Kruger, Steven. 1992. *Dreaming in the Middle Ages*. Cambridge: Cambridge University Press.
La Garanderie, Marie-Madeleine de. 1990. "'Vous arrive-t-il parfois de rêver des astres?' ou Quelques pages curieuses de Jules-César Scaliger." In *Le songe à la Renaissance*, edited by Charpentier, 33–9.
Lahire, Bernard. 2020. *The Sociological Interpretation of Dreams*. Translated by Helen Morrison. Cambridge: Polity.
Lamoreaux, John C. 2002. *The Early Muslim Tradition of Dream Interpretation*. Albany: SUNY Press.
Lanternari, Vittorio. 1981a. "Sogno/visione." In *Enciclopedia*, vol. 13, 94–126. Turin: Einaudi.
Lanternari, Vittorio 1981b. "Sonno/sogno." In *Enciclopedia*, vol. 13, 227–43. Turin: Einaudi.
La Via, Stefano. 1997. "'Natura delle cadenze' e 'natura contraria delli modi': Punti di convergenza fra teoria e prassi nel madrigale cinquecentesco." *Il Saggiatore musicale* 4: 5–51.
Le Brun, Jacques. 1994. "Jérôme Cardan et l'interprétation des songes." In *Girolamo Cardano: Philosoph, Naturforscher, Artzt*, edited by Eckhard Kessler, 185–205. Wiesbaden: Harrassowitz.
Légasse, Simon and Martine Dulaey. 1990. "Songes-rêves." In *Dictionnaire de spiritualité*, vol. 14, cols 1054–66. Paris: Beauchesne.
Le Goff, Jacques. 1980a. "The Medieval West and the Indian Ocean. An Oneiric Horizon" (1970). In Id., *Time, Work and Culture in the Middle Ages*. Translated by Arthur Goldhammer, 189–200. Chicago: University of Chicago Press.
Le Goff, Jacques 1980b. "Dreams in the Culture and Collective Psychology of the Medieval West" (1971). In Id., *Time, Work and Culture in the Middle Ages*. Translated by Arthur Goldhammer, 201–4. Chicago: University of Chicago Press.
Le Goff, Jacques 1985. "Le christianisme et les rêves (IIe-VIIe siècles)." In *I sogni nel Medioevo*, edited by Gregory, 171–218.

Leroux, Virginie, Nicoletta Palmieri and Christine Pigné, eds. 2015. *Le sommeil: approches philosophiques et médicales de l'Antiquité à la Renaissance*. Paris: Champion.
Levin, Carole. 2008. *Dreaming the English Renaissance: Politics and Desire in Court and Culture*. New York: Palgrave Macmillan.
Lochert, Véronique and Jean de Guardia, eds. 2012. *Théâtre et imaginaire. Images scéniques et répresentations mentales (XVI*^{e}*-XVIII*^{e} *siècle)*. Dijon: Éditions Universitaires de Dijon.
Lombroso, Cesare. 1855. "Su la pazzia di Cardano." *Gazzetta medica italiana – Lombardia. Appendice psichiatrica*, 40: 341–5.
Mac Carthy, Ita, Kirsti Sellevold and Olivia Smith, eds. 2016. *Cognitive Confusions: Dreams Delusions and Illusions in Early Modern Culture*. Cambridge: Legenda, Modern Humanities Research Association.
Mack, Peter. 2004. "Early Modern Ideas of Imagination: The Rhetorical Tradition." In *Imagination in the later Middle Ages and Early Modern times*, edited by Lodi Nauta and Detlev Pätzold, 59–76. Leuven: Peeters.
Macrobius. 1952. *Commentary on the Dream of Scipio*. Translated by William Harris Stahl. New York: Columbia University Press.
Macrobius 2007. *Commento al Sogno di Scipione*. "Translated into Italian" or "Italian translation" by Moreno Neri. Milan: Bompiani.
Mageo, Jeanette Marie. 2003. *Dreaming and the Self: New Perspectives on Subjectivity, Identity and Emotion*. New York: State University of New York Press.
Maggi, Armando. 2008. "Interpretare i sogni." In *Il Rinascimento italiano e l'Europa. 5: Le scienze*, edited by Antonio Clericuzio and Germana Ernst, 261–80. Costabissara: Colla.
Maggi, Armando 2009. "Il significato del concetto di figlio nel pensiero di Girolamo Cardano." *Bruniana & Campanelliana* 15: 81–100.
Maggi, Armando 2010. "The Dialogue between the Living and the Dead in Cardano's Thought." *Bruniana & Campanelliana* 16: 473–80.
Mancia, Mauro. 2003. "Il pensiero di Cardano come cerniera tra le idee antiche e moderne sul sogno." In *Cardano e la tradizione dei saperi*, edited by Marialuisa Baldi and Guido Canziani, 35–41. Milan: FrancoAngeli.
Marchetti, Valerio. 1982. "Le désir et la règle. Recherches sur le *Dialogo dei giochi* de Girolamo Bargagli (1572)." In *Les jeux à la Renaissance*, edited by Philippe Ariès and Jean-Claude Margolin, 163–83. Paris: Vrin.
Marr, Alexander. 2016. "Richard Haydocke's *Oneirologia*: A Manuscript Treatise on Sleep and Dreams, including the 'Arguments' of King James I." *Erudition and the Republic of Letters* 2.
Martines, Lauro. 2004. *An Italian Renaissance Sextet: Six Tales in Historical Context*. Translated by Murtha Baca. Toronto: University of Toronto Press.
Massing, Jean Michel. 1986. "Dürer's Dreams." *Journal of the Warburg and Courtauld Institutes* 49: 238–44.
Mathieu-Castellani, Gisèle. 1990. "Veiller en dormant, dormir en veillant. Le songe dans les *Essais*." In *Le songe à la Renaissance*, edited by Charpentier, 231–8.
Maus de Rolley, Thibaut. 2007. "La part du diable: Jean Wier et la fabrique de l'illusion diabolique." In *Fictions du diable*, edited by Françoise Lavocat, Pierre Kapitaniak and Marianne Closson, 109–30. Droz: Geneva.

Mavroudi, Maria. 2002. *A Byzantine Book on Dream Interpretation: The Oneirocriticon of Achmet and its Arabic sources*. Leiden: Brill.
Max, Frédéric. 1993. "Les premières controverses sur la réalité du sabbat dans l'Italie du XVIe siècle. In *Le sabbat des sorciers (XVe-XVIIIe siècles)*, edited by Jacques-Chaquin and Préaud, 55–62.
Mazurel, Hervé. 2022. *L'inconscient ou l'oubli de l'histoire: profondeurs, métamorphoses et révolutions de la vie affective*. Paris: La Découverte.
Mazzolini, Silvestro. 1518. *Summa summarum que Sylvestrina dicitur*. Strasbourg: J. Grieninger.
Mazzoni, Jacopo. 2017. *Della difesa della Comedia di Dante* (1587), edited by Claudio Moreschini and Luigia Businarolo. Cesena: Società di studi romagnoli.
McClure, George. 2013. *Parlour Games and the Public Life of Women in Renaissance Italy*. Toronto: University of Toronto Press.
McGowan, Margaret M. 2008. *Dance in the Renaissance: European Fashion, French Obsession*. New Haven: Yale University Press.
McGowan, Margaret M. 2012. *La danse à la Renaissance: sources livresques et albums d'images*. Paris: Bibliothèque nationale de France.
Medici, Sisto. 1561. "Disputatio de somniis." Venice, Biblioteca Nazionale Marciana, ms Lat. XIV.59 (4239): 156–85.
Ménager, Daniel. 2005. *La Renaissance et la nuit*. Geneva: Droz.
Meschini, Franco Aurelio. 1988. "Della Barba, Pompeo." In *Dizionario biografico degli italiani*, vol. 36. Rome: Treccani (now online).
Meurget, Michel. 1993. "Plantes à illusion: l'interprétation pharmacologique du sabbat." In *Le sabbat des sorciers (XVe-XVIIIe siècles)*, edited by Jacques-Chaquin and Préaud, 369–82.
Michelini Tocci, Franco. 1985. "Teoria e interpretazione dei sogni nella cultura ebraica medievale." In *I sogni nel Medioevo*, edited by Gregory, 261–90.
Miegge, Mario. 2005. "Sogno e profezia." In *Sogno e sogni*, edited by Mimma Bresciani Califano, 41–54. Florence: Leo S. Olschki.
Miller, Patricia Cox. 1994. *Dreams in Late Antiquity: Studies in the Imagination of a Culture*. Princeton: Princeton University Press.
Milne, Louise S. 2011. *Carnivals and Dreams: Pieter Bruegel and the History of the Imagination*, revised edn. London: Monochrome.
Mitchell, W.J.T. 1994. *Picture Theory*. Chicago: University of Chicago Press.
Montaigne, Michel de. 1603. *The Essayes or morall, politike and millitarie discourses*. Translated by John Florio. London: V. Sims.
Montanari, Anna Maria. 2022. "'Such stuff as dreams are made on': Prophetic Dreams and Dreams of Death from Classical Antiquity to Italian Renaissance Drama and Shakespeare's Plays." *Strumenti critici* 37: 333–61.
Monticini, Francesco, ed. 2023. *Il Trattato sui sogni di Sinesio di Cirene e il commento di Niceforo Gregora*. Genoa: Genova University Press.
Morelli, Giovanni di Pagolo. 2019. *Ricordi*, edited by Claudia Tripodi. Florence: Firenze University Press.
Moss, Ann. 1996. *Printed Commonplace-Books and the Structuring of Renaissance Thought*. Oxford: Clarendon.
Niccoli, Ottavia. 1990. *Prophecy and People in Renaissance Italy*. Translated by Lydia G. Cochrane. Princeton: Princeton University Press.

Nicephorus. 1980. *Libro dei sogni*, edited and translated by Giulio Guidorizzi. Naples: M. D'Auria.
Niehoff, Maren. 1992. "A Dream which is not Interpreted is like a Letter which is not Read." *Journal of Jewish Studies* 43: 58–84.
Oberhelman, Steven M. 1983. "Galen, *On Diagnosis from Dreams.*" *Journal of the History of Medicine* 38: 36–47.
Oberhelman, Steven M. 1991. *The* Oneirocriticon *Of Achmet: A Medieval Greek and Arabic Treatise on the Interpretation of Dreams*. Lubbock: Texas Tech University Press.
Oberhelman, Steven M. 2008. *Dreambooks in Byzantium: Six Oneirocritica in Translation, with Commentary and Introduction*. Aldershot: Ashgate.
Olsan, Lea T. 2010. "Enchantment in medieval literature." In *The Unorthodox Imagination in Late Medieval Britain*, edited by Sophie Page, 166–92. Manchester: Manchester University Press.
Ortalli, Gherardo. 2013–2014. "Sixteenth-Century Courts and Salons: *Giochi di veglia.*" *Ludica* 19–20: 61–86.
Paoli, Marco. 2011. "Sognare nel Cinquecento: saggio su un microgenere editoriale tra Rinascimento e Controriforma: i trattati sul sogno." *Rara volumina* 1–2: 29–57.
Park, Katharine S. 1974. "The Imagination in Renaissance Psychology." Unpublished MPhil diss., University of London.
Parlato, Enrico. 2011. "Sogno e conoscenza nella Venezia del Cinquecento: Daniele Barbaro, alias Hypneo da Schio, e Francesco Marcolini." In *Forme e storia. Scritti di arte medievale e moderna per Francesco Gandolfo*, edited by Walter Angelelli and Francesca Pomarici, 505–14. Rome: Artemide.
Perec, Georges. 2012. *La Boutique Obscure*. Translated by Daniel Levin Becker. New York: Melville House Publishing.
Pererius, Benedictus. 1592. *Adversus fallaces et superstitiosas artes*. Lyon: heirs Giunta.
Perrus, Claude, ed. 1997. *Rêves et récits de rêve (Arzanà 4)*. Paris: Presses de la Sorbonne nouvelle.
Petrarca, Francesco. 1579. *Phisicke against Fortune*. Translated by Thomas Twyne. London: R. Watkyns.
Pigeaud, Jackie. 1981. "Le rêve érotique dans l'Antiquité gréco-romaine: l'oneirogmos." *Littérature, médecine, société* 3: 10–23.
Pigeaud, Jackie 1995. "Introduction." In Aristote, *La Vérité des songes*, 9–112. Translated and edited by Jackie Pigeaud. Paris: Rivages.
Pick, Daniel and Lyndal Roper, eds. 2004. *Dreams and History*. London: Routledge.
Pigman, G.W., III. 2019. *Conceptions of Dreaming from Homer to 1800*. London: Anthem Press.
Plane, Ann Marie. 2014. *Dreams and the Invisible World in Colonial New England*. Philadelphia: University of Pennsylvania Press.
Plane, Ann Marie and Leslie Tuttle, eds. 2013a. *Dreams, Dreamers, and Visions: The Early Modern Atlantic World*. Philadelphia: University of Pennsylvania Press.
Plane, Ann Marie and Leslie Tuttle, eds. 2013b. "Introduction: The Literatures of Dreaming." In *Dreams, Dreamers, and Visions: The Early Modern Atlantic World*, edited by Plane and Tuttle, 1–30 (incorporated and expanded in "Review Essay: Dreams and Dreamers in the Early Modern World." *Renaissance Studies* 67 (2014): 917-31).

Poesche, Joachim. 1994. "Dürers 'Traumgesicht'." In *Traum und Träumen: Inhalt, Darstellung, Funktionen einer Lebenserfahrung in Mittelalter und Renaissance*, edited by Rudolf Hiestand, 187–206. Düsseldorf: Droste.
Ponzetti, Ferdinando. 1515. *Tertia pars Naturalis phylosophie*. Rome: G. Mazzocchi.
Préaud, Maxime. 1988. "Le rêve du sabbat." In *Revue des Sciences Humaines*, edited by Gautier, 103–13.
Price, S.R.F. 1986. "The Future of Dreams: From Freud to Artemidorus." *Past & Present* 113: 3–37.
Prins, Jacomien. 2017. "Carl Gustav Jung's Interpretation of Girolamo Cardano's Dreams." *I Tatti Studies in the Italian Renaissance* 20.2: 391–413.
Prins, Jacomien 2020. "Heavenly Journeys: Marsilio Ficino and Girolamo Cardano on *Scipio's Dream*." *Aither* International issue no. 7: 40–57.
Prosperi, Adriano, ed. 2010. *Dizionario storico dell'Inquisizione*. 5 vols. Pisa: Edizioni della Normale.
Quakelbeen, Julien. 1995. "Freud et les psychanalistes devant les rêves de Descartes." In *Les Olympiques de Descartes*, edited by Hallyn, 113–26.
Rabb, Theodore K. 2006. *The Last Days of the Renaissance and the March to Modernity*. New York: Basic Books.
Rabbi Bernard, Chiara, Alessandro Cecchi and Yves Hersant, eds. 2013. *Il sogno nel Rinascimento*. Livorno: Sillabe [also published in French].
Richter, Isabel. 2014. "Dreams in Cultural History: Dream Narratives and the History of Subjectivity." *Cultural History* 3: 126–47.
Ricoeur, Paul. 1970. *Freud and Philosophy: An Essay on Interpretation*. Translated by Denis Savage. New Haven: Yale University Press.
Rivière, Janine. 2017. *Dreams in Early Modern England: "Visions of the Night"*. London and New York: Routledge.
Robb, Alice. 2020. "Why Are My Dreams So Vivid Right Now?" *The Cut*, 2 April.
Rochon, André. 1974. "Une date importante dans l'histoire de la *beffa*: la *Nouvelle du Grasso legnaiuolo*." In *Formes et significations de la "beffa" dans la littérature italienne de la Renaissance*, edited by Marina Marietti, Danielle Boillet, José Guidi and André Rochon, vol. 2, 211–376. Paris: Université de la Sorbonne Nouvelle.
Roper, Lyndal. 1994. *Oedipus and the Devil: Witchcraft, Sexuality and Religion in Early Modern Europe*. London: Routledge.
Roper, Lyndal 2021. *Living I Was Your Plague: Martin Luther's World and Legacy*. Princeton: Princeton University Press.
Rosaccio, Giuseppe. 1600. *Il microcosmo*. Florence: F. Tosi.
Roselli, Amneris. 1995. "I *Sogni* di Ippocrate nell'interpretazione di Giulio Cesare Scaligero." In *Il sogno raccontato*, edited by Nicola Merola and Caterina Verbaro, 137–50. Vibo Valentia: Monteleone.
Rosenwein, Barbara H. 2022. *Love: A History in Five Fantasies*. Cambridge: Polity.
Ruggiero, Guido. 2015. *The Renaissance in Italy: A Social and Cultural History of the Rinascimento*. New York: Cambridge University Press.
Rupprecht, Carol Schreier. 1993. "Divinity, Insanity, Creativity: A Renaissance Contribution to the History and Theory of Dream/text(s)." In *The Dream and the Text: Essays on Literature and Language*, edited by Carol Schreier Rupprecht, 112–32. Albany: State University of New York Press.
Russell, Donald A. and Heinz-Günther Nesselrath, eds. 2014. *On Prophecy, Dreams and Human Imagination: Synesius*, De insomniis. Tübingen: Mohr Siebeck.

Ruvoldt, Maria. 2004. *The Italian Renaissance Imagery of Inspiration: Metaphors of Sex, Sleep, and Dreams.* Cambridge: Cambridge University Press.

Saunders, David T., Chris A. Roe, Graham Smith and Helen Clegg. 2016. "Lucid dreaming incidence: A quality effects meta-analysis of 50 years of research." *Consciousness and Cognition* 43: 197–215.

Sbriccoli, Mario, ed. 1991a. *La notte. Ordine, sicurezza e disciplinamento in età moderna.* Florence: Ponte alle Grazie.

Sbriccoli, Mario 1991b. "Nox quia nocet. I giuristi, l'ordine e la normalizzazione dell'immaginario." In *La notte. Ordine, sicurezza e disciplinamento in età moderna*, edited by Sbriccoli, 9–19.

Schalk, Fritz. 1955. *Somnium und verwandte Wörter in den romanischen Sprachen.* Cologne: Westdeutscher Verlag.

Schick, Hartmut. 2016. "*O sonno.* Cipriano de Rores Spätstil und die Florentiner Camerata." In *Cipriano de Rore: New Perspectives on his Life and Music*, edited by Jessie Ann Owens and Katelijne Schiltz, 331–56. Turnhout: Brepols.

Schmitt, Jean-Claude. 1985. "Rêver au XIIe siècle." In *I sogni nel Medioevo, Lessico Intelletuale Europeo XXXV*, edited by Gregory, 291–316 (repr. as chapter 11 of Schmitt 2001).

Schmitt, Jean-Claude. 1998. *Ghosts in the Middle Ages: The Living and the Dead in Medieval Society.* Translated by Teresa Lavender Fagan. Chicago: University of Chicago Press [original title: *Les revenants*].

Schmitt, Jean-Claude. 1999. "The Liminality and Centrality of Dreams in the Medieval West." In *Dream cultures: Explorations in the comparative history of dreaming*, edited by Shulman and Stroumsa, 274–87 (repr. in French as chapter 12 of Schmitt 2001).

Schmitt, Jean-Claude. 2001. *Le corps, les rites, les rêves, le temps: essais d'anthropologie médiévale.* Paris: Gallimard.

Schmitt, Jean-Claude. 2002a. "Hildegarde de Bingen ou le refus du rêve" [originally published in German in 2000]. In *Le corps des images: essais sur la culture visuelle au moyen âge*, edited by Schmitt, 323–44.

Schmitt, Jean-Claude. 2002b. "L'iconographie des rêves" [originally published in German in 1987]. In *Le corps des images: essais sur la culture visuelle au moyen âge*, edited by Schmitt, 297–321.

Schmitt, Jean-Claude. 2002c. *Le corps des images: essais sur la culture visuelle au moyen âge.* Paris: Gallimard.

Schmitt, Jean-Claude. 2007. "Postface. Du 'moi' du rêve au 'je' du récit et de l'image." In *Le rêve médiéval*, edited by Alain Corbellari and Jean-Yves Tilliette, 232–42. Geneva: Droz.

Schmitt, Jean-Claude. 2010. *The Conversion of Hermann the Jew.* Translated by Alek J. Novikoff. Philadelphia: University of Pennsylvania Press.

Schmitt, Jean-Claude. 2016. "Les clés des songes au Moyen Âge." In *Clés des songes et sciences des rêves de l'Antiquité à Freud*, edited by Carroy and Lancel, 61–71.

Schmitt, Jean-Claude, Gisèle Besson, Alban Bensa and Andreas Mayer. 2018. "Table ronde autour de *Rêver de soi. Les songes autobiographiques au Moyen Âge.* Entretien des auteurs Jean-Claude Schmitt et Gisèle Besson avec Alban Bensa et Andreas Mayer". *Sensibilités* 4, "La société des rêves".

Scholler, Dietrich and Jing Xuan, eds. 2020. *Traumwissen und Traumpoetik von Dante bis Descartes.* Göttingen: Vandenhoeck & Ruprecht-Mainz University Press.

Schutte, Anne Jacobson. 1983. *Printed Italian Vernacular Religious Books 1465-1550: A Finding List*. Geneva: Droz.
Sellevold, Kirsti. 2016. "'Imagine this Place': Doni's Utopian Dream." In *Cognitive Confusions. Dreams, Delusions and Illusions in Early Modern Culture*, edited by Mac Carthy, Sellevold and Smith, 147–162. Oxford: Oxford Legenda.
Semeraro, Martino. 2002. *Il Libro dei sogni di Daniele. Storia di un testo "proibito" nel Medioevo*. Rome: Viella.
Seretti, Marina. 2021. *Endormis: le sommeil profond et ses métaphores dans l'art de la Renaissance*. Dijon: Presses du réel.
Short-title Catalogue. 1958. *Short-title Catalogue of Books printed in Italy and of Italian Books printed in other countries from 1465 to 1600 now in the British Museum*. London: British Museum.
Shulman, David and Guy G. Stroumsa, eds. 1999. *Dream Cultures: Explorations in the Comparative History of Dreaming*. New York: Oxford University Press.
Simon, Gérard. 1995. "Les Olympica dans le premier dix-septième siècle." In *Les Olympiques de Descartes*, edited by Hallyn, 141–57.
Simpson-Younger, Nancy L. and Margaret Simon, eds. 2020. *Forming Sleep: Representing Consciousness in the English Renaissance*. University Park: Pennsylvania State University Press.
Siraisi, Nancy. 1997. *The Clock and the Mirror: Girolamo Cardano and Renaissance Medicine*. Princeton: Princeton University Press.
Sluhovsky, Moshe. 2007. *Believe Not Every Spirit: Possession, Mysticism, and Discernment in Early Modern Catholicism*. Chicago: University of Chicago Press.
Small, Graeme. 2020. "Epilogue: From Herfstij to Autumntide." In Huizinga, 538–79.
Sorge, Valeria. 2016. "Introduzione." In Agostino Nifo, *Sui sogni*. Translated and edited by Valeria Sorge, 7–60. Milan: Mimesis.
Sörlin, Per. 2008. "Child Witches and the Construction of the Witches' Sabbath: The Swedish Blåkulla Story." In *Witchcraft Mythologies and Persecutions*, edited by Éva Pócs and Gábor Klaniczay, 99–126. Budapest and New York: Central European University Press.
Stavru, Alessandro. 2018. "Ekphrasis." In *International Lexicon of Aesthetics*, vol. 1. Milan: Mimesis.
Stephens, Walter. 2011. "Sex, Popular Beliefs, and Culture: 'In the Waie of Lecherie'." In *A Cultural History of Sexuality in the Renaissance*, edited by Bette Talvacchia, 137–56. London: Bloomsbury Academic.
Storper Perez, Danielleand Henri Cohen-Solal. 1997. "'Tout songe non interprété est comme une lettre non lue': Approche anthropologique et psychanalytique de l'interprétation des rêves dans le Traité Berakhot du Talmud de Babulone." In *Le corps du texte: Pour une anthropologie des textes de la tradition juive*, edited by Florence Heymann and Danielle Storper Perez, 225–55. Paris: CNRS Éditions.
Sugarman, Susan. 2023. *Freud's Interpretation of Dreams: A Reappraisal*. Cambridge: Cambridge University Press.
Synesius. 2004. *Opuscules*, edited by Jacques Lamoureux. Translated by Noël Aujoulat, vol. 1. Paris: Belles Lettres.
Thompson, Stith. 1955–57. *Motif-Index of Folk Literature*, revised and enlarged edn. 6 vols. Copenhagen.

Thonemann, Peter. 2020a. *An Ancient Dream Manual: Artemidorus'* The Interpretation of Dreams. Oxford: Oxford University Press.
Thonemann, Peter 2020b. "Introduction." In Artemidorus, XI–XXVIII.
Timotin, Andrei. 2016. "Techniques d'interprétation dans les clés des songes byzantines." In *Clés des songes et sciences des rêves de l'antiquité à Freud*, edited by Carroy and Lancel, 47–60. Paris.
Tiraqueau, André. 1986. *De poenis temperandis* [1559]. Translated into French by André Laingui. Paris: Economica.
Tommasino, Pier Mattia. 2018. *The Venetian Qur'an: A Renaissance Companion to Islam*. Translated by Sylvia Notini. Philadelphia: University of Pennsylvania Press.
Trachtenberg, Joshua. 2004. *Jewish Magic and Superstition: A Study in Folk Religion* [1939]. Philadelphia: University of Pennsylvania Press.
Ulbricht, Otto. 2001. "Ich-Erfahrung. Individualität in Autobiographien." In *Entdeckung des Ich: Die Geschichte der Individualisierung vom Mittelalter bis zur Gegenwart*, edited by Richard van Dülmen, 109–44. Cologne: Böhlau.
Valente, Michaela. 2022. *Johann Wier: Debating the Devil and Witches in Early Modern Europe*. Translated by Theresa Federici. Amsterdam: Amsterdam University Press.
Van Deusen, Nancy, ed. 2010. *Dreams and Visions: An Interdisciplinary Enquiry*. Leiden: Brill.
Vasoli, Cesare. 1999. "Ficino e la rivelazione onirica." *Academia. Revue de la Société Marsile Ficin* 1: 67–75.
Vermigli, Pietro Martire. 1564. *Most Fruitfull and Learned Commentaries*. London: J. Day.
Vermigli, Pietro Martire 1583. *The Common Places*. Translated by Anthony Marten. London.
Wagner, Kevin. 2019. "Synesius of Cyrene and Neoplatonic Dream Theory." In *Dreams, Virtue and Divine Knowledge in Early Christian Egypt*, edited by Bronwen Neil, Doru Costache and Kevin Wagner, 116–68. Cambridge: Cambridge University Press.
Wallace, Anthony F.C. 1958. "Dreams and the Wishes of the Soul: A Type of Psychoanalytic Theory among the Seventeenth Century Iroquois." *American Anthropologist* 60: 234–48.
Wiseman, S.J. 2008. "Introduction: Reading the Early Modern Dream." In *Reading the Early Modern Dream*, edited by Hodgkin, O'Callaghan and Wiseman, 1–13.
Wirth, Jean. 1976. "Le rêve de Dürer." In *Symboles de la Renaissance*, vol. 1, edited by Daniel Arasse, 105–18. Paris: Éditions Rue d'Ulm (online 2012).
Yourcenar, Marguerite. 1992. "On a Dream of Dürer's." In Ead., *That Mighty Sculptor, Time*. Translated by Walter Kaiser, 63–9. New York: Farrar, Straus and Giroux.
Yver, Jacques. 2015. *Le Printemps d'Yver* [1572], edited by Marie-Ange Maignan. Geneva: Droz.
Zambrini, Francesco, ed. 1862. *Dodici conti morali d'anonimo senese; testo inedito del sec. XIII*. Bologna: G. Romagnoli.

INDEX

Pages in *italics* refer to figures and pages followed by "n" refer to notes.

Abû Ma'sar al-Falakî (Albumasar, Apomasar) 30
academies 59, 61, 63–4, 71–2, 75, 80–2, 84, 109; Academy of the arts of drawing, Florence *16*
Achmet 30, 32, 45, 65, 109
Agrippa von Nettesheim, Heinrich Cornelius 43–4, 76–7
alchemy 51, 67, 110
Alcionio, Pietro 70
Alcmaeon of Croton 19
Aldrovandi, Ulisse 96
Alexander the Great 54, 75
Alfonso V, King of Aragon and Naples 55
Alighieri, Dante 20, 64, 100, 106
Apostolius, Michael 29
Aquinas *see* Thomas Aquinas
Aragona, Giovanni d' 55
Argenterio, Giovanni 19
Aristotle 12, 19, 22, 32, 38, 40, 59–61, 63–4, 69–72, 77, 79, 94n2, 107–8
Artemidorus 12, 24, 27–32, 38–9, 52, 65, 83, 85, 107–8
astrology 32, 37, 41, 45, 48, 51, 58, 65, 69–70, 76–8, 84, 104
Augustine 20, 32, 63, 79
autobiography 32, 48–9, 56, 104–6
Averroism 64
Avicenna *see* Ibn Sina
Azpilcueta, Martín de 41

Bacon, Francis 89
Barbaro, Daniele 59, 71–2, 75
Barbaro, Ermolao 71, 94n2
Bargagli, Girolamo 80–2
Barlacchi, Tommaso 33
Bastide, Roger 111
Bayle, Pierre 56
Beatrizet, Nicolas 33
beffa (practical joke) 7–8
Bellini, Giovanni 68
Beradt, Charlotte 119
Bessarion 29
Besson, Gisèle 104
Boccaccio, Giovanni 61, 82–4
Boccadiferro, Lodovico 59, 78
Bodin, Jean 44
Bokdam, Sylviane 114
Bonifacio, Giovanni 82–4
Borges, Jorge Luis 52
Borromeo family 50
Bosch, Hieronymus 97
Brucioli, Antonio 70
Bruegel, Pieter the Elder 97
Brunelleschi, Filippo 7–8
Buddhism 46
Buonaccorsi, Filippo 109
Buonarroti, Michelangelo 9, *16*, 17, 75
Burckhardt, Jacob 104
Burke, Peter 2, 88, 112–14, 118n2
Burton, Robert 29–31, 47n6, 88, 109

Caesar, Julius 53
Caillois, Roger 7, 111–12
Cairns, Douglas 1
Calderón de la Barca, Pedro 6–7, 112
Caldwell, Ian 67
Calpurnia 53, 61
Calvin, John 76
Camporesi, Piero 36–7, 87
Caravaggio (Michelangelo Merisi) 97
Cardano, Girolamo 28–9, 39, 47n2, 48–56, 89, 95, 100, 103, 110
Cariero, Alessandro 63–4
carnival 46, 97–8
Carpaccio, Vittore 68
Carracci, Annibale 86
Castiglione, Baldassarre 9, 81
casuistry *see* sin and confession
Catherine of Alexandria 106
cauchemar 14
Cavallo, Sandra 18
Cellini, Benvenuto 56
chimera, chimerizzare 13
chiromancy 48, 77
Christianity 32–4, 40–2, 64, 79, 106–7
Cicero 26–7, 77; *Dream of Scipio (Somnium Scipionis)* 12, 26–7, 52, 61, 70–1
Cima da Conegliano, Giovanni Battista 73
Ciruelo, Pedro 41
Clark, Stuart 60, 90
Colonna, Francesco, *Hypnerotomachia Poliphili* 58, 66–8, 95
commonplace books 78–9
confession of sins *see* sin and confession
conjecture 77
conversation 59, 63, 80
Cosimo I, grand duke of Tuscany 71
Cranmer, Thomas 79
Crasso, Leonardo 66
Croce, Giulio Cesare 86–7

dance 101
Daniel 31–2, 96
Dante *see* Alighieri, Dante
death, the dead 7, 17, 39, 50, 63, 97, 104
Decius Mus, Publius 61
Dee, John 65n2
delirium 13, 37, 60, 77
Della Barba, Pompeo 71
Della Casa, Giovanni 80, 102
Della Porta, Giovan Battista 39, 47n6, 89
Demaules, Mireille 114–15

demonology 8, 42, 90
demons, devil 6, 12, 14, 21, 32, 35, 40–1, 63, 70, 78–9, 88–9, 101, 104–6
Descartes, René 8, 90–3, 112, 114
dialogue 61–2
Dieterle, Bernard 116–17
Diogenes 19
divination 27–8, 32, 41–2, 45, 48, 58, 64, 69, 77–8, 84, 104, 109
Dodds, Eric 112
Dolce, Lodovico 72
Domenichi, Lodovico 76
Domitian, Roman emperor 84
Donatello 7
Doni, Anton Francesco 9
dorveille 13
Dottori, Benedetto 36, 59–61, 64
drama 6, 8, 61, 100–1
dream (English word) 13
dreamers (Anabaptist sect) 106
dream(s), dreaming: and self-knowledge 9–10, 28, 52, 82, 91, 105–6, 108–9; as deception 6–8; diaries 28, 106, 120; drugs 89; epidemics 88; erotic 37–8; fast 43; keys of 31, 42, 52, 65, 82, 84–5; lucid 71, 120; other dream-books 37; royal 23, 32; sonnets 56; and vision(s) 2, 12, 20–1, 53, 56, 79, 89, 106–7
droom 13
Dumora, Florence 114, 116
Dürer, Albrecht 98–100
Dürr, Hans Peter 89

ecstasy 21, 53
Ekirch, Roger 18
ekphrasis 95
Eliade, Mircea 111
emotions 1, 95, 99
Empedocles 19
enargeia 95
Engel, Manfred 38, 103, 116–17
enýpnion 12
ephialtes 12
Erasmus 9
Erastus, Thomas 88
Este family 64; Ercole II 101

fantasma(ta) see phàntasma
fantasy *see* imagination
Febvre, Lucien 31
Ferdinand I of Aragon, King of Naples 55
Ferrier, Auger 32

Ficino, Marsilio 17, 21, 50, 55, 71, 75
Florio, John 13, 74, 77
folklore 85–7
Foucault, Michel 52, 93
Frederick the Wise 107
Freud, Sigmund 4n1, 38, 46, 51, 92, 102n1, 115–16, 118n2
Fumi, Bartolomeo 40

Galen 18, 19, 22, 25, 36–8, 63, 79
Galilei, Galileo 62, 102
Galilei, Vincenzo 102
Gantet, Claire 108–9, 117
Garzoni, Tommaso 59, 76–8
gender 90–1, 98, 109
genius 55–6
Gentilcore, David 36
gesture 47, 62, 82–5
Giambelli, Cipriano 18, 61–3
Gideon 79
Giglioni, Guido 22, 75
Grafton, Antony 67
Grassi, Paolo 44–5, 64, 88
grasso legnaiuolo (novella) 7–8
Gregory I, pope 41
Grunebaum, G.E. von 111
Guglielmo Gonzaga, Duke of Mantua 59
Guidobaldo da Montefeltro 66
Guillaume de Machaut 13

hallucination 20, 38, 56
Hamilton, Alexander, Eliza and Philip 48
Hassan-i-Sabbah 7
Haydocke, Richard 37
health *see* medicine
Hegel, Georg Wilhelm Friedrich 56
Henry VIII 69
Herberstein, Sigismund von 45
Hermeticism 77, 97
Herder, Johann Gottfried von 56
Hildegard of Bingen 21
Hill, Thomas 65, 65n2
Hippocratic Corpus 12, 18, 22, 24–6, 36–8, 79, 83, 108
Homer 12, 23, 47n1, 95
Hsia, Ronnie Po-chia 46
Huizinga, Johan 9
humours *see* medicine, melancholy
hýpnos 12

Iamblichus 21
Ibn Sina 22
idolatry 32, 42

idolum 53
illusion 13, 21, 40, 72, 74, 89, 93, 101, 114, 118
images 95–101
imaginatio 22
imagination 22, 29, 39, 53, 59, 65, 79, 100
incubation 34, 42, 79, 104
Incubus 35, 39, 88
Index of prohibited books 45, 77
indigenous, non-European dream cultures 44–7, 104
Inquisition 42, 45, 54, 62, 69–71, 76
Insanity: and culpability 17; *see also* madness
insomnia 7, 49, 102
insomnium 12
Isidore of Seville 27
Islam 21

James I, King of Scotland and England 37
Javelli, Giovanni Crisostomo 70
Joseph 31–2, 33, 44, 79, 83, 96
Joyce, James 67
Judaism 21, 42–5
Jung, Carl Gustav 50–1, 118n2

Kabbalah 43
Kepler, Johannes 45
kerygma 21
Keskiaho, Jesse 114
Koselleck, Reinhart 21
Kruger, Steven 114, 116

Laetus, Pomponius 109
Lahire, Bernard 2
Lascaris, Janus 29
Laud, William 113
Le Goff, Jacques 112–13, 118n1
Leonardo da Vinci 51, 100, 110
León, Lucrecia de 69
Leonico Tomeo, Niccolò 70
Leo X, pope 16
Lessing, Gotthold Ephraim 56
Livy 61
Lombroso, Cesare 56
Löwenklau, Johannes (Leunclavius) 30
Luther, Martin 20, 41, 106–7

Machiavelli, Niccolò 9
Macrobius 12, 23, 27–8, 47n4, 55, 63, 70–1, 74, 108

madness 56, 74
magic 41–2, 45, 48, 76–7, 85
Mancini, Celso 64, 88
Mantegna, Andrea 68
Manuel I Komnenos, Emperor of the East 30
Manuzio, Aldo 28, 66, 107, 123
Marcolini, Francesco 72
Marenzio, Luca 102
Marinoni, Prospero 50
Martinengo, Fortunato 72
Martin, Henri-Jean 31
Maximilian II, Emperor of Germany 30
Maximus, Valerius 61
Marx, Karl 51
maya 6
Mazurel, Hervé 2, 119–20
Mazzolini, Silvestro 41
Mazzoni, Jacopo 20
Medici, Giuliano de', Duke of Nemours 16
Medici, Lorenzo de', the Magnificent 29, 109
Medici, Lorenzo di Pierfrancesco de' 109
medicine 18–9, 24–5, 34–9, 58, 69, 83, 86
Medici, Sisto 58–9
melancholy 26, 34–9, 70, 75, 100
Melanchthon, Philip 106
memory, art of 78, 96
memory books (egodocuments) 106
memory (faculty) 22, 60, 74, 95
Menocchio (Domenico Scandella) 30
Mérimée, Prosper 112
Merli, Cesare 64–5, 88
Michelangelo *see* Buonarroti, Michelangelo
Michelet, Jules 89
microcosm and macrocosm 25, 109
Miller, Patricia Cox 114
Milne, Louise 97–8
Miranda, Lin-Manuel 48
missions, Catholic 42
Monica 63
monsters and prodigies 76–8
Montaigne, Michel de 8, 13, 90
Monteverdi, Claudio 101
Morelli, Giovanni 106
More, Thomas 9
Moretto da Brescia 72
Moses 20
music 101–2

Napoleon 18
Nashe, Thomas 65

Naudé, Gabriel 56
Nazari, Giovan Battista 67
Nebuchadnezzar 32
Neoplatonism 8, 17, 21–2, 27–8, 32, 64, 70–2, 75, 97
Nero 45
news 63
Nietzsche, Friedrich 51
Nifo, Agostino 70
night and darkness 15–7, 74, 97, 119
nightmare 7, 12, 14, 35, 37, 65, 74
novella 85–6

occult 42, 51, 67, 77–8
ónar 12
óneiros 12
oraculum 12, 53
Orphic hymns 17, 75

parlour games 80–1
Passavanti, Jacopo 33, 38
Passeri, Marco Antonio 59
Perec, Georges 120
Pereira, Benito 41–2
Petrarch (Francesco Petrarca) 6–7, 93, 101–2
Petronius 39
phantasia 22
phàntasma 11, 21
Philip II, King of Spain 69
physiognomics 35, 48, 76–7, 84
Piccolomini, Marcantonio 80–1
Pinturicchio 68
Pious V, pope 45
Plane, Anne Marie 45–6
Plato 19, 27, 77; Platonic love 71
play and games 72, 79–82
Pliny, the Elder 44
Poliziano, Agnolo 29
pollution, nocturnal 38
Polo, Marco 7, 112
Ponzetti, Ferdinando 58, 63, 65n4
Ponzinibio, Gianfrancesco 88–9
printing and book market 3, 65, 107–8
prophecy 5–6, 20–1, 25–6, 32, 40, 53, 55, 58, 69–70, 77, 79, 107
psychoanalysis 2, 51, 92, 104, 113, 120
Pythagoras 77

Quintilian 95

Rabelais, François 17, 23, 67
Raimondi, Marcantonio 33
Raphael (Raffaello Sanzio) 33, 62

reason (faculty) 7, 17, 22, 59, 75
Reformation 3, 79–80, 97, 106–7
Renaissance (concept, movement) 3, 10, 16, 24, 31, 70, 80, 93, 95–6, 105, 109
rêve 13, 115
rêverie 13
rhetoric 95–6
Ricoeur, Paul 51
Rigault, Nicolas 30
Rore, Cipriano de 101–2
Rosaccio, Giuseppe 35
Rosenwein, Barbara 5
Rubens, Peter Paul 61–2
Ruggiero, Guido 9
Ryff, Andreas 96

Scaliger, Julius Caesar 25, 48, 108
scepticism 71, 76, 90
Schmitt, Jean-Claude 21, 47n4, 98, 104, 113
Schopenhauer, Arthur 6, 26
Scipio Aemilianus 27
Scipio Africanus 27
Segni, Giovanni Battista 34, 40–1, 63–4, 88
senses and perception 22, 25–6, 53, 57, 60, 70, 90, 95, 107
Sepúlveda, Juan Ginés de 70
Serin, Élizabeth 120
Sextus Empiricus 90
Shakespeare, William 6, 61, 67, 95, 100–1
shamanism 45, 88–9, 111
siesta 94n1
Simonides of Ceos 61
sin and confession 30–2, 40–2, 64–5; original sin 72
Siraisi, Nancy 49
sleep and wakefulness 7, 12–3, 17–9, 24–6, 37–9, 53, 58, 60–1, 63, 65, 70, 72–5, 78, 81, 86–7, 92–3, 97–8, 100–1, 109, 115, 119
sleepwalking 37
snoring 19, 86
sogno, sognare 13
somnambulism 37, 74
Somniale Danielis 31, 65, 85, 110
somnium 12, 17
somnus 17
songe 12–3

Sozzini, Fausto 80–1
Sozzini, Lelio 80
Spada-Veralli family 18
Spina, Bartolomeo 89
Spinello Aretino 105
stoicism 19
Storey, Tessa 18
storytelling 81–2
Strozzi, Giovanni Battista 102
Suda 28
Suetonius 44
superstition 40–2, 56, 65, 76–7, 90
Synesius 12, 28, 52, 75, 77, 95, 107

theatre *see* drama
Themistius 94n2
Thomas Aquinas 20, 32–3, 70
Thomas, Keith 85, 113
Thomason, Dustin 67
Tiraqueau, André 17, 37
Titian (Tiziano Vecellio) 9
Traum 13
Tricasso, Patrizio 30
Tuscus, Leo 30, 109

Ugoni, Stefano Maria 59, 72–5
unconscious 2, 51
utopia 9

Valdés, Juan de 94n3
Van Mander, Karel 100
Vasari, Giorgio 105
Vatable, François 70
Vermigli, Pietro Martire 41, 47n3, 79
Virgil 23
visio 12
visum 12
Vives, Juan Luis 71
vocabulary, oneiric 11–4

Wallington, Nehemiah 37
Wier, Johan 88–9
witchcraft, witches 14, 39, 41–2, 88–90, 98

Yourcenar, Marguerite 100
Yver, Jacques 81–2

Zacchia, Paolo 36–7
Zambrini, Francesco 86
Zsámboky, János (Sambucus) 29–30, 39